Taking Freshwater Game Fish

A Treasury of Expert Advice

Taking Freshwater Game Fish

A Treasury of Expert Advice

Edited by Todd Swainbank and Eric Seidler
Illustrated by Patricia Witten

The Countryman Press
Woodstock, Vermont

Chapters 1–5, 8, and 9 originally appeared in *Taking Game Fish* (The Crossing Press, 1980) and have been carefully reviewed and updated for this edition. Many of the illustrations in this book are based on original artwork by Gordon L. Eggleston that appeared in *Taking Game Fish*.

Published by the Countryman Press, Inc.
Woodstock, Vermont 05091

Printed in the United States of America
Cover photograph by Jill Kimball
Cover design by Kathy Robinson
Book design by Leslie Fry

Library of Congress Cataloging-in-Publication Data

Taking freshwater game fish : a treasury of expert advice / edited by
   Todd Swainbank and Eric Seidler ; illustrated by Patricia Witten.
      p.   cm.
   Rev. ed. of: Taking game fish. c1980.
   Includes index.
   ISBN 0-88150-113-1 (pbk.) : $14.95
   1. Fishing.   2. Fishes, Fresh-water.   I. Swainbank, Todd.
II. Seidler, Eric, 1954–   III. Taking game fish.
SH441.T33 1988
799.1'1—dc19   88-28319
                                                                              CIP

Photographs on pages 49, 62, and 228 by Bill Butler; pages 26 and 34 by Judy Butler; pages 88 and 92 by Gordon Eggleston; page 73 by Niles Eggleston; page 101 by Todd Swainbank; pages 139, 144, and 152 by Jill Kimball; page 153 by J. Michael Kimball; page 157 by Kris Lee; page 168 by Katherine Seidler; page 183 by Jean Lebanowski; pages 187, 190, 198, 199, 216, 218, and 220 by Ernie Lantiegne; page 225 by Carol Lantiegne; page 205 by J. Goerg, New York State Department of Environmental Conservation; page 234 by Roy Gray; and pages 129 and 175 by Dr. Edward Brothers.

Contents

Introduction: About this Book   **7**

1/Largemouth Bass Basics   **11**
Bill Butler

2/Tackle, Tips, and Techniques for Smallmouth Bass   **36**
Todd Swainbank

3/Fishing for the Wily Walleye   **60**
Todd Swainbank

4/Trophy Northerns and How to Take Them   **70**
Gordon L. Eggleston

5/Garpin' for Carp   **98**
Todd Swainbank

6/Introduction to Fly-fishing   **102**
Eric Seidler

7/Streamer Seasons   **128**
Eric Seidler

8/Nymph Fishing to Non-Surface-Feeding Trout   **138**
J. Michael Kimball

9/Nymph Fishing to Surface-Feeding Trout   **147**
J. Michael Kimball

10/Landlocks in a Nutshell   **167**
Eric Seidler

11/Deep-Water Trolling   **184**
Capt. Ernie Lantiegne

Appendixes:
Getting Kids Started in Fishing   **227**
Todd Swainbank
Dream Trips   **232**
Todd Swainbank

Index   **237**

Dedication

This book is dedicated to all the good people who share the roar of the waterfall, the shade of the Royal Palm, and the fight against the hydropower project at Ithaca Falls in Fall Creek, New York.

Ithaca, NY 1988

About this Book

The basic concept of this book began during a gloomy winter spent mostly around the coffee pot in my now-defunct tackle shop, The Compleat Angler, in Ithaca, New York. There was something about that shop that attracted anglers, and some of those anglers were very good fishermen and women. It is their experience and knowledge of fish and fishing that inspired and made *Taking Freshwater Game Fish*.

Since the first edition (published as *Taking Game Fish*) came out in 1980, change has affected all of the authors. The second edition has changed too, reflecting the increased experience of the individual writers. Some have traveled extensively and caught new species of fish in exciting and challenging locations. Some have stayed closer to home and expanded their angling versatility or fine-tuned their specialties. The present edition also includes several chapters by new authors who did not appear in the earlier book.

Just as the sport of fishing offers something of value to all participants, I believe that *Taking Freshwater Game Fish* offers something of value to any angler or reader, regardless of where his or her current fishing interest lies. The contributors have conveyed a great amount of relevant information on tackle and technique for a wide variety of fish. This information is not limited to any one section of the country, because game fish have similar preferences wherever they are found.

The keys to angling success are knowledge and versatility. By reading this book and practicing what it preaches, you will catch more fish and have more fun doing so. Good luck, and good fishing!

—T.S.

About the Authors

The seven contributors to this book have been anglers their entire lives and in most cases teachers of the sport for many years.

Todd Swainbank

Todd's angling career began thirty years ago under Ithaca Falls in Fall Creek, New York. Since then he has guided professionally in New York, Vermont, and Alaska. A Cornell University graduate, Todd has written numerous books and articles on fishing and hunting. For several years he operated The Compleat Angler, a tackle shop in Ithaca, and wrote articles for *The Grapevine,* a Finger Lakes region news and opinion weekly. Currently Todd is an Orvis fly-fishing and wing-shooting instructor in Manchester, Vermont. In the wintertime he is a professional guide in the Bahamas.

Bill Butler

Bill is a bass fisherman, a veteran of the professional bass tournament trail. He has enjoyed tremendous success in catching bass on northern lakes as well as southern reservoirs. In addition, Bill has worked as a representative of several major fishing-tackle companies. Bill's true love is fishing for trophy largemouths, smallmouths, and northern pike. He lives in Massachusetts and is vice president of Weetabix, a large corporation.

Gordon Eggleston

Gordon is a professor of physical education at Ithaca College, in Ithaca, New York. He was born and brought up on a farm near Cooperstown, New York. His fishing exploits began at age ten and have included fishing northern New York State and Canada for walleyes and northern pike as well as fly-fishing for trout and salmon throughout the Northeast. An avid outdoorsman, Gordon has instructed physical education majors in archery, wilderness canoe camping, survival camping, fly-fishing, and fly tying. He has also written on these subjects and is a commercial artist, fish taxidermist, and fly tier. Gordon prepared the illustrations for the original edition of *Taking Game Fish,* on which many of the illustrations in this book are based.

J. Michael Kimball

Mike is a real-estate developer who makes his home in Ithaca, New York, and has fished extensively throughout the eastern and western United States and Canada, the Caribbean, Mexico, and Europe. He has been fly-fishing for close to thirty years and has been a nymph specialist almost exclusively for over twenty. While still in his early twenties, Mike taught fly-fishing and fly tying, and he has acted as a guide and instructor for the Federation of Fly Fishermen. He has also done extensive graduate work at Cornell in fisheries biology and aquatic ecology. Mike has contributed to and been featured in numerous outdoor magazines and books. His methods of fishing and tying the nymph have received special recognition in *Fly Fisherman Magazine*.

Eric Seidler

Eric began fishing on Spy Pond in Massachusetts. When a family move took him to Philadelphia, he fished the Schuylkill River. Another move brought him to Ithaca, New York, placing him firmly in the heart of the Finger Lakes region, and vice versa. Eric has focused his fishing energies on the Finger Lakes and their tributary rivers, taking rainbow, brown, brook, and lake trout, landlocked Atlantic salmon, and smallmouth bass. He alternates with the seasons and the fish runs between fly-fishing the streams and windfishing the lakes from his canoe. A musician, Eric is a member of the Ithaca-based rhythm-and-blues band Moxie. He also writes articles and essays on fly-fishing, fisheries management, and water-resources management in the Finger Lakes region.

Capt. Ernie Lantiegne

Ernie is a Coast Guard-licensed charter-fishing captain and has operated Fish Doctor Charters on Lake Ontario since 1977. He has a broad background in the charter-fishing business, with twenty years' experience in the Finger Lakes, Lake Champlain, and Lake George. Ernie took his first game fish, a brook trout, at the age of six, handlined his first laker from an Adirondack lake when he was only eight, and has deep-water trolling experience ranging from a hand-held lead-core trolling line to today's sophisticated electronic gear. In addition to his many years of fishing in waters throughout New York, Ernie has worked as a fisheries biologist and manager for the New York State Department of Environmental Conservation for twenty-two years.

Ernie and his wife, Carol, also a licensed charter captain, operate Fish Doctor Charters out of the Little Salmon River in the Mexico Bay area of Lake Ontario. They also operate the "Gone Fish-Inn" for sportsmen. They can be reached at RD #1, Box 213, Oswego, New York 13126.

Patricia Witten (Illustrator)

Patti is a freelance illustrator and graphic designer, and a fly-fisher. In 1984 she set up her one-woman studio, Wisteria Graphics, in Ithaca, New York. This is her first fishing book.

1/Largemouth Bass Basics

by Bill Butler

I t has often been stated that 10% of the fishermen catch 90% of the fish. That may be an exaggerated estimate, but it is a fact that certain anglers always are successful, while others experience mixed results at best. The reason for this is not some new secret lure or technique. Successful bass fishermen—for that matter, *all* successful fishermen—are engaged in a never-ending learning process; the most important tool a bass angler has is intelligence. Every fishing trip should be viewed as a new learning experience. The successful bass fisherman learns to apply his accumulated knowledge to the methods he uses.

The largemouth bass is a product of its environment in each different body of water. What this means is that environmental factors such as amount of cover, depth, water clarity, *etc.* will cause bass to behave differently in one lake from the way they behave in another. Therefore, the same largemouth that school up in 30 feet of water on a submerged point in a deep, clear impoundment like Table Rock Lake in Missouri might be found in 6 to 10 feet of water on weedlines in Oneida Lake in upstate New York. The bass in each body of water adapt to the conditions around them. The ability to read these conditions enables the successful fisherman to find the fish on any given lake or river. The ability to analyze the salient environmental factors leads the successful bass angler to correct lure selection and presentation. When he begins to catch fish, he is establishing the pattern for that particular day. Catching the fish becomes the easy part. *Locating* them is what separates the very successful angler from the others.

Factors that Influence Success

Many different factors are taken into consideration by the successful bass fisherman. We will examine some of these and discuss how they relate to the largemouth bass population from lake to lake.

Season of the Year. This is a primary factor in determining where the bass should be. Each season will cause the fish to move to a new location on most bodies of water.

Type of Lake. Bass in a deep, clear lake will not be found in the same places as they will be on a shallow, weedy body of water.

Size of Lake. Obviously a larger lake offers more possibilities and choices in searching for bass. Small farm ponds often will have one or two primary holding points for the bass population, while a large lake such as Lake Champlain offers never-ending possibilities for both the fisherman and the fish.

While discussing types and sizes of lakes, let's list the basic categories that are generally found in the United States:

Deep, clear, natural lakes. Lakes with depths of over 50 feet, predominately rock or gravel bottom, with aquatic vegetation found along shorelines and in coves. Good examples of this type would be the Finger Lakes in upstate New York. These lakes usually have populations of both largemouth and smallmouth bass, as well as other game fish.

Shallow, natural lakes. This type of lake, seldom exceeding 30 feet in depth, has far more aquatic vegetation. The bottom varies from rock to mud, and the bottom contour variations are less extreme than on the deeper lakes. Good examples of this type are Oneida Lake in upstate New York and certain portions of Lake Champlain.

Natural, "dishpan" lakes. Extremely shallow, with very heavy vegetation and a muck bottom with little variation. Lake Toho in Florida is an excellent example of a "dishpan" lake, with miles and miles of 4- to 6-foot deep water filled with heavy aquatic vegetation.

Man-made reservoirs. These are common in the South and West. They are generally created by construction of a dam across an existing river or stream, when the surrounding terrain is permanently flooded. Because of this, man-made impoundments offer various types of cover and *structure* (that is, irregularities in the terrain of the lake bottom) not found in natural lakes. Standing timber, old roads and railroads, and entire fields of bushes and shrubs are covered by water in these impoundments and create fishing conditions unlike any found on natural bodies of water. Most reservoirs have both very shallow and very deep sections. Aquatic vegetation is not as common as on natural lakes.

Other factors to consider when locating bass:

Water Temperature. Bass are cold blooded, with their body temperature and metabolism fluctuating with the water temperature. When the water temperature is below 50 degrees, bass are extremely sluggish and do not feed actively. At 55 degrees bass become more active, and when the water temperature reaches 65 to 70 degrees in the spring, bass will be very active. Their preferred temperature range in the summer is 68 to 74 degrees, and they will hold at whatever depth is necessary to be in approximately that range. However, bass will frequent 80-degree and warmer shallows in midsummer at certain times when feeding. The preferred temperature range is not without exceptions, but it is a good base to begin with in understanding how water temperature can affect your fishing success.

Aquatic Vegetation. Lily pads, reeds, bulrushes and various weedlines all are used by bass as protective cover at various times. The type and amount of vegetation where you are fishing will help determine your bait selection and presentation.

Shoreline Type. Some shorelines will attract bass better than others. Fallen trees, boat docks, and overhanging bushes will be much more productive under most circumstances than a beach or barren mudbank.

Amount of Sunlight. Since bass don't have eyelids, they are sensitive to bright light. As a result, on extremely sunny days they will seek protection from the sun.

Water Clarity. This should help determine what color lure you choose as well as how close you can fish to whatever cover you have in mind. Extremely clear water means using a lighter test line. It is a fact that on clear bodies of water a fisherman using 6-pound test line will generally have better success than someone in the same boat using 20-pound line.

Food Availability. There is an old saying on the bass tournament trail that goes, "Find the food, find the fish." What it means is that the most promising area on a lake will be devoid of bass unless natural forage (such as minnows, crayfish, frogs, insects, *etc.*) is available.

If you find a good-looking bay or cove and you see schools of minnows, chances are you will find that bass are in the area at some time during the day. Game fish such as bass follow their food supply. That is why on southern reservoirs a common practice is to search for schools of shad, which is the primary forage fish for bass. I have also applied this technique to northern bodies of water like Lake Champlain, where I located bass and northern pike that were chasing giant schools of shiners or yellow perch.

Bottom Structure. This is a key factor to consider when searching for bass. Are there dropoffs or underwater knolls on the lake you are fishing? The underwater contours of the lake, along with the time of year, are the two most important factors to analyze when bass fishing. Good topographical maps are as important to the modern bass fisherman as anything that can be bought in a tackle store. A tournament bass fisherman would not think of seriously fishing without a good map. The best maps are published by United States government agencies such as the Army Corps of Engineers or the U.S. Geological Survey. These maps provide information concerning depth, dropoffs, ridges, sharp rises, points, holes, and other bottom structures where fish love to live. By checking the obvious places on the map, you can begin to put together a pattern even on a lake you are visiting for the first time.

Other factors, such as the amount of boat traffic, water quality, bottom composition, and time of day all enter into the bass-fishing picture.

Cover and Structure

Now that we have looked at the various factors that should be considered when fishing, let's discuss specific types of cover and structure frequented by largemouth bass on both natural lakes and artificial reservoirs. Remember, bass like cover and structure because they harbor food and provide protection.

Natural Lakes

Primary and Secondary Dropoffs. The average lake will slope gradually from shore from 0 to 10 feet, then quickly drop to 15- or 20 feet. That quick drop to 20 feet is the primary dropoff and is generally the end of the primary food zone as well as of most aquatic vegetation. Then, further out, there is an additional dropoff to 30 or 40 feet. This second ledge is the secondary dropoff. In most lakes largemouth bass are found on the primary dropoff but not the secondary. The primary food zone is where most of your fishing efforts should be focused.

Shallow, Weedy Bays. This is an ideal spot to find largemouth in the spring. Depending on the consistency of the bottom, bass may spawn in such locations. Once spring is past bass may move in to feed in the early morning or evening, but during the rest of the day this type of bay won't be very productive. (See Figure 2.)

In the spring these areas should be extensively fished using shallow-water or top-water baits, as well as plastic worms. Small openings in the middle of visible grass or pads should not be ignored. Bass will often use these

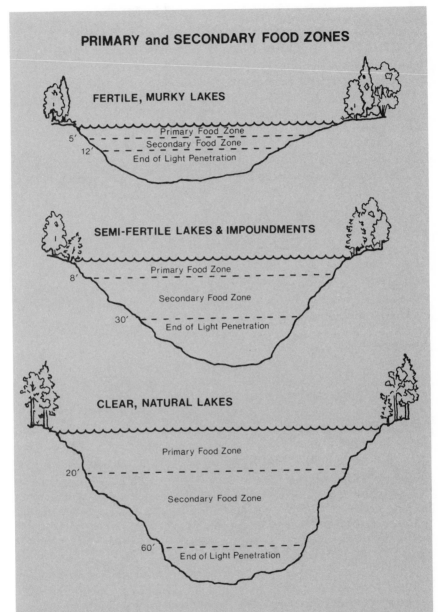

The diagrams above illustrate the location of Primary and Secondary food zones on the basic types of lakes. Most largemouth bass fishing success will be in the Primary food zone regardless of which lake you are on.

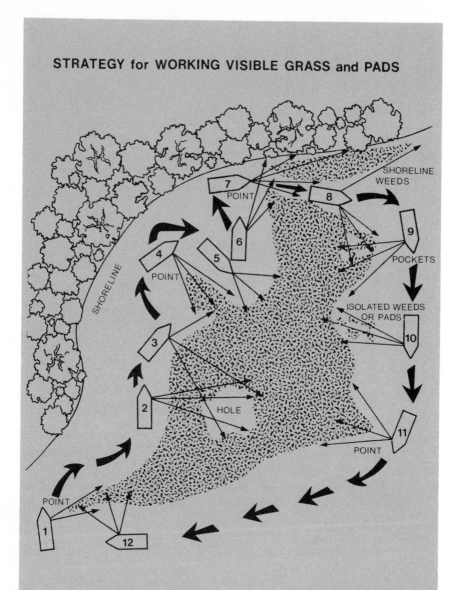

Fish all points, edges, and openings in visible grass or pads. This is very good cover for bass, especially during the early season.

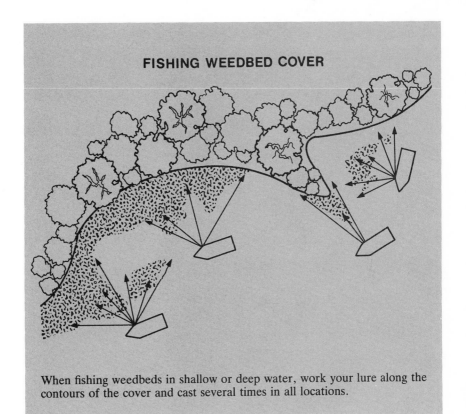

FISHING WEEDBED COVER

When fishing weedbeds in shallow or deep water, work your lure along the contours of the cover and cast several times in all locations.

spots as ambush points for baitfish. Common types of vegetation in these bays are lily pads, reeds, bulrushes, and milfoil.

Weedbeds in Deeper Water. Weeds growing in deeper water, such as combomba, cabbage weed, or coontail weeds, offer excellent bass cover and should always be carefully fished. Combomba and cabbage weeds can grow in water as deep as 20 feet, while coontail stops at about 8 to 10 feet. These weedbeds should be fished on all sides along with any open pockets in the middle of the bed.

Isolated Deep Hole. Especially on a very shallow lake, deeper holes will attract bass because they afford refuge from light, surface noise, and boating disturbances.

Submerged Reefs. Underwater rockpiles are well-known smallmouth-bass hangouts, but largemouth bass will also frequent these spots, especially if they are no deeper than 30 feet.

Weedlines. The weedline is generally considered the outside edge of the weed growth coming out from the shoreline. As stated earlier this outside

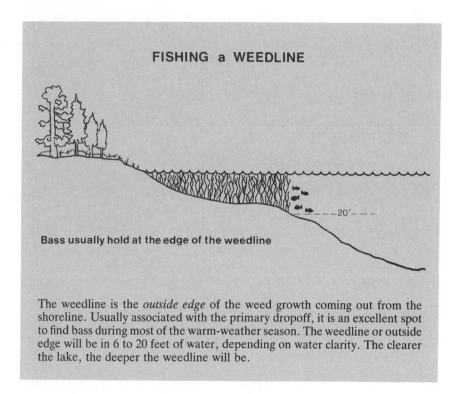

FISHING a WEEDLINE

Bass usually hold at the edge of the weedline

—20′—

The weedline is the *outside edge* of the weed growth coming out from the shoreline. Usually associated with the primary dropoff, it is an excellent spot to find bass during most of the warm-weather season. The weedline or outside edge will be in 6 to 20 feet of water, depending on water clarity. The clearer the lake, the deeper the weedline will be.

edge is often right at or near the primary dropoff and generally is no deeper than 20 feet. The outside edge of the weedline provides protection and a point of ambush for bass in their search for food. This is a primary area for bass in the summer when the shallows are warmer than the preferred temperature range. On natural lakes weedlines are key features to look for when searching for bass.

Underwater Saddles or Trenches. These depressions in the bottom are good spots in summertime on natural lakes, especially if some type of cover, such as deep weedbeds, is nearby to attract baitfish.

Mouths of Creeks and Rivers. In early spring largemouth will congregate where feeder streams enter the lake, because of the warmer water moving in. This is usually a pre-spawn condition however, and once the lake temperature reaches 65 degrees these areas no longer seem to hold the fish.

Submerged Weedbeds. If you have a depthfinder you can often find weedbeds that do not appear on the surface. These areas generally hold fish because they offer protection, good depth, and baitfish.

Fallen Trees or Brush in Water. Usually found along the shoreline or in coves, this type of cover offers excellent protection and usually attracts

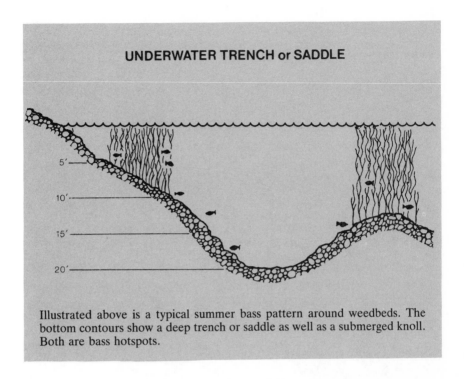

UNDERWATER TRENCH or SADDLE

Illustrated above is a typical summer bass pattern around weedbeds. The bottom contours show a deep trench or saddle as well as a submerged knoll. Both are bass hotspots.

baitfish. If the surrounding water is less than 5 feet deep, this area may only be productive in the spring. If the water has sufficient depth, however, fish will generally hold there all season. Even if found in shallow water, this spot could produce all summer in the very early morning.

Rubble-rock or Riprap. Usually found along structures such as bridges, marinas, or roadways running along water. This is an excellent spring haunt for bass. The rocks tend to heat up and warm the water, providing a great home for crayfish, a favorite in the bass diet. If sufficiently deep water is nearby, bass will use this riprap as a feeding area all season.

Piers, Boat Docks and Boat Houses. These offer cover and attract baitfish. They are especially productive in the spring, but if the water is at least 5 to 6 feet deep they can hold fish all year long.

Underwater Points. These are points extending from the shoreline toward deeper water. Bass move up on a point to feed and can generally be found off the deeper end of certain points all season long, once spawning is completed.

Bridges and Bridge Pilings. Depending on the depth of the surrounding water, bass will use these constructions for cover and protection. This type of cover should be fished vertically, to cover all depths available.

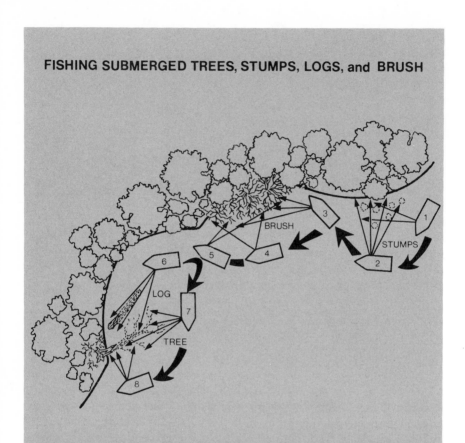

FISHING SUBMERGED TREES, STUMPS, LOGS, and BRUSH

When fishing fallen trees, submerged logs, stumps, and brush, cast parallel repeatedly along the cover. Work all sides and angles of the obstacles. If it is a bright day, *always* fish the shady side first, because bass will avoid bright sunlight.

Artificial Reservoirs

Some of the cover on artificial reservoirs is very obvious, such as standing timber. The problem with obvious cover is that it gets fished by everyone on the lake. Also, only a small portion of standing timber will actually hold fish. Usually the best spots will be the heaviest cover next to water deep enough to offer bass a sense of security.

Other hotspots are not so obvious but can be very productive. A good topographic map and depthfinder are needed to locate these areas, but the

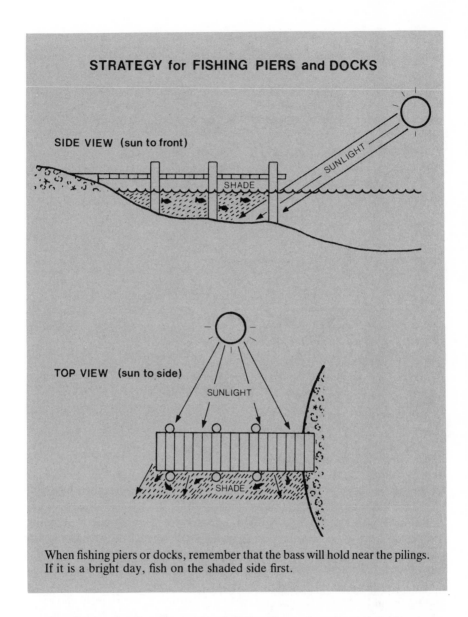

STRATEGY for FISHING PIERS and DOCKS

SIDE VIEW (sun to front)

SUNLIGHT

SHADE

TOP VIEW (sun to side)

SUNLIGHT

SHADE

When fishing piers or docks, remember that the bass will hold near the pilings. If it is a bright day, fish on the shaded side first.

results often make the efforts worthwhile. Examples of potential hotspots on artificial reservoirs include:

Old River or Creek Bed. When the reservoir was constructed, the original river or creek was dammed up and the surrounding area flooded. However, the bed of that original river or creek, with all of its bends,

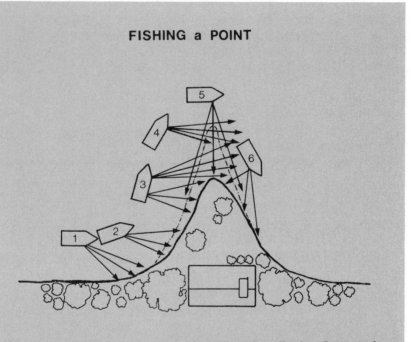

FISHING a POINT

When fishing a point, a crankbait or jig will be very effective. Saturate the entire area, and be sure to remember that the point extends out toward open water.

holes, and configurations, is still a prime bass area because it is like a deep trench that winds its way throughout the impoundment.

Where creek beds meet the river bed are key spots, because bass will use these beds as migratory paths.

Stump Fields. Before many of the reservoirs were flooded, standing timber was cut to prevent boating problems. However, the remaining underwater stumps and roots are usually very productive, depending on the depth of the water. Any small trees or brush left uncut becomes great bass cover once the area is flooded.

Old Road Beds and Drainage Ditches. Most roads are slightly elevated, with ditches on either side. When underwater, these represent good fish-holding structure and should be checked out.

Underwater Points or Saddles. These variations in the bottom contour hold both catfish and bass. They can be excellent summer and winter spots to fish.

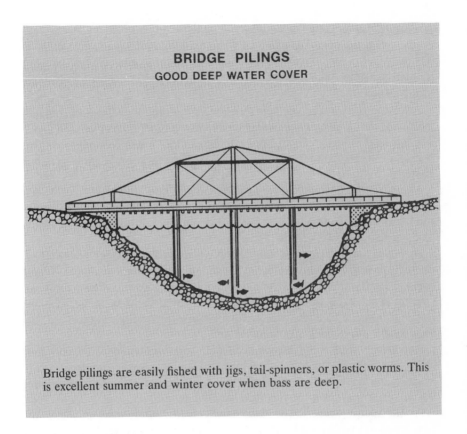

BRIDGE PILINGS
GOOD DEEP WATER COVER

Bridge pilings are easily fished with jigs, tail-spinners, or plastic worms. This is excellent summer and winter cover when bass are deep.

Seasonal Patterns

Beginning with the end of winter, the early-spring movement of large-mouth bass is from deep water to the warmest available areas. During this period bass will seek out shallow, weedy bays and coves, boat docks, or gradually sloping shorelines.

As the water continues to warm up with the coming of spring, the fish will seek out nesting areas. Largemouth prefer a slightly hard bottom for their nests, but they will use a tangle of roots or vegetation if nothing better is available. Spawning time is controlled by weather conditions and water temperature. In northern waters bass generally spawn from mid-May into June. Obviously, the spawning period is earlier the farther south you travel.

For the spawn to begin, the water temperature usually must be at least 65 degrees. Fishing for spawning bass is shallow-water fishing—you can often see the fish guarding the nest. Fish caught during this period, in my opinion, should always be released. This will help protect your fishing resource for future years.

After the spawn, summer patterns begin. As the weedlines become established, the largemouth congregate at locations offering cover and access to deep water. They will still migrate to shallow-water feeding areas, but pounding the bank in 2 feet of water in midafternoon is now usually a waste of time.

This is the mistake made by most beginning bass anglers—that lily-pad field or fallen tree in 2 feet of water that was so productive in early spring still looks great, and the novice bass fisherman spends hours casting surface plugs or spinnerbaits at this type of cover.

However, in the summer the bass have moved to deeper water where the temperature is in the preferred range and cover is still available. Weedlines, dropoffs, points, underwater weedbeds, *etc.* now are the haunts you have to seek out if you want to be successful. Even in summer, in very early morning or at night, the bass will move to the shallows to feed, but then they'll move back to deeper water.

As summer ends, the largemouth will begin to frequent the shallows again as the water cools down. They also seem to sense the approach of winter; an angler can get great catches in fall because the fish are feeding heavily in preparation for the lean months ahead.

As the temperature drops consistently below 40 degrees at night, the bass move out of the shallows and school up in their winter home, usually along dropoffs and points in at least 15 feet of water, if it is available. They can be caught at this time, but they are sluggish, and the bait must be worked very slowly.

Basic Bass Lures

Plastic Worms

The plastic worm was first introduced about thirty years ago. It is probably the most popular bass bait, although it is a difficult bait for some anglers to fish effectively. A keen sense of feel must be developed; the good worm fisherman can feel with his hands exactly what the worm is doing as he crawls it over, around, and through various types of cover.

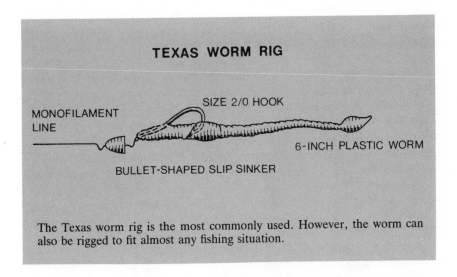

TEXAS WORM RIG

MONOFILAMENT LINE

SIZE 2/0 HOOK

6-INCH PLASTIC WORM

BULLET-SHAPED SLIP SINKER

The Texas worm rig is the most commonly used. However, the worm can also be rigged to fit almost any fishing situation.

The worm can be fished shallow or deep and can be rigged in many different ways. The most popular worm rig is the Texas-style rig, where the hook point is turned back into the worm to make it weedless.

The sinker used with a plastic worm should be as light as possible, and the hook size should increase or decrease with the size of the worm. Generally accepted hook and worm match-ups are as follows:

Worm	Hook
4″	1
6″	1/0-2/0
7″	2/0-3/0
9″	4/0-5/0

Also important when worm fishing is keeping slack out of your line and watching the point where your line enters the water for any telltale taps that you can't feel. Many bass caught on worms are caught because the angler saw his line move, even though he didn't feel anything. Set the hook immediately, as it is a fact that a bass can inhale and exhale a worm in less than one second. The rod you use when worm fishing should be stiff enough to allow you to solidly set the hook. Graphite rods are very popular for worm fishing because of their sensitivity and power.

Plastic worms come in a rainbow of colors and many different sizes and styles. The most popular colors on the pro bass Tournament circuit are purple, black, blue, brown, and strawberry. Are colors important? Yes, colors can make a difference depending on particular fishing conditions.

The author with a lunker largemouth he caught while fishing a plastic worm around dock pilings in the spring.

In very clear water, blue is a good choice. Black is good in virtually all conditions. In very muddy water many of the pros use yellowish colors. Purple offers excellent contrast with the surrounding cover.

When you are worm fishing, try to develop your sense of feel, and watch your line. The hook should be set immediately when anything is seen or felt. Another thing to remember is *never* to work the rod and reel at the same time. Take your rod tip from about 9 o'clock to 11, and then reel in the slack. Repeat this process, crawling the worm along the bottom. This is a good basic retrieve for learning how to fish the plastic worm. However, the worm can also be hopped, jiggled, or rapidly crawled. There is no one standard way to fish this bait, which is why it is so much fun.

The most popular sizes for worms are 4, 6, 7, 8, and 9 inch, with 6 inch being a good size to start with. Recently plastic lizards, which are generally fished the same way, have become very popular.

The worm is a great bait in all seasons of the year and can be rigged so many different ways it can be applied to almost any fishing situation.

Spinnerbaits

The basic spinnerbait concept is a V-shaped, safety-pin-type wire frame with one or two spinners on the top wire and a hair, rubber, or vinyl skirt around the hook on the bottom wire. Spinnerbaits are easily the second-most popular bass bait, behind the plastic worm. There are many different versions and sizes on the market today: the angler can choose baits with large blades, small blades, the new propeller-style buzzing blades, single blades, and tandem spins.

The vinyl- or rubber-skirted versions are more popular than hair. The most popular sizes are ⅛, ¼, ⅜, and ½ ounce, with ¼ ounce being a good all-around size. Colors that are popular include chartreuse, white, black, and yellow. A general rule for colors is to use a bright lure on a bright day and a dark lure on a dark day.

Some spinnerbait terms are:

Buzzing. This is a very popular method of retrieving a lure, where the bait is retrieved on or just under the surface, and the blades or propellers create a very noticeable wake on the surface. Recently, special spinnerbaits called buzz baits have been developed especially for this style of fishing. Instead of standard blades, they feature a large propeller to churn up the surface.

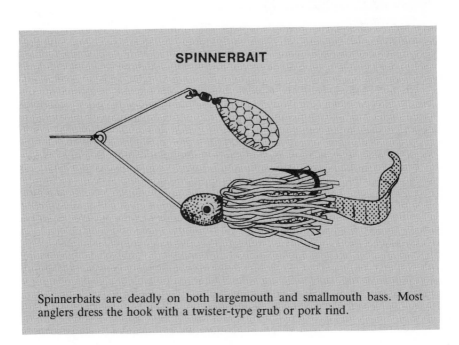

SPINNERBAIT

Spinnerbaits are deadly on both largemouth and smallmouth bass. Most anglers dress the hook with a twister-type grub or pork rind.

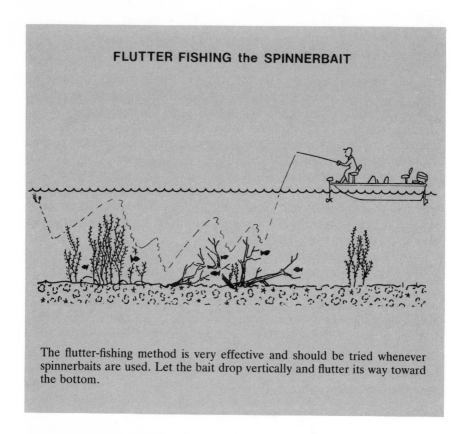

FLUTTER FISHING the SPINNERBAIT

The flutter-fishing method is very effective and should be tried whenever spinnerbaits are used. Let the bait drop vertically and flutter its way toward the bottom.

Drop-fishing or Flutter Fishing. This is a very good technique to use around fallen trees, docks, bridge pilings, or in open spaces in weeds or pads. The spinnerbait is allowed to fall freely toward the bottom, which will cause the blade or blades to revolve. Most of the pros use a short-armed single spin type of spinnerbait for this technique. (See Figure 12.)

Trailer Hook. A good way to make sure you hook your fish is to use a trailer hook. The eye of a second hook is slipped over the first hook, giving you double hooking capacity.

Tuning your Spinnerbait. Make sure the upper arm with the blades is directly over the top of the hook. The bait should not lean to either side when retrieved. Spinnerbaits can be used all year long, but they are especially effective when the bass are shallow in spring and fall. The standard retrieve is to reel the bait back about 12 inches under the surface, so it is still visible. As discussed earlier, it can also be drop-fished or buzzed on the surface. An added feature of the spinnerbait is that it is a very good bait for fishing in weeds or logs, because the top arm protects the hook.

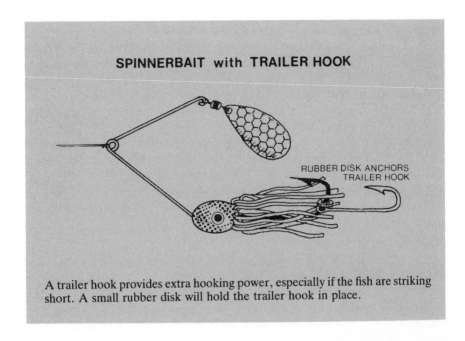

SPINNERBAIT with TRAILER HOOK

RUBBER DISK ANCHORS
TRAILER HOOK

A trailer hook provides extra hooking power, especially if the fish are striking short. A small rubber disk will hold the trailer hook in place.

It can actually be crawled over and through fallen trees without getting hung up when the rod is in the hands of a skilled angler.

When casting a spinnerbait at a stump or group of pads, be sure to cast beyond the target and bring the bait back past it. If you cast directly at the target area, the resulting splash may scare off the fish. Another helpful idea is to use a twister tail on your spinnerbait for added action. Both the plastic twister worms or pork-rind strips are excellent for this purpose.

The biggest mistake you can make when using a spinnerbait is to use only one type of retrieve. Experiment with different techniques, and you will find that one retrieve will work best on one day whereas the very next day something else will be better.

Also, develop the ability to work that spinnerbait through the thickest cover you can find. Old Ironjaw is in there waiting for you!

Crankbait

The growth in popularity experienced in recent years by crankbaits can be traced to a lure called the Big O, developed in Tennessee in the early 1970's. This original plug looked like a pregnant minnow, floated at rest, and when retrieved would wiggle its way back about 6 feet under the surface. Crankbaits are any plug following this same basic concept. They come in various sizes, shapes, and colors; the depth to which they will dive on retrieve is dependent on the size and angle of slant of the lip on the bait.

Today you can buy crankbaits that swim inches under the surface or dive to 15 feet. They are made of plastic or balsa wood. The most popular sizes for bass are ⅛, ¼, ⅜, and ½ ounce.

Some of the more popular crankbaits are the Rebel Wee-R, Mann's Deep Pig, Norman's Deep N and Little N, and Bagley's Balsa B's.

Crankbaits can be fished rapidly or just crawled along. The fisherman who is successful with these lures continually varies his retrieve.

Use crankbaits all season long. Choose the appropriate type for the depth you are fishing, and go get 'em!

Grubs and Leadhead Jigs

The small plastic grub was initially developed as a bait for salt-water speckled trout. However the tournament bass pros consider the grub and jighead combination to be one of the best baits that can be used.

Jigging is similar to worm fishing because you must develop a keen sense of feel and watch your line very closely. In jigging you raise and lower

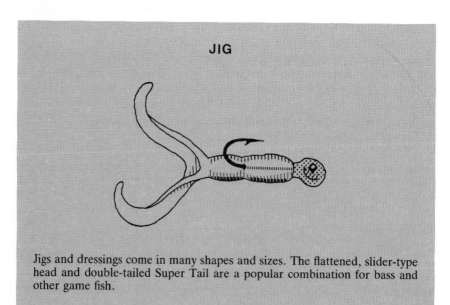

JIG

Jigs and dressings come in many shapes and sizes. The flattened, slider-type head and double-tailed Super Tail are a popular combination for bass and other game fish.

your rod tip so the bait rises and falls repeatedly, bobbing on and then off the lake bottom.

About 90% of the time, bass will hit a grub on the fall. The only indication of the strike will be a very slight movement at the point where the line enters the water. The hook should be immediately set.

Grub fishing is especially effective for vertically jigging bridge pilings or deep structure such as rockpiles or sunken depressions or points. Jigging is productive all season long if done properly.

The most popular sizes for bassing are 2- to 4-inch grubs on a ⅛- to ½-ounce leadhead jig, depending on what depth you are fishing.

The twister-tail-style grub is a very good choice because the tail has quite a bit of extra action. Because these baits are small, 6- to 12-pound line is the best choice. Because of the light line, most of the pros favor open-faced spinning reels and a light 5½- to 6-foot spinning rod, rather than heavy bait-casting equipment.

The Jig 'n' Pig combination so popular today with bass fishermen is simply a dressed-up version of a type of jig used for both stripers and sea trout for many years. It is an especially good lure for taking big fish, because it can be dropped quietly into very heavy cover where big bass are often found. The most popular sizes are ⅜-ounce and ½-ounce jigs with pork-rind dressings.

Surface Baits

The old standby top-water plug provides exciting fishing, primarily in shallow water. Slowly worked across the surface, top-water plugs can be literally knocked out of the water by Old Ironjaw. They can be used with bait-casting or spinning gear. Popular top-water plugs include the Jitterbug, Hula Popper, and Zara Spook.

Spoons

Both standard and weedless spoons are deadly baits for taking large-mouth. Jigging spoons over deep-water structure is a popular technique on southern reservoirs, while on natural lakes weedless spoons like the Johnson Silver Minnow are very effective when worked around and through heavy cover, especially weeds and lily pads. A good trick is to add a twister tail or pork-rind strip to the hook of a Johnson spoon for added action.

A very productive technique is skittering a spoon over milfoil or pads.

JOHNSON SPOON

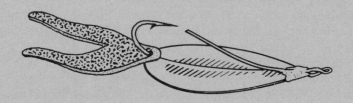

Skittering a Johnson spoon with pork-rind or plastic dressing across lily pads and other vegetation can produce violent strikes from largemouth bass and northern pike.

SKITTERING A SPOON OVER SURFACE WEEDS

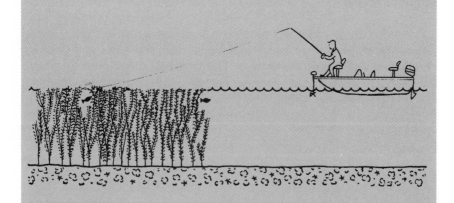

By holding your rod tip high, you can retrieve a weedless spoon over the top of heavy vegetation. Skittering offers very exciting fishing as bass explode through the weeds to take the spoon.

This involves a steady retrieve holding the rod tip high, so the spoon skitters over the top of the vegetation.

Rod and Reel Selection

A properly equipped bass fisherman should have a light-action rod, plus a stiff rod. The light-action rod should be used when fishing with grubs or under tough circumstances when the use of light line and small baits is required.

Bait-casting and spinning tackle each have their advantages. Just be sure to use quality brand-name gear; nothing is more disappointing than losing a big fish because of poorly made discount equipment.

Most bass fishermen use different line sizes depending on the fishing situation. Your light rod should have 4-, 6-, or 8-pound test line, while standard bass tackle usually means using 12- to 20-pound line. If you are fishing in heavy cover, you need strong line to pull that trophy out of there!

For fishing heavy cover a special rod called a "flippin' stick" has been developed. This very stiff, 7½- to 8½-foot rod for a level-wind (bait casting type) reel is ideal for flipping underhand casts with jigs and worms into pockets in snag-filled waters.

Boats and Equipment

Modern bass boats today are equipped with a trolling motor, depthfinder, and other electronic gear designed with one thing in mind: *fishing!*

However, even if your idea of a fishing boat is a 10-foot aluminum johnboat, a trolling motor is an extremely valuable tool. It allows you to maneuver silently from spot to spot; and motoring is a heck of a lot easier than rowing. A portable depthfinder can also be added to any boat so the angler can read bottom structure. This is a real necessity if you plan to fish anywhere other than the shoreline. Learning to read the various signals on the depthfinder takes practice, but eventually the angler can determine where there are underwater weedbeds, stumps, rockpiles, dropoffs, and other structures. Therefore, the depthfinder is an invaluable aid to the serious fisherman.

Today the serious angler can choose from a variety of types of depthfinders: flashers, liquid crystal readouts (LCR's), or graph units are available in a wide range of prices. Which unit is right for you will depend on your boat style and the types of fishing you'll be doing.

Modern bass boats, equipped with elevated seats, depth finders, electric trolling motor and aerated live-wells are designed with fishing in mind. Pictured below is the author with a well-equipped bass boat fishing a shallow bay in early spring.

Basic Bassing Tips

Keep your lure where the fish are. You should fish parallel rather than perpendicular to fallen trees, logs, weedlines, and undercut banks. That way the entire retrieve is around the cover, rather than only the first few feet.

When catching fish, stay snagged. Never unsnag a lure that's hung up if it means spooking fish. Let me give an example. You are working a spinnerbait through fallen trees, and in a few minutes you've taken two nice bass. Your next cast gets hung on a branch. Rather than going in with the boat and spooking the remaining fish, put that rod down and continue to fish with your spare until you're satisfied that the area has been thoroughly fished. Then retrieve your snagged lure.

Check your line for frays. Fishing in heavy cover will damage your line, and it should be re-tied often in the course of the day.

Keep equipment and lures handy. Valuable fishing time is lost every time you fumble around the boat looking for pliers, spare baits, snap swivels, *etc.*

Fish coves outside-in. Work your way into quiet coves rather than blasting in with your boat to fish the inside shoreline. Fish the outside first, and work your way in.

Be quiet and careful in your approach. Although voices don't seem to frighten bass, other noises do—banging oars, dropping tackleboxes or pliers. So try the silent approach for better results.

Fish the shaded side first. Bass have fixed pupils and are extremely sensitive to bright sunlight. Regardless of the type of cover, cast to the shaded side on your first try.

Avoid waves. When a strong wind blows up, especially in shallow water, shut down your fishing and try to find sheltered water.

Find the pattern and then stick with it. You're on a strange lake, and by analyzing the factors we've discussed earlier, you decide that the bass should be on weedlines in 10 to 15 feet of water. You check a couple of these weedlines and find fish. When you are sure of the pattern, stay with it. Concentrate all of your efforts on similar weedlines until the bass stop hitting. If bass are found on one weedline, pattern fishing tells you they will be found also on others.

Release bass gently and quickly. Hold a bass by the bottom jaw, quickly take it off the hook, and if you are going to release it, do so promptly. Never throw a fish back in the lake; release it gently.

This chapter started with an explanation of the various factors to analyze when seeking out the elusive largemouth. We have also discussed types of structure and cover as well as basic bass lures. Applying this information will definitely improve your bass fishing. However, never forget that each fishing trip should be a learning experience. Many pro anglers keep a diary, recording valuable information such as depth at which fish were caught, time of day, water temperature, lures that were productive, *etc.* This information is very useful, even when you are on a different body of water. Often successful techniques from previous trips can be used again if you learned what was done correctly the first time.

So apply what you've learned, keep casting, and remember that the ultimate thrill in bass fishing is not just catching fish but being skilled enough to locate them consistently.

2/Tackle, Tips, and Techniques for Smallmouth Bass

by Todd Swainbank

One of the most highly prized game fish found in North America is the smallmouth bass. The bronzeback or brownie, as smallmouth are called by legions of admirers from coast to coast, is a triple treat to anglers.

First, smallmouth bass are extremely tasty table fare. This bass's preference for cool, clear, and clean water contributes to a firm and sweet-tasting flesh. Next, the smallmouth's reputation as a battling and acrobatic sportfish cannot be denied. These fish, when hooked on light tackle, often amaze anglers with their stamina. Sometimes smaller specimens will fool even experienced anglers into thinking they've hooked a lunker, because they fight so hard. Compared to their slower but heavier cousins, the largemouth bass, bronzebacks are truly longwinded, rock-hard, battle-ready middleweights. Lastly, lunker smallmouths (over 4 pounds), as is true of most large specimens of freshwater game fish, are often extremely wary and offer the serious angler a worthy challenge. Any angler who is consistently successful in taking smallmouths on artificial lures is likely to be very versatile.

Where Are They Found?

Originally the range of the smallmouth bass was restricted to eastern-central North America. Now, fortunately for anglers everywhere, the range has been expanded through the western states to California, as well as south into Alabama.

Life History and Spawning Habits

Smallmouth bass are spring spawners throughout most of their range. Spawning may occur as late as the end of June in southern Canada and as early as April near the southern limit of their range in Alabama. The spawning ritual, which I have witnessed many times in Cayuga Lake in Ithaca, New York, usually takes place when spring water temperatures reach 60 degrees.

Smallmouth bass, and their cousins the largemouth and spotted bass, are members of the sunfish family, and the spawning habits of all these species involve the digging of a shallow nest by the male. The smallmouth usually selects a nest site with a firm, gravel-covered bottom, often very near a protecting bank, log, or boulder in shallow water. The completed nest, which is saucer shaped and 2 to 3 feet in diameter, is easily observed by watchful anglers. Digging is accomplished by vigorous use of mouth, fins, and tail. The male then brings one or more females to the nest for spawning. The eggs stick to the bottom of the nest and are closely and aggressively guarded by the male. Eggs hatch a few days after they are laid, and the tiny bass, called fry, quickly leave the nest to begin feeding on their own.

Growth rates depend on many factors such as forage quality and quantity and the length of the high-metabolism growing season. Growth rates in many large mid-southern reservoirs are better than in colder and often less fertile northern waters. Average growth rates for typical northern waters might approximate the following: one year old, 3½ to 4 inches; two years, 5½ to 6½ inches; three years, 8 to 9 inches; four years, 10 to 11 inches; five years, 12½ to 13½ inches; six years, 13½ to 14 inches; seven years, 15 to 16½ inches.*

As with most fish, very few smallmouth bass fry survive the many hazards of early life to become adults. A true lunker smallmouth of over 20 inches and 4 pounds in weight could be as much as eight to ten years old, and such a fish would be a trophy throughout most of the smallmouth's geographic range.

The world record** weighed a tremendous 11 pounds, 15 ounces and was caught in one of the most famous smallmouth lakes in the country, Dale Hollow Lake in Kentucky. It was caught July 9, 1955, by David L. Hayes.

*K. Lagler, *Freshwater Fishery Biology* (Dubuque, Iowa: Wm. Brown Co.), p. 51.
**"Fish of the month; The Smallmouth Bass," *Fishing Facts Magazine* (July 1976), p. 100.

Habitats Preferred by Smallmouth

The smallmouth bass is an adaptable species that thrives best in rivers and lakes that offer gravel, rock, or other firm bottoms and fairly clear, clean, and cool water. The bodies of water that I primarily fish for small-mouth bass can be divided into two types of lakes.

The first type is termed an *oligotrophic* lake. The term refers to the youngest geological stage in the life of a lake. Oligotrophic waters are characterized by relatively small amounts of plant life and a fairly small number of pounds of fish-per-acre yield. Lakes of this type are usually very large and very deep, with clear, clean water. These lakes are relatively infertile, with clean, rocky bottoms. Such lakes very often are populated with many trout and salmon species and are found in the areas of the country that underwent intense glaciation—for example Lake George, Lake Ontario, and the Finger Lakes of New York's southern tier. My home lake is Cayuga; it is 40 miles long with an average depth of 175 feet and a maximum depth of 435 feet. Cayuga and nearby Seneca Lake, with a maximum depth of 618 feet, are, with the exception of the Great Lakes, the two deepest lakes east of the Rocky Mountains.

The second kind of lake is a more common type found across the country. These lakes are also large but fairly shallow and usually discolored. They are characterized by much higher concentrations of plant life and higher yields of pounds of fish per acre. They are *mesotrophic* lakes and contain large numbers and species of warm-water game fish such as walleye pike, largemouth bass, and northern pike, plus many panfish and rough-fish species (e.g., carp, suckers).

Examples of mesotrophic lakes that I regularly fish are Oneida Lake and the Inland Sea, Lake Champlain, both found in New York State. Oneida is the largest lake completely within the borders of the state and covers over 50,000 acres with a maximum depth of only 55 feet. Over half the lake is less than 35 feet deep.

Champlain is more like an ocean, over 100 miles long and up to 12 miles wide, forming about two thirds of the New York–Vermont border. Although Champlain has some *very* deep stretches (300–400 feet), they are many miles from the areas I fish. (A lake of this size actually exhibits many different environments.) The areas I fish are primarily bays and coves with less than 40-foot depths.

Large lakes offer the angler a number of benefits that smaller water bodies do not. First, during the spring of the year when smallmouths are migrating to spawn, very large schools will concentrate on the prime spawning areas. Finding the spawning grounds on large lakes can take some time and effort but will reward the angler with potentially tremendous success. Next, big lakes offer a higher potential for *consistently* producing large numbers of lunker-sized fish.

Fishing the big lakes regularly seems to improve an angler's skill in other aspects of fishing. Big lakes, such as the ones mentioned, can be very dangerous, demanding equipment and nautical skills superior to those needed by anglers who fish small sheltered streams, rivers, or lakes.

An angler who fishes big lakes regularly finds it easy to locate fish quickly when fishing a smaller, unknown lake or river, because he has been exposed to many different situations. The reverse is not always true for the fisherman who spends most of his time on smaller bodies of water. The fisherman used to small lakes may have considerable difficulty locating fish on lakes of the size that I speak of.

Outfitting for Big-Lake Bassin'

The equipment available to the bass fisherman of today is considerably more diverse than that which was available fifteen years ago. The boom in the popularity of bass, together with the formation of major sportsmen's organizations like the Bass Anglers Sportsman Society (B.A.S.S.) and the advent of big-money tournaments, have encouraged tremendous product expansion, experimentation, research, and development geared primarily to the bass fisherman.

The major components of what is considered today to be standard equipment on a boat rigged for serious big-lake bass fishing in our part of the country would be somewhat as follows:

Bass Boat. It should be at least 15 feet long with a wide beam; should possess one (or more) adjustable swiveling pedestal fishing seat; and should be rated for at least a 40-H.P. outboard motor. The hull design would probably be semi-vee or trihull with aluminum or fiberglass construction and upright flotation. All required safety equipment would be included.

The boat I used for many years was an aluminum 16½-foot Sea Nymph Fishing Machine with two aerated live wells, two raised-deck pedestal seats, a 7-foot long rod-and-tackle locker, and a steering console. Rated to 70 H.P., the boat handled guide parties of up to three people comfortably and safely.

Outboard Motors. Although foreign imports are showing up more and more, I and most of my fishing friends still prefer motors produced by the big three: Johnson, Evinrude, and Mercury. I use an electric-start 60-H.P.

Evinrude with power tilt (to make shallow water less hazardous). Mounted beside that, a 5-H.P. Evinrude motor comes in handy for trolling and as an emergency spare.

Electric Motor. An electric motor, whether bow- or stern mounted, enables silent and easy maneuvering of the boat, and once one has been used, most anglers will want to continue using it. The motor should be a variable-speed unit which is powerful enough to hold the boat in position against a breeze.

I favor a foot-controlled, bow-mounted motor that can be operated easily while I'm fishing. This keeps my hands free for what they do best and enjoy most—catching fish! For silently maneuvering the boat around fishy-looking cover and structure, your motor, especially when used in conjunction with a depth sounder, is equipment whose importance cannot be emphasized too much.

Depth Sounders. For pinpointing schools of fish, locating underwater structure, and aiding navigation, a "sonar" is a must. It should be operable at fairly high boat speed and give bright, clear signals. Placement and mounting technique depends on type of boat material and the manufacturer's operating instructions.

The transducer for my unit is mounted directly into the water off the transom via a homemade aluminum bracket. This produces very good slow- to medium-speed signals, although it requires periodic cleaning of algae buildups when the boat is left in the water for long periods.

Most bass anglers favor Humminbird or Lowrance units, mounted on the steering console so they may be easily read while operating the boat. The unit can be reversed so it can be read while sitting on the front pedestal seat operating the electric motor.

Graph units and the newer LCR's are very popular depthfinders. It is best to research the specifics of electronics through manufacturer's brochures to determine which unit will be best suited to your craft and the type of fishing you'll be doing.

Electric Trolling Motor Battery. The constant draining and re-charging of the battery used to power the electric trolling motor will ruin a typical car battery. Get a special deep cycle battery made by Gould, Sears, or others, and your fishing will be much happier. Get a good battery charger also. Bass Pro Shops offers a great catalog of special-interest items to bass anglers.

Marker Buoys. When a school of fish or a particularly good-looking structure is found on the depth sounder, I throw over marker buoys to mark off the area and then begin a systematic fan-casting approach to effectively fish the spot (see illustrations in Chapter 1).

Buoys are particularly effective to use when you need pinpoint boat control, such as in marking sudden dropoffs or sunken islands, especially on windy days. The angler can make a trolling or casting pass and easily return to the exact spot where fish were caught. Very often, especially in midsummer on clear lakes, smallmouths will be tightly grouped in small areas in deep water. If these small schools aren't pinpointed accurately by using the depth sounder and marker buoys, a lot of time can be wasted.

Markers also come in handy when trolling, letting me make repeated passes exactly where I took a fish. Throw them to one side of a school of fish so they won't be spooked. My markers are high-visibility yellow and have 70 feet of line attached to a 6-ounce lead weight. Markers can be easily made from empty plastic bottles or something similar.

Topographical Maps. Every angler who fishes big lakes should purchase the "topo" maps available for the lake in question. Maps are valuable navigational aids and provide enough detailed information so an angler can, by using landmarks and a depth sounder, check the more interesting structures and cover in short order. The cast-for-cash tournament pros wouldn't think of venturing out for tournament practice days without the most detailed maps they can find. Often a skilled angler used to reading topo maps can, with a surprising degree of accuracy, pinpoint hotspots without ever having been on the lake.

Maps of nearby lakes are occasionally found in tackle stores or outdoor-sports stores. The best source of information is the U.S. Geological Survey, Box 25286, Federal Center, Denver, Colorado 80225 (303-236-7477).

Large Landing Net. We are very fortunate in the Northeast to have lakes that are populated by a number of large game-fish species. Walleyes, northerns, muskies, big trout and salmon inhabit many waters with smallmouth bass. Although even large bass can be fairly easily landed by using the paralyzing lower-jaw grip or small nets, I prefer to carry one of the large nets favored by pike anglers. I may go out fishing with a 20-inch smallmouth bass on my mind, but if a 40-inch pike decides to pay a visit I want to be prepared to receive him in proper style. A big net, within easy reach and not buried under a pile of tackle, is worth anything to the angler who is fighting the fish of a lifetime, especially if he is alone in the boat.

Pliers. Smallmouth bass are a hardy species and can be released unharmed even after fairly rough handling. I prefer to make the release of a fish as easy on both of us as possible. Pliers speed up the process of unhooking a well-hooked fish, especially in cold weather. I find needlenose pliers work best.

Anchor Mate. This clever invention for anchor-line storage and retrieval is a blessing to the deep-water jig fisherman. (Some are even made that automatically retrieve the anchor by battery power.) Mine is manually operated by a crank retriever. It saves my back from the strain of handlining an anchor up from deep water and is a less dangerous method of anchor retrieval when you're in rough water. Also on cold days, the Anchor Mate is a most welcome accessory, because it lets you take in your anchor without handling the cold, wet line.

For anchors I have an 18-pound typical double-prong naval type that grabs well on uneven bottoms and on windy days in deep water. I use a smaller 15-pound mushroom anchor when maintaining boat position is less critical or when the boat is over soft bottoms. I have at least 60 feet of nylon cord for use on each anchor.

Rod Holders. I don't often troll for smallmouth bass, but sometimes it can be a very productive technique. The rod holders preferred by anyone who trolls regularly have to be heavy duty, and they must secure the rod firmly and attach to the boat tightly. The best I've used are Down-Easters, both the D10 and double-locking S10 version. They release quickly with a firm upward pull of the rod when you're setting the hook on a striking fish and can be tightened very securely against the boat's gunnels. I wouldn't trust my rod to dime-store-quality holders.

Log Book. Even anglers blessed with a good memory should keep a log book to record important data that might aid them on future trips. Information such as weather conditions, water temperature, locations, and lures that produced action, *etc.* can be valuable in producing a better understanding of the factors governing success on each body of water.

Rainsuit. Nothing ruins a day's fishing like getting soaked in a rainstorm. An easily rolled, two-piece Gore-Tex rainsuit can be stored in the boat until needed. It should be big enough to fit over a fully clothed angler.

Tackle to Tackle Smallmouths

With all the numerous improvements each year in rods, reels, and lines, it can be difficult to stay abreast of the best equipment. Suffice it to say that standard equipment for smallmouth tackle leaves considerable room for personal preference. Many bass fishermen have a number of matched rods and reels rigged and ready in the boat to be prepared for any situation. This saves time when different lures and techniques are called for.

The Jig Outfit. About 75% of my smallmouth fishing is done with one rod. A good spinning jig rod should be either high-quality fiberglass or graphite and have a straight cork handle without a fixed reel seat. I mount the reel on the rod using black electrician's tape; this makes a secure, comfortable, and warm grip.

My favorite jig rod is a two-piece, light-action custom rod made from

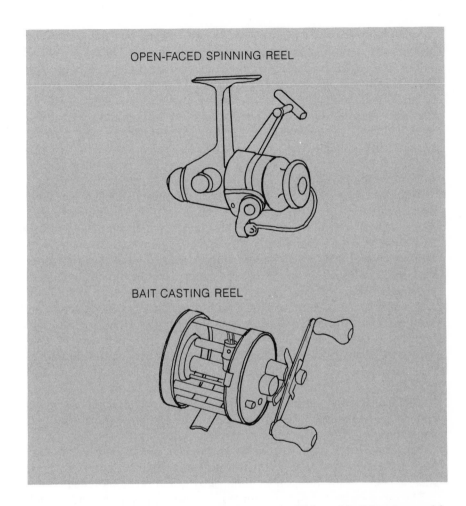

OPEN-FACED SPINNING REEL

BAIT CASTING REEL

an Eagle Claw Blue Diamond graphite blank. This rod is 7 feet long with Lews single-foot Fuji speed guides and is perfect for throwing the ⅛- to ¼-ounce jigs I use. Graphite, with its superior sensitivity to fiberglass, makes an ideal rod to feel the often subtle taps associated with jig fishing. Sensitivity is a *must* in jig fishing.

Many high-quality light spinning reels are available from Daiwa, Shimano, and others. Unfortunately the reels I use are no longer available. The original, Swedish-made and Zebco-imported, Cardinal 3 and the others in that series were generally acknowledged as the finest spinning reels obtainable, and although these reels have been unavailable for many years, the number of them still in service with serious anglers nationwide is noteworthy.

Suitable reels should offer a fast 5:1 gear ratio and a quickly reached and, ideally, *rear-mounted* drag.

The least expensive but most important component of a jig outfit is the line. A high-visibility line is required so that those often subtle taps can be easily seen and acted upon by a line-watching angler. An invisible line that can't easily be seen by the angler is useless in jig fishing. Many times when guiding I've seen clients get strikes that they never knew they had because they either weren't paying attention or simply couldn't see their line clearly. Berkley High VIS and Stren in 4- to 8-pound test are very well suited for jig fishing.

Multiple-Use Outfit. This outfit should be able to handle just about everything an angler faces in smallmouth fishing. A rod-and-reel combination of this type can be used for fishing larger, more water-resistant baits like crankbaits and can handle the heavier jigging spoons such as the Mannolure and Slabspoon. This combination can also be used for trolling baits such as Rapalas and Rebels and other baits that come through the water easily.

Again I favor a 7-foot rod, now with a medium-fast taper action and fixed-reel seat. Mine is a Shakespeare Purist with Carbaloy guides. The reel should be able to handle 8- to 10-pound test line, and two spools will be needed if any trolling is to be done. Berkley High Vis and Stren both are excellent lines for this multipurpose outfit and are also suitable for light trolling.

The Bait-Casting Outfit. Although the casting combination has limited application in the fishing I do, I've used some that were sporty, fast, and enjoyable.

The bait-casting outfit should be lightweight and built to handle light lines and small lures. This outfit will probably see most action in tossing small crankbaits around points, cliffs, shoals, and other shoreline cover.

The rod should be a light-action graphite with a pistol grip and a length between 5 and 6 feet. Mine is a Bass Pro Shops Graphite 96 light-action 5½ footer. The reel should be one of the smaller high-speed, narrow-spool reels available. The Shimano Bantam and the smaller Daiwas are excellent choices.

A high-visibility line isn't required for crankbait fishing, since the strikes are almost always obvious rod-tip benders. Garcia Royal Bonnyl in brown is a good choice in discolored or neutral-colored water. The more invisible lines are well suited to crankbait fishing.

Lures and How to Choose Them. Literally thousands of lures are made in this country and overseas. The investment in lures by avid anglers often exceeds $500, usually with mixed results. Many anglers also seek out lures

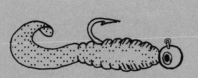

The most productive lures I've found for smallmouth bass are the small Mister Twister grubs fished on ⅛-ounce and ¼-ounce jigheads. These lures are also deadly on walleyes.

with magical powers that out-produce all others at all times. Unfortunately magic lures don't exist. The only magic in fishing is in the fisherman.

A representative selection of smallmouth lures that cover most situations would include lures in the following six categories:

1. *Leadhead jigs* in ⅛-ounce and ¼-ounce weights made with size-1 and 1/0 Eagle Claw 575 hooks for use with 3- and 4-inch plastic Mister Twister grubs, Super Tails, *etc.* Colors for plastic baits should include chartreuse, blue, black, brown, purple, yellow, and white.

The best shape of the jig is a matter of opinion; they *all* get snagged on the bottom, especially if you are fishing them right. Charlie Brewer's Slider Heads, stand-up heads, and round-ball heads are my favorites.

I might add that anyone who fishes a lot of jigs properly is going to lose a lot of jigs. A mold for pouring your own lead jigs can save a lot of money.

The line is always tied *directly* to the hookeye of the jig. Smallmouth bass don't have the line-cutting teeth that pike possess, and a simple improved clinch knot is all that's needed. (See Figure 8, Chapter 6.) This group of lures is among the most consistent producers of smallmouths that exists.

2. *Small crankbaits.* Smallmouth bass show a definite preference for small baits. Small crankbaits are extremely effective when bass are in shallow rocky areas and actively feeding. These baits should be either tied directly to the line or used with a small snap that doesn't impede the action of the lure.

Crankbaits that fail to run true through the water can be correctly tuned by adjusting the line eye of the lure with a pair of needlenose pliers. The eye should be aligned vertically and placed in the center of the lip or nose of the lure to get proper action.

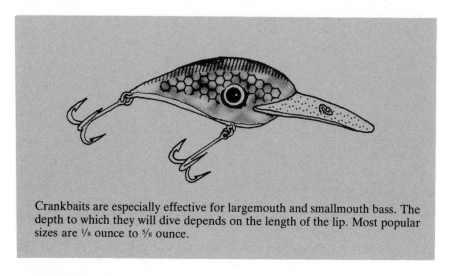

Crankbaits are especially effective for largemouth and smallmouth bass. The depth to which they will dive depends on the length of the lip. Most popular sizes are ⅛ ounce to ⅝ ounce.

An excellent small crankbait selection would include lures on the following list:

Natural Ike ¼ ounce and ⅛ ounce by Lazy Ike
Tiny Deep N ⅛ ounce by Bill Norman
Deep Baby N ¼ ounce and Reflect N by Norman
Bagley's Honeybee ¼ ounce by Bagley Baits
Small Mudbugs ¼ ounce by Arbogast
Deep Piglet ⅛ ounce by Manns Baits
Teeny R ⅛ ounce by Rebel
Shallow R ⅛ ounce by Rebel
Humpback Rattler by Rebel
Floating Rapala size 5, 7, 9, 11
Countdown Rapala size 5, 7, 9
Broken back Rapala size 9

3. *Larger and deeper diving crankbaits*. The larger baits are very effective for fishing deeper waters and for getting down along the edge of a weedline. They also work well when fast retrieved so the lip of the lure bumps and grinds on a rocky bottom. This sends out easily located sounds to nearby fish and prompts them to investigate, especially in discolored water.

A good selection of these baits would include lures on the following list:

Rapala Fat Rap size 5
Rebel Super R
Rebel Deep Wee R
Mann's Deep Pig
Bomber Model A
Bomber Water Dog

Original Bomber
Norman Super Scooper
Bagley's Divin' B
Bagley's Killer B II
Medium Size Natural Ike
Medium Size Mud Bugs
Big O Cordell
Deep Big O Cordell
Deep Mini R Rebel

4. *Small spinnerbaits.* Smaller safety-pin-style, single-hook spinnerbaits can be devastating on bass around shallow shoreline cover and flutter-fished around pilings, weedlines and riprap. Because they sink more slowly than jigs, they can be very effective in discolored water where visibility is shortened.

Most anglers tie these lures directly to the line and dress the hook with a small plastic twister-type grub or pork strip.

A good selection of these lures would include ones from the following list:

Mini Rats $1/16$ ounce, $1/8$ ounce by Bass Pro Shops
Shannon Super Twin $1/4$ ounce
Shannon Twin Spin $1/4$ ounce
Squirmin' Worm $1/8$ ounce, $1/4$ ounce by Bass Pro Shops
Stump Jumper $1/8$ ounce
Small Hustler Buzz Bug $1/4$ ounce
Small Bush Hogs $1/4$ ounce

5. *Structure spoons and tail-spinners.* These lures are especially effective when bass have retreated to deep water dropoffs in midsummer to early fall or when fishing in rough water or heavy current. They can be cast long distances and jigged back or yoyoed vertically under the boat for suspended fish. Lures should be tied directly with a high-visibility line.

A good selection would include lures from the following list:

Mannolure $1/2$ ounce by Mann's Baits
Swedish Pimple $3/8$ ounce, $1/2$ ounce
Hopkins Shorty $1/2$ ounce
Little George $1/4$ ounce, $3/8$ ounce by Mann's Baits
Bomber Slab Spoon $1/2$ ounce

6. *Trolling lures.* Trolling can be very effective on smallmouths, especially when checking out large areas at specified depths. Lures can be trolled as they are or weighted with sinkers ahead of them to attain a deeper run.

An angler seriously interested in trolling for bass should purchase a non-stretch monofilament line such as Buck Perry's No Bo and a stiffer rod than the one described as the multipurpose outfit.

A good trolling-lure selection would include lures on the following list:
Rapala Floating size 9, 11
Rapala Countdown 9, 11
Rapala Brokenback 11
Rebel D1000 Series Spoon Bill Diver
Rebel 1000 Series Brokenback F
Buck's Spoon Plugs, size 500–100
Heddon Clatter Tad
Flatfish Helin
Twin Minnow
Bomber Waterdog

Locating Seasonal Bass Patterns on Different Lake Types

A good way to learn more about the habits and movements of small-mouth bass is by comparing bass behavior in two different lakes (one oligotrophic and the other mesotrophic) and at different times of the year. In this way the angler can become more aware of the Big Picture involved in locating those relatively small "honey holes" where bass will concentrate in large numbers. More important he will understand why the fish move as they do.

May 1–June 30

This is the favorite time of the year for the bass angler. Smallmouths will be found grouped in large numbers in shallow water and are easily caught at this time. Fishing can be fast and furious, and multiple-lunker potential is excellent.

Pre-season and Early-Season Patterns for Oneida and Other Shallow Lakes. Shallow Oneida Lake warms faster than the deep Finger Lakes of New York State. This is an extremely important fact. Spring smallmouth fishing is excellent in lakes similar to Oneida at least two weeks earlier than in the deeper and colder Finger Lakes.

Tributary streams and rivers are often several degrees warmer than their receiving waters in early spring. The largest and most fishable tributary to Oneida Lake is the Oneida River, located at the western end of the lake. The river offers warmer water, outstanding spawning and feeding habitat,

The author with a chunky Oneida River smallmouth taken on a small Norman crankbait.

and extensive shoreline cover such as boat docks, boat houses, bridge abutments and riprap. The extensive riprap areas draw tremendous concentrations of fish in May and early June. Oneida Lake is also an outstanding walleye fishery. During the spring this species gets almost all the attention of fishermen. It is a rarity to encounter another bass angler enjoying preseason, catch-and-release sport in the river. Consistent large catches of 2- to 4-pound fish can be expected, and an occasional 5-pounder is also caught. Although New York State bass season doesn't open until mid-June, a bass angler interested in *sport* can find it in and around major lake tributaries in the spring.

We will make three or four trips to Oneida starting around May 1 when water temperature hovers around 50 degrees. The cold waters make the bass slower and more sluggish than in midsummer. Jigs are by far the most effective lures at this time. As the summer approaches and waters warm, spinnerbaits and crankbaits become effective.

Pre-season and Early-Season Patterns for Cayuga Lake and Other Deep Lakes. Though early May finds Cayuga Lake pressured by trout and salmon anglers, little pre-season attention is given the battling bronzeback. Although Cayuga has much less extensive shoal areas and smaller tributaries than Oneida Lake, similar patterns can be found. Excellent pre-season smallmouth fishing is usually two weeks later than in Oneida Lake due to colder water.

Tributaries such as Fall Creek, Six Mile Creek, Cayuga Inlet, Taughannock Creek, and Salmon Creek all get smallmouth runs, with fish seeking gravel spawning grounds. These tributaries can be easily fished from shore, and they contain large numbers of fish. They are found on the southern end of the lake. Productive shallow-lake shoal areas exist on the north and south ends of the lake.

Cayuga Lake smallmouths, especially lunker specimens, often spawn on the limited shoal areas available. Large schools of bass spread out over the shoals in mid-May and concentrate around good shoreline cover, primarily sunken boulders, docks, pilings, and rock cribs. A jig cast next to cover and allowed to flutter down will often be intercepted by a striking smallmouth. By the end of May and into June small crankbaits (⅛ to ¼ ounces) fished on light lines (6-pound test) are very effective. The only time I ever caught two bass on one cast came in June on a small crankbait in Cayuga.

July 1–September 30

Mid-Season Patterns on Oneida and Other Shallow Lakes. By early July the majority of the smallmouth bass that entered the river have deserted the area for suitable sites in the lake. Water temperature in the river will rise well over 70 degrees in midsummer, and although there are always a few bass in the river, most of them retreat to deeper, cooler waters. There is one very notable exception to this migration, however. The Oneida River has a lock system whereby boaters can travel to Cross Lake and Lake Ontario. Many spring-run bass pass through these locks in May and remain above them throughout the season. Catching a lunker there is rare, but tremendous angling potential exists for fish in the 12- to 16-inch range. The bass above the lock are usually long and lean and jump repeatedly when hooked. (River bass, wherever I've caught them, always seem to outjump their lake counterparts.)

The river water has a brownish tint, and small brightly colored crankbaits and small spinnerbaits are devastating on the river bass. The bass above the lock concentrate around the obvious shoreline cover like docks, cribs, and rockpiles, showing preference for cover that is well shaded from the midday sun.

For the angler searching the main lake, the extensive midlake shoal area called Shakleton Shoals is a well-known smallmouth spot, offering good deep-water rock structure. Trolling with Rapalas and jigging are both productive there.

Submerged rock bars near islands and the island dropoffs are good midsummer smallmouth producers. Occasionally on Oneida in midsummer an oxygen deficiency will exist when many rough fish and panfish can be observed washed up dead on the shore. With a depth sounder, an angler often can find schools of suspended fish near the surface. If only deep-water fishing tactics are used, these fish will be missed. Spinnerbaits and crankbaits work well on shallow suspended fish.

Mid-Season Patterns on Cayuga and Other Deep Lakes. This is traditionally the toughest time of the year on the clear Finger Lakes. A number of very difficult situations face the angler.

For a few weeks each year in late June and early July, swarms of alewifes (sawbellies) move into shallow water to spawn. Game fish such as bass gorge themselves on these easily caught forage fish, and with so much food available at this time, catching smallmouths can be extremely difficult, though small silver crankbaits and silver Rapalas *sometimes* work well. By Mid-July the majority of smallmouth bass, especially larger ones, have deserted the quickly warming tributaries and shallow shoals. Shallow-water fishing tapers off when temperatures pass 65 degrees.

Periodic shallow-water fish movements occur throughout the summer but are limited usually to the hours around dawn and dusk and to times of stormy skies and rough water conditions. Night fishing can be productive, as smallmouths move into the shallows under the protective cloak of darkness to feed. Spinnerbaits and Rapalas are excellent baits for night fishing, and so are small surface plugs. Outside edges of weedlines bordering deeper water, fished with the deeper diving crankbaits, can yield good catches.

During daylight hours on bright, sunny, calm days, smallmouths will be *very* deep. Occasionally, some are caught by downrigger trout fishermen trolling depths greater than 60 feet. Deep-water structure fishing is the key to success at such times. Underwater points extending into deep water and sharp dropoffs in 20- to 60-foot depths get most of my attention. I often spend considerable time cruising and watching the depth sounder for flashes of suspended fish or particularly good looking structure.

The heavier spoons and tail-spinners can be very effective for these deep-water bass. Many bass anglers never fish deeper than 15-foot depths, but in the Finger Lakes to stay on smallmouth bass consistently an angler has to be versatile. The two biggest smallmouth bass I caught in Cayuga one year were in 55 feet of water suspended along an even deeper dropoff. Both fish were over 4½ pounds, and I lost two more that were probably over 5 pounds. The Mannolure is my favorite lure for deep-water jigging. Unlike the plastic twister jigs, which require almost no rod action to catch fish, the jigging spoons work best with vigorous rod-pumping motions. The development of a sensitive touch is definitely helpful when fishing down that deep.

October 1–November 15

Late-Season Patterns on Oneida and Other Shallow Lakes. As lake temperatures drop, smallmouths again group up and approach the shallows for extended feeding forays. Visible shoreline cover becomes productive once again as smallmouths, seemingly sensing the approach of winter, go on their last feeding binge of the season. It was in early October on Lake Champlain that Bill Butler and I caught over a hundred smallmouths in six hours on crankbaits along rock cliffs and rubble banks in shallow 1- to 4-foot depths. Fall fishing can be *fantastic,* and on many lakes solitude is almost guaranteed at that time of year.

Shallow-water migrations occur dramatically in lakes like Oneida and Champlain in the fall. When water temperatures fall to the 55- to 65-degree range, and if the water is somewhat discolored, smallmouths will spend extended periods feeding around shallow rocky shoals.

Before the water drops below 50 degrees, a productive technique is to use a small, deep-diving crankbait and a fast retrieve causing the lure to dig up the bottom and bounce off small rocks. This sends up small mud clouds, and the sounds and sights produced draw bass to investigate from quite a distance.

By mid-November smallmouth bass will often move to faster-breaking structure in deeper water. The deep edge of green weedlines can also be productive, and spinnerbaits and crankbaits retrieved slowly work well. After the water cools to below 50 degrees, the jig is once again the primary weapon in the bass angler's arsenal. Strikes will become very soft in cold water, much as they do in early spring.

Late-Season Patterns of Cayuga Lake and Other Deep Lakes. The fall feeding frenzy takes place on the Finger Lakes also, but because the water is often crystal clear, shallow-water movements occur usually on dark, rainy days when light penetration in the water is at a minimum.

Anglers will do best on bright, calm days in the 20- to 40-foot depth range. On darker days, 10- to 20-foot depths will be most productive. In October and November rainbow trout and smallmouth bass are often found in the same areas and depths, and trolling Rapalas can take outstanding mixed bags. At this time trolling becomes a major part of my fishing game plan. Plastic-grub jigs and jigging spoons are also very effective for fishing dropoffs and other deeper structures. Cruising the lake in search of the last green weedbeds can also be a shortcut to finding fish concentrations. In the fall, weeds die off and turn brown, but just as all deciduous tree leaves don't change color at the same time, neither do weedbeds. Baitfish and predator fish will often concentrate around the last green, oxygen-producing weedbeds. Bait-size, young-of-the year sawbellies occur in huge schools at this time and congregate around weedbeds for protection from predators. Trolling and spot casting with silver crankbaits to bass actively chasing sawbellies can be deadly. (Matching artificial lures to the primary forage is sometimes as important to the lake bass fisherman as is matching the hatch to the stream fly angler.)

Fall is the most overlooked time of the year for fishing. Pleasure boaters and water skiers disappear when the weather cools. Fair-weather anglers desert the lakes for more comfortable pursuits. The veteran angler knows this is the time to grab his tackle, jump in his boat, and hightail it down the big blue highway. Solitude and success always await die-hard anglers.

Six of the Best Smallmouth Bass Spots I Have Found*

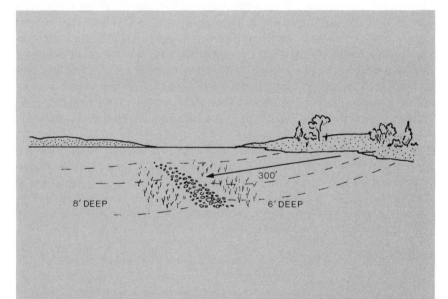

This illustration shows one of the most unusual and productive smallmouth spots I've ever found. It's in Lake Champlain. Because the shoreline markers keep changing, it is becoming harder and harder to find this spot.

How the cobblestone reef emerged so far from shore I'll never know. Maybe thousands of years ago a glacier deposited the cobblestone there, or maybe some hard-working fisherman built up the reef over the years.

Whatever the origin of the reef, we give thanks—it's a lunker hotspot! The reef is about 50 yards long bordered on both sides by extensive tobacco weedbeds. A downwind approach casting crankbaits parallel to the reef often produces smallmouths of trophy size. On overcast days the bass will move up on top of the reef to feed, and the area will be alive with rising and slashing bass and northern pike. I hope we can find this spot next time we go to Champlain!

---

*A variety of other game fish can be caught from typical bass cover and structures. Anglers interested in identifying potential hotspots for other species should refer to the section on Cover and Structure in Chapter 1, "Largemouth Bass Basics."

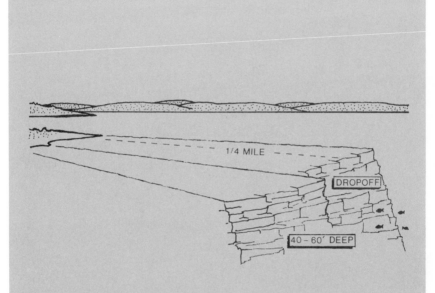

This is an illustration of one of my favorite deep-water-structure spots for smallmouth on Cayuga Lake. You'll notice that the dropoff to deep water is a long way from shore. This is the something special that makes this spot a smallmouth magnet. Cayuga Lake is *extremely* deep, and throughout most of the lake the main dropoffs are close to shore. This spot is one of the few exceptions. Smallmouths and other game fish seek out this ledge in midsummer under bright skies. On overcast or stormy days in summer, spring, or fall, fish are likely to be scattered over the top of this extensive shoal area on the inside of the dropoff.

I fish here mostly in midsummer. The first cast I ever made in this spot yielded a lunker 4-pounder caught on a Mannolure in about 50 feet of water! The key to success at this time of year is pinpoint boat control and a depth sounder. Bass will tend to school in tight groups along the stair-step projecting rock ledges along the dropoff. The heavier jigging spoons or trolling with lead-core line or a downrigger will produce the best results.

Occasionally, deep-water forage fish like smelt or sawbellies school near this dropoff. Once I was anchored on the spot when this happened; bait was chased right to the surface by smallmouths, and the action was fast and furious. Such spots often produce mixed bags of bass, trout, and pike. I *always* have big-fish fever when fishing deep-water structure such as this.

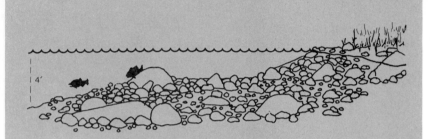

This illustration shows an outstanding early- to midseason smallmouth spot on Cayuga Lake. The rocky rubble provides excellent spawning grounds for bass, and the scattered boulders provide cover. This is the kind of spot I often guide inexperienced anglers to so they can learn the finer points of jig and crankbait fishing.

In May and June, and on overcast or stormy days in July, this kind of spot is always good for a few bass. Under bright sunlight, bass will hang *very* close to the boulders, and a jig allowed to flutter down along the shadowy side of the boulder often receives a jolting smash.

It was in this spot that I caught the only double of my fishing career: two bass on one cast with a small crankbait. This type of spot is also good at night in midsummer.

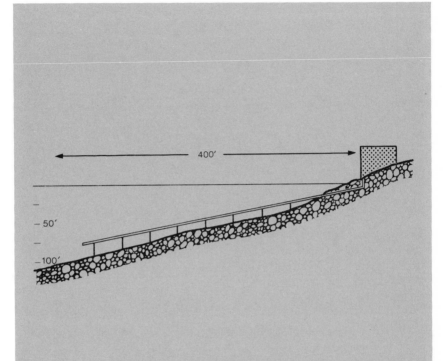

This illustration shows how *on occasion* the activities of engineers indirectly aid the angler.

Pictured is what the intake pipe of a water-treatment plant looks like. Game fish began schooling in this area shortly after the completion of the project. The pipe and supports offer cover from shallow to very deep water for a variety of game fish.

A depth sounder is needed to pinpoint such structures, and a variety of depths can be easily checked along the pipe's length with jigs and jigging spoons. This type of structure is a tackle graveyard. I once lost six jigs on six casts there, but the good fishing can make up for lost tackle in a hurry!

This type of spot always seems best for bass in the late summer to fall period. The fish seem to prefer 20- to 40-foot depths.

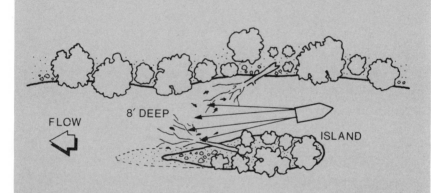

This illustration shows a classic early-season smallmouth spot in the Oneida River. The boat pictured is fishing the inside of a small island. The bottom composition is gravel and small stones, providing excellent spawning habitat for bass. Overhanging trees provide shade, and scattered deadfalls provide protection for bedding bass.

The inside of the island is very narrow. A quiet approach and accurate presentation of your bait are needed to take fish in this situation.

Although small spinnerbaits and crankbaits will do well there, we usually fish plastic-grub jigs because of the likelihood of getting snagged up. I'd rather lose a half a dozen jigs than a half a dozen crankbaits. If we get hung up, we simply break off and re-tie without moving in to try to salvage the lure. Moving in on snags in this kind of spot will definitely spook the fish.

There is often a strong current in the spring, and boat control can be the critical factor in fishing success. A trick we use sometimes is to make the current work for us by fishing a floating Rapala downstream. We cast the lure downstream as close to the bank and stickups as possible. The current carries the lure over a likely looking spot. Then we twitch it. The lure will hover over the spot we want to fish until its presence can be tolerated by a bass no longer. This is a great way to force a bedding lunker into trying to destroy the irritating minnow that refuses to swim away.

This illustration shows a cliff-bank situation common on Lake Champlain and the St. Lawrence River. Boulders and chunk rocks extend well out from the shoreline, providing excellent bottom conditions for smallmouth bass. Notice also that there are definite inside and outside edges to the weedbed.

In spring and fall, bass are likely to be on the inside edge of the weeds all the way to the cliff bank. In summer, bass are more likely to be located on the outside weed edge in deeper water or scattered well beyond the first major dropoff.

It was in this type of spot that Bill Butler and I had our greatest bass action ever on Lake Champlain in October. An extensive cliff area such as this produced over a hundred smallmouths in only half a day's fishing.

All the fish were caught on ¼-ounce Norman crankbaits on the inside weed edge. The water temperature was 60 degrees, and the sky was very heavily overcast. We didn't see another fisherman all day!

3/Fishing for the Wily Walleye

by Todd Swainbank

The walleye pike is the largest member of the perch family in North America. This large, delicious, and widely distributed game fish is popular throughout this country and Canada. A shore dinner of freshly caught walleye fillets is the specialty of Canadian fishing guides.

Walleyes were originally found in the northern states and Canada. By extensive stocking they are now found throughout the U.S. except for a few Far West and Deep South states. The walleye is easily reared in hatcheries, and many hatcheries produce only this species.

The walleye has a reputation as a feast-or-famine species. During some periods of the year, primarily in the spring, walleyes may be easily caught in large numbers and then suddenly disappear. Some years will find lakes with fantastic numbers of fish; other years the fishing may seem very poor. This has led many anglers to regard the walleye as a difficult fish to catch. On the contrary: anglers who complain of difficulty in taking walleyes throughout the fishing season simply fail to be versatile in their fishing approach.

As in fishing for any game fish, there is no one best way to fish for walleyes. Versatility is the key to taking walleyes consistently. Let's take a closer look at the wily walleye, and maybe you'll be more likely to catch this species—regarded by many as being the best tasting freshwater fish.

Spawning Habits

Walleyes are spring spawners. Male fish will seek suitable spawning sites when water temperature warms to the 45- to 50-degree range. Males await the larger females on gravel and rubble lake shoals or in tributary streams and rivers. Preferred spawning sites will have current or wave action present. Walleyes are prolific, producing eggs on an average of 25,000–50,000 per pound of body weight.

Spawning takes place at night, in shallow 1- to 5-foot depths. Eggs fall to the bottom and are abandoned. Depending on water temperature the eggs hatch three to four weeks later.

Growth Rates

Walleyes thrive best in large rivers and medium- to large-size lakes. Those found in northern waters grow slower but live longer than fish found in southern rivers and impoundments. A 15- to 16-inch fish found in a fertile impoundment may be only two years old.* A similar size fish from Canadian waters might be four to five years old. The life expectancy, however, is six to seven years for southern walleyes and twelve to fifteen years for slower growing northern fish. The world-record walleye, which weighed 25 pounds, was caught in Old Hickory Lake, Tennessee by Mabry Harper, August 1, 1960.

Tackle and Tips for Walleyes

Walleyes are school fish, like their cousins the yellow perch. When you find one, your chances of catching others are excellent. The walleye's diet consists primarily of other fish. Minnow-imitating lures are very popular for trolling and casting. I often catch walleyes when jigging or crankbaiting for bass. Walleyes often lie in the deeper water bordering good smallmouth-bass cover and structure.** Bait and lure presentations should be made deep, as these fish lie very close to bottom much of the time.

A medium-action spinning rod and freshwater-size spinning reel make a fine combination for casting and jigging for walleyes. The same rods and reels mentioned in the chapter on smallmouth bass will handle walleyes

---

*A. J. McClane, *1974 New Standard Fishing Encyclopedia* (New York: Holt, Rinehart and Winston).

**A variety of other game fish can be caught from typical bass cover and structures. Anglers interested in identifying potential hotspots for other species should refer to the section on Cover and Structure in Chapter 1, "Largemouth Bass Basics."

adequately. Although walleyes can reach large size in many waters and are dogged fighters, they can be landed easily with light tackle in open water. A stiffer casting or trolling rod used with a level-wind reel is suggested for those interested in trolling for walleyes.

Trolling

There are two types of trollers: people who troll without any idea of what is under the boat or at what depth the lures are running, and those who troll to eliminate unproductive water in a searching pattern to find fishy cover or structure and, they hope, fish.

This second type of troller probably uses a depth sounder of some kind and is keenly aware of depth changes, bottom contours, and changes in bottom composition. He is aware of daily and seasonal weather and light changes and how his presentation should vary accordingly. This troller *knows* almost to the inch how deep his lures run, and he probes whatever depths are necessary to take whatever species of fish he pursues. He doesn't depend on luck to find and catch fish, and he is versatile.

This lunker walleye was taken in the swift water below a dam off Lake Champlain on a small Norman crankbait.

The top illustration shows a good rig for trolling a floating Rapala for a variety of game fish. A regular three-way swivel or a branch swivel can be used to keep the lure and weight away from each other. Often the line section with the sinker attached is lighter in strength than the main line to the rod. That way, if the sinker becomes snagged, the lure and swivel might be saved. The floating lure will ride up off the bottom like this.

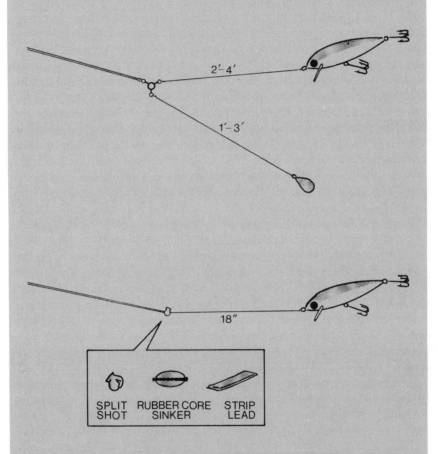

SPLIT SHOT RUBBER CORE SINKER STRIP LEAD

The bottom illustration shows the proper setup for casting or shallow trolling a floating Rapala. Split shot, rubber-core sinkers, or strip lead can provide the necessary weight. Notice both rigs are used *without* snap swivels. The direct line tie yields the best action from this type of lure.

A troller in search of walleyes may need a number of different types of line to meet the situations faced throughout the year. A non-stretch monofilament line like Buck's No Bo is an excellent all-around trolling line. Walleyes often move to deep water in summer, especially in clear lakes. Lead-core line and small-diameter stainless-steel line are very effective trolling lines when deep-water depth control is needed. Downriggers also have fishing value for a lot more than just trout and salmon fishing; they can be used effectively for other game fish.

Depth and speed control are the two most important factors governing success or failure in trolling for any species of game fish. The old saying "Troll as slowly as possible for walleyes, then cut the speed in half" is often true, but high-speed trolling can also turn fish on. It's best to experiment. At whatever speed you troll, occasionally pump the rod to suddenly give the lure a burst of speed followed by a pause. This sudden change of pace often prompts a strike. Stalling the outboard momentarily and then quickly picking up the pace has the same effect. Incidentally, Rapalas, Rebels, and June Bug spinners with worms are excellent trolling-lure choices.

While on the subject of trolling, I might add that very often in midsummer I see anglers trolling the same depths and locations that they fish during the spring spawning run. That gravel bar or shallow rock shoal which is red-hot in April or May will probably be devoid of walleyes in July and August. It makes no sense to troll the same spot day after day if it stops producing. Don't come back empty handed and say, "The fish weren't biting." Go find the fish and make them bite! Walleyes are famous for moving great distances in large lakes seeking the large schools of baitfish needed to support them. Once they have decimated baitfish populations in one area, they will move to another. The *consistently* successful walleye angler is a predator who will move around in search of walleye concentrations in the areas where baitfish and walleyes are most likely to congregate.

Underwater points, deep-water rockpiles, rock ledges, and deep weedbeds are good summer spots. The tailraces below dams will hold fish throughout the summer if deep, cool water (60 to 70 degrees) is available. The deep-water holes in rivers and the drop-offs near islands are the places to try.

Back Trolling

This method of live-bait presentation is very popular in the upper Midwestern states. The system consists of a live-bait rig such as a snelled hook,

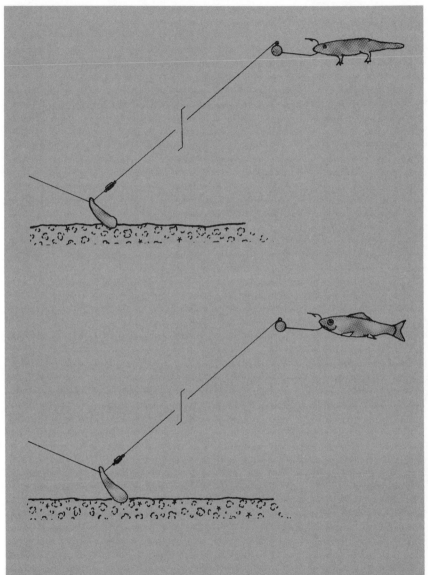

These illustrations show popular Midwestern live-bait rigs. The sinker shown is a walking slip sinker, allowing a striking walleye to move off with the bait without feeling the sinker drag.

The floating jigheads keep preferred bait like leeches, minnows, and salamanders up off the bottom and easily visible to nearby fish.

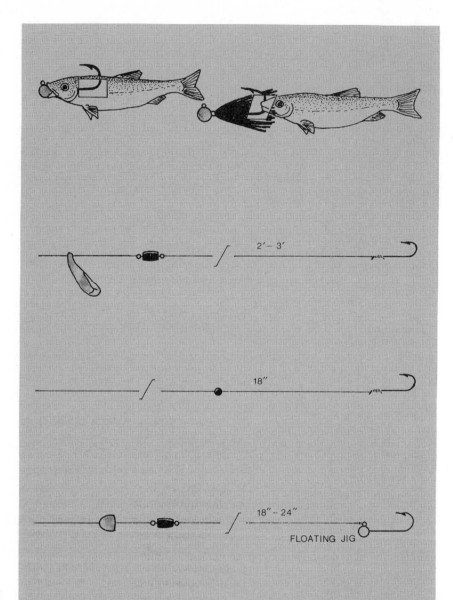

2' – 3'

18"

18" – 24"

FLOATING JIG

The top illustration shows "bait-sweetened" jigs very effective on walleye pike when they don't seem interested in artificial lures. This rig often turns on bass and northern pike, too.

Other illustrations show a variety of live-bait rigs for bottom bumping or back trolling.

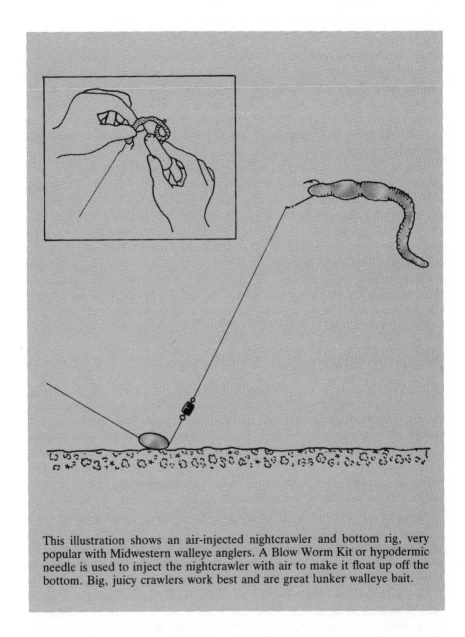

This illustration shows an air-injected nightcrawler and bottom rig, very popular with Midwestern walleye anglers. A Blow Worm Kit or hypodermic needle is used to inject the nightcrawler with air to make it float up off the bottom. Big, juicy crawlers work best and are great lunker walleye bait.

swivel, and sliding-bullet weight or walking sinker. The hole in the weight lets the line run freely through when a fish takes the bait. A swivel prevents the weight from slipping down on the hook. The bail on the spinning reel is kept open, with the index finger tapping the spool to prevent the line from running out, so no unnatural sinker drag or line friction is felt by the often subtly biting walleye.

Back trolling is just that—trolling with your outboard in reverse gear, usually into the wind. This enables the skipper to maintain very slow speeds or even hover in place. Anglers' lines are thus well ahead of the boat and well away from the propeller. Pinpoint depth and speed control can be maintained using this technique, and repeated passes can be made over productive structures.

The live-bait presentation can be made with very light lines (4- to 6-pound test) and tiny hooks without the need of wire leaders. Although walleyes have needle-sharp teeth, the teeth are smooth sided and well spaced, and I've *never* had one bite through my line. Using light line and fine wire hooks will also improve your catch, as walleyes can be shy of heavy monofilament, and their mouths are easily torn. Check the line often and re-tie if any nicks develop.

Back trolling using air-injected nightcrawlers or floating jig and worm combinations are very productive for walleyes. Give the fish plenty of time before you strike since walleyes often take bait slowly and deliberately.

Night Fishing for Walleyes

Walleyes are very active night feeders, often moving in schools to shallow shoals, weedbeds, and sandbars. Trolling a large Rapala can locate fish quickly, and then they can be cast to. Mister Twister grubs on ⅛- and ¼-ounce lead jigheads and the popular bass-pattern crankbaits are very effective on walleyes, as are bucktail and marabou jigs. Let the jig flutter and fall over the dropoffs. Walleyes cruise along dropoffs in search of food, ever watchful for a stray crayfish or minnow.

Night fishing can produce fast action, especially on clear lakes in mid-summer. During the cool evening hours walleyes will move from their midday, deep-water haunts and spread out to feed actively. Lunker potential is excellent on summer nights. Jigs are outstanding daytime lures too.

So where are the best spots for walleyes? Good waters are common in Manitoba and Ontario. In this country lakes and rivers in the Dakotas, Minnesota, Tennessee, and New York boast excellent walleye fishing. Remember one thing in your walleye quests: the best walleye lake in the world is no better than the anglers on it. So be versatile, experiment, and maybe you'll find that the walleye isn't so wily after all.

Batter-Fried Bass or Walleyes

This is *the* recipe for those people that think they hate fish. Bass and walleye fillets cook up crisp and crunchy, not unlike fish served in popular fast-food fish-and-chips establishments.

Batter:
2 cups Bisquick
2 eggs
1 cup beer

Beat ingredients with hand beater until batter is smooth. Dip fillets in batter and cover each piece completely. Deep fry in *hot* oil, when puffy they are ready to eat, normally in about two minutes. Tastes super!

4/Trophy Northerns and How to Take Them

by Gordon L. Eggleston

E*sox lucius*. Sounds sinister, doesn't it? The great northern pike *is* sinister—any true pike fisherman will agree *Esox* is a freshwater "Jaws," an incredible predator. To the angler who connects with a mature member of the species, this is a tackle-busting knuckle-bruiser with power to spare. When these fish get to be 36 to 39 inches long, they are prize adult specimens. The ones measuring 40 inches or more are in a class by themselves: trophy fish. Whenever one of these old mossbacks hooks up and makes its first power run, the angler is never sure whether it's the fish or himself who's directing the battle.

This chapter is intended to help you gain knowledge and skill in challenging trophy-size northern pike with rod and reel. I will deal primarily with the use of artificial lures, both spin and bait-casting, using the tactics and insights gained from twenty-five extended fishing trips to the St. Lawrence River and the rivers of Ontario and Quebec in Canada. Though this information is based on northern lakes and rivers, I feel it will apply also to pike waters elsewhere in the United States and Canada.

The Fish and Its Characteristics

The northern pike is a very adaptable fish which prefers water temperatures of from 55 to 65 degrees with lower and upper tolerances in the lower 40's to mid 70's respectively. They are found in both clear and tannic-acid-darkened waters (primarily between the latitudes of 36 degrees and 52 degrees) and, depending upon the depth of the water, thrive at both shallow and intermediate levels. Like most fish northern pike are carnivorous. They will readily attack any fish, reptile, bird or animal which they can swallow whole; *e.g.,* fallfish, shiners, suckers, small sturgeon, walleye pike, small northerns, frogs, mice, muskrats, ducklings, *etc.*

Spawning takes place during the spring of the year, March through June depending upon latitude. Unlike many fish species which build a bed or nest, the female northern deposits her eggs over a shallow, soft-bottomed river cove or lakeside bay near an inflowing stream. The male will accompany the female to fertilize the eggs as they spawn close to shore. Breeding temperature range is from 45 degrees to 55 degrees.

North American northern pike come in two varieties, one with white rectangular markings along their olive-green sides and the other with multiple white spots (like the markings on a lake trout) along their bluish-green sides. These bluish-green fish are sometimes called blue or silver pike. They are far rarer than the olive-green variety, and they rarely come in trophy size. Of this type taken in the past number of years by our group while fishing Canadian waters, only one was of trophy size.

For years the world record for northern pike taken via rod and reel was held by Peter Dubuc. The fish was taken from the Sacandaga Reservoir in New York State on September 15, 1940. It measured 52½ inches and weighed 46 pounds 2 ounces. Although it no longer remains as a world record, it still holds as the United States record. The officially recognized world-record northern stands at 55 pounds 1 ounce and was taken in West Germany during October of 1986. Unverified reports, as researched by Keith Gardner* claim a Finnish record pike of 56 pounds (1905), a Scottish record of just over 70 pounds (early 1900's) and a 55-pounder claimed to have been taken from the waters of Alberta, Canada, in recent years. The official Canadian record-breaking northern pike was taken in Saskatchewan, weighing 42 pounds 12 ounces. Despite their size and ferocity, northern pike (in their natural habitat) are generally not long-lived fish. However, pike have attained a life span of 75 years (and weights of over 100 pounds) in Europe when kept in large aquariums.**

Mature pike of 36 inches or over fight in a totally different manner from those of immature age and size. Big pike often fight to the point of total exhaustion before being landed. At such times even careful handling and proper reviving may fail.

Unlike a feeding walleye pike, which tends to either tailgate or swim in on its prey from the side, a northern on the take will suck in and crush, or slash its prey. Generally a feeding northern will wait in ambush from cover (weedbed, submerged tree, rock ledge) or will cruise about openly

*Keith Gardner, "Field Testing the Leader-Free Pike Lure," *Fishing World Magazine,* May/June 1978.
**K. L. Lagler, *Freshwater Fishery Biology,* (Dubuque, Iowa: Wm. C. Brown, Co., 1973), p. 38.

in search of a meal. Often the attack will be from beneath and to the side, but seldom will it be directed head-on. It is amazing how gracefully and swiftly an old mossback can overtake its prey (natural or artificial) once the attack begins. Upon reaching its target the fish opens its mouth as the gill covers and cheeks flare, creating a suction which impedes escape of the prey. Generally, upon impact the mouth crushes shut as the head turns in a slashing movement. The prey is often dead upon impact. The prey may be held and crushed as the momentum of the pike's attacking rush subsides before being carried to the bottom or to cover where it will be gradually turned and swallowed head first. There are also times when a pike will attack and continue the run, without pause, while crushing the prey between jaws, tongue, and roof of mouth. Once well away from the scene and in deeper water, the pike will turn the prey and swallow it. Should the fish wish to reject its prey, it may either open its mouth and shake its head free or, in some cases involving smaller hard or foreign objects, it may discharge them through the flared gills. One look at the massive head and jaws, the three distinctly different sets of teeth (each designed for a specific task) as well as the streamlined, elongated body justifies the pike's reputation as an accomplished killer.

Although typical pike habitat may include a few northerns in attendance, pike are not considered to be a school fish. I have found that prime feeding areas of perhaps 75 yards in length by 50 yards in width may possess as many as six or eight large adult northerns at one time.

Unlike their close relative, the muskellunge (musky), which may live a lifetime as an inhabitant of a specific area, adult northerns tend to cover ground. Much as an African lion may follow a herd of waterbuck or impala until the urge to dine prompts an attack, so an adult northern pike moves with a school of fish until succumbing to the urge to feed. This is why an angler is wise to linger for five to ten minutes at a spot where fish (for instance, a school of walleyes) which have been hitting on nearly every cast suddenly stop abruptly. This should be acknowledged as a signal to the angler that one of two things has taken place down below: the school has moved on, or a big northern has moved in. At such times the angler should slip on a pike lure and wire leader and be ready for a take by a northern. Certainly pike will frequent a particular area which has proven rich in prey. However, the angler in search of trophy pike must keep in mind that they will range to a large extent. This observation is based upon research and encounters experienced by our party while fishing the prime Chibougamau waters in Quebec. For three years we marked each fish caught and released *via* a paper hole-punch, each year punching a different fin. Some such fish were recaught at different locations. Also, two experiences regarding a northern's tendency to roam substantiate this observation:

Gordon Eggleston and his nephew Tom display a brace of trophy northerns taken at the edge of a weedy river cove. The combined weight of the two fish was 42 pounds 4 ounces.

1) During a seven-day fishing trip a trophy-size northern was lost after taking a large fallfish bait on a monofilament rig. After cutting the mono on the strike, the pike apparently moved upstream from the river site. The following day the rig with dead fallfish was found floating near shore one mile above where it had broken free.

2) Just last year my brother caught a trophy northern from a weedy lake bay. It still held in its cheek the black jig which was lost in the fish while jigging for walleyes on the preceding day a mile and a quarter away. That the jig was lost by another angler was not possible, since our party was the only one to portage back into this area to fish.

Fishing for northern pike is much like fishing for any other species in that the angler should heed and react to his gut feelings about lure selection. Typical haunts frequented by trophy pike are best presented by a description (and accompanying diagrams) of those river and lake feeding areas which have proven most successful for me over the years. The actual names of the rivers and lakes have been omitted, but for the most part they are located within the Chibougamau Preserve of upper Quebec. Our party has adopted a policy of naming each location to assist in pinpointing and gathering statistics on fish caught. These names will, along with relevant statistics gained over a nine-year period, appear with each description.

Identification of Prime Trophy Northern Pike Haunts

1) River Coves. *Example:* High Hopes. High Hopes has produced seventy-two pike of 30 inches or over for us. Over the years this small cove has never let us down. It has become our number-1 producer of adult northerns. Any pike fisherman could immediately recognize the spot as possessing all the necessary ingredients which spell success.

Located alongside the main inlet stream of the large lake (about 300 yards from its entrance), the cove contains a weedbed which runs outward some 25 yards from its inner shoreline. All the weeds of this cove are long, slender and a yellowish-green; we refer to them as pike weed. They are limp in structure, reaching to and beyond the surface with about 12 inches lying on top of the water during normal water-level conditions. The shoreline pike weeds are nearly impenetrable, with heavy surface growth, a mass of tiny yellow buds. Finally, some 75 yards from the inner shoreline, the weeds thin to only a patch here and there across the mouth of the cove. The bottom is silt over coarse gravel and rock. The water is dark in color as the result of the high tannic-acid concentration. The depth is approximately 4 feet at the outer edge of the thick weed strip, 6 feet among the intermediate weeds, and from 10 to 12 feet at the center of the river. When

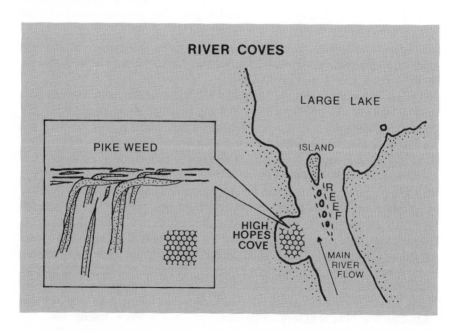

it comes to pike fishing, High Hopes is my favorite type of setting. Moderately shallow water, a sizable bed of pike weed, and a deeper water flow immediately adjacent affording cover (reef, boulders or bottom rocks, sunken trees or logs, *etc.*) that draws fish. Although always fishable due to its sheltered location, High Hopes presents ideal conditions when 1) the surface is calm and sky is overcast, and 2) when a slight breeze slowly drifts the angler parallel to the inner shoreline. When fishing, the angler should work his way inward gradually on drift. Casts are best made with the grain of the weeds through open lanes and open pockets, using accurate, short casts.

2) River Weedbeds. *Example:* Big Ben. Big Ben has produced twenty-seven pike of 30 inches or over for us. Big Ben received its name because a house-sized boulder lies submerged (reaching just inches beneath the surface under normal water-level conditions) nearly at midstream at the river's bend. The river at this point is about 50 yards wide, and the current is slow. It is always an especially good spot for walleyes and fallfish, both a favorite diet of pike. Immediately below the boulder at the river bend is a large, thick, underwater tobacco-cabbage weedbed. When both lighting and water conditions allow, the angler can also see a narrow strip of pike weed whose tops float upon the surface. Also, there is a small patch of pike weed growing in about 4 feet of water between the shoreline and the tobacco-cabbage weeds.

Although a few large northerns have been taken over the years from

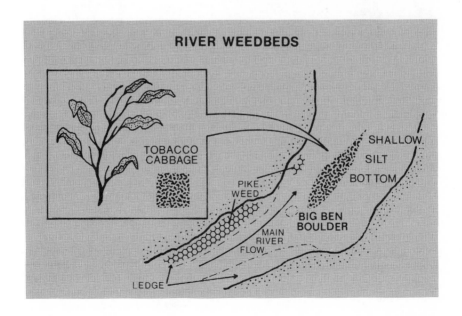

along the rocky ledge above Big Ben, the majority come from both the pike weed and tobacco cabbage at the current's edge. While casting to the pike weeds and above the submerged tobacco cabbage produces best results from the shallower inside-current edge, trolling upstream just off the tobacco cabbage within the main current produces the best results at this location.

3) River Sandbars and Adjacent Holes. *Example:* Hotspot No. 3. This river location produced seventeen pike of 30 inches or over for our party. Hotspot No. 3 also contains fallfish and lake whitefish in good numbers and, as previously mentioned, wherever walleyes, fallfish and whitefish are gathered, the setting is right for trophy northerns as well. On one side of the river hole is a large rock which slopes down to the water where its

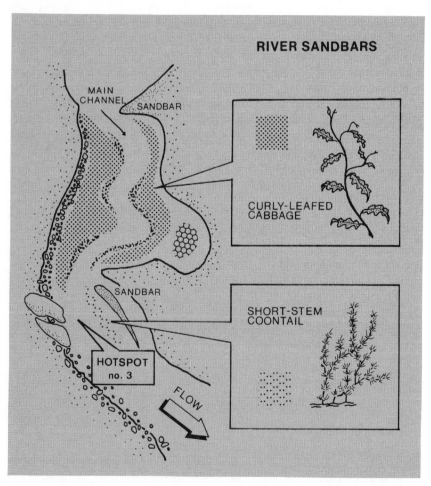

RIVER SANDBARS

MAIN CHANNEL

SANDBAR

CURLY-LEAFED CABBAGE

SANDBAR

SHORT-STEM COONTAIL

HOTSPOT no. 3

FLOW

upstream side immediately drops off to a depth of 8 feet. The other side of the river contains a long sandbar. Under normal conditions a strip of the bar is about 1 foot above the water and is separated from the inner shoreline by shallows. Immediately to the current side of the strip the bar drops offs quickly to a depth of 8 to 10 feet. The river bottom is mainly sand and, along the bottom paralleling the sandbar dropoff, there is a thick, short-stemmed coontail weedbed. The current flow through this area is slow. Above Hotspot No. 3 the current winds slowly through a wide spot in the river, flanked on both sides by curly-leafed cabbage weed. The channel through this weedbed is edged with tobacco cabbage, and the water is about 5 feet deep. The channel is approximately 10 to 12 yards wide and 6 feet deep at its center. While only small pike in large numbers have been taken from the weeds and channel above Hotspot No. 3, trophy pike

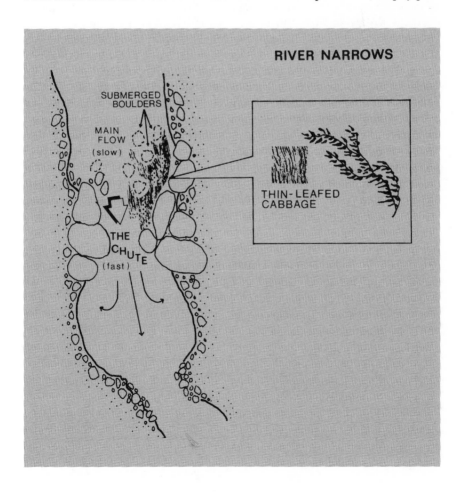

have often come from the hole between the sandbar and the sloping rock where, at midstream, the water depth is 12 feet. The best way to take these fish is to anchor at the sandbar dropoff and fish the hole and weedbed. Downstream wind trolling and upstream motor trolling with plugs are also good ways of fishing the area.

4) River Narrows. *Example:* The Chute. The Chute has produced seven pike of 30 inches or over for our party. It is the narrowest point in the main tributary of the river. Huge boulders on each side force the river flow to funnel through an opening 8 feet wide. Immediately below, the current swirls over a rocky bottom 8 feet deep. The force of the water through the opening is so great that rooster tails 3 to 4 feet high roll and splash. However, the approaching flow is slow as it passes over scattered submerged boulders. These boulders are in 5 feet of water, with submerged curly-leafed cabbage weeds growing about their base. The shoreline along one side is very shallow and rocky with curly-leafed cabbage, and thin-leafed cabbage extending out to nearly midstream. The opposite shoreline forms part of the main current as the water flows over rocks at a depth of 4 feet. The main channel is 5 feet deep with a hard bottom.

The Chute is an ideal haunt for feeding northerns, as any crippled or weak fish will be carried through the restricted area. It is interesting to note that, once hooked, the northern will avoid running downstream through the chute, preferring to fight it out within the confines of the narrow channel. Walleyes, fallfish, and small pike are often taken from the varied pool current just below the chute. However, such fish have always proven to be small in size and quite thin from fighting the current. Any narrow restriction to a river's flow may work equally well if conditions are right.

5) Lakeside Reefs. *Example:* Bar & Grill. This reef has produced twenty-one pike of 30 inches or over for us. There is no outward appearance which would prompt a passing angler to stop and fish this area. In fact it is one of those places which is best discovered through the use of a sonar probe unit, as its virtues rest more on what is beneath the water than what is visible above. Bar & Grill is located about halfway down a big lake. It consists of a long, rocky, underwater bar or reef which extends some 75 yards into the lake at a right angle to the mainland. The bar is approximately 10 yards wide and slopes very gradually from the shoreline to a depth of 8 feet. The lead edge drops abruptly to the lake bottom at a depth of 8 to 15 feet. The bottom appears to be composed of silt and gravel with occasional rock projections here and there. The only weed cover in the area is a scattering of sandgrass.

The major problem faced in fishing the area, as is often the case in open-lake angling, is maintaining position in rough water conditions. At such times trolling is much easier than stationary fishing, because it prevents

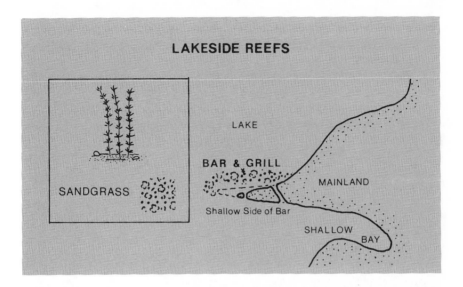

LAKESIDE REEFS

SANDGRASS

LAKE

BAR & GRILL

MAINLAND

Shallow Side of Bar

SHALLOW BAY

slack line from becoming a handicap to the angler. When starting to fish the Bar & Grill we generally troll just off the bar on the deeper side using a crankbait in order to locate walleyes. Once fish are located, we anchor within casting distance of the reef and work jigs. As previously mentioned, if the walleyes stop abruptly or if a northern makes his presence known, we switch to a spoon such as a Dardevlet, attached to a 6-inch wire leader, and spend five to ten minutes casting the lure before repeating the fish-locating troll.

6) Weedy Lake Bays. *Example:* Battlefield Bay. Battlefield Bay has produced fifty-two pike of 30 inches or over for our party, nine of which were trophies of 40 inches or longer. Battlefield Bay is well named for the many campaigns which have taken place within its weedbeds between its powerful fighting pike and members of our party. In one year alone we landed fifteen fish of 30 inches or better in our seven-day trip. The bay is situated about halfway down a lake much like the one we camp on except it has fewer shoreline bays and less variable cover. Although small in size, this bay is one of the two best on the lake. It also ranks as the second-best all-time producer of lunker northerns for our party. The bay is about 75 yards across by 100 yards wide at the mouth, possessing a mixture of pike weed, tobacco cabbage and a few long-stemmed pads. Generally the thinner pike weed along the lake shore edge have proven the most productive over the years. The inner and middle bay bottom is silt over sand, and the outer bottom is sand. A tiny stream enters the bay at its innermost point. What makes the bay a hotspot is not the entrance of the tiny stream

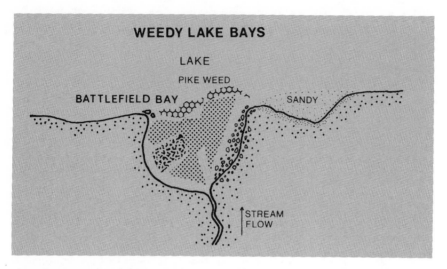

WEEDY LAKE BAYS

but the favorable (although shallow) water depth and temperature, abundant cover, immediately adjacent deep-lake waters, and, lastly, an abundance of small baitfish of various kinds. From the bay's mouth the sand bottom gradually slopes lakeward some distance before dropping noticeably to a depth of 12 to 15 feet, well within the lake itself. The bay is best fished in the same manner as explained earlier under River Coves.

7) Lake Lagoons. *Example:* Old Folks' Home. This spot has produced thirty-three pike of 30 inches or over for our party. Of these seven were of trophy size, with my largest measuring 45 inches and weighing 23 pounds, 9 ounces. Old Folks' Home received its name in dedication to the numerous old mossbacks that have been encountered (but not all landed) while fishing this massive, shallow and weedy location. It is situated at the extreme end of the large lake along the edge of a big bay and is approximately 125 yards long by 60 yards wide. A stream enters the end of the lagoon and broadens to flow more slowly through a long, wide field of pike weed to empty into the bay. For the most part, the bed of pike weed is thick with a few pads and curly-leafed cabbage at its downstream conclusion followed by a bottom cover of sandgrass along the entire mouth of the lagoon. The water depth over the whole width of the area is 5 feet. However, at the entrance to the bay there is a buildup of silt with a water depth of only 3½ feet. The stream offers high oxygen content, cold water, and a haven for small baitfish, which walleyes and fallfish will seek during the evening hours. Pike can be found among the weeds of the lagoon. Skittering spoons over the thicker weeds or working with the grain of the weeds, through lanes and pockets employing a slow-steady retrieve has proven to be the most effective fishing technique. It should also be mentioned that lagoons

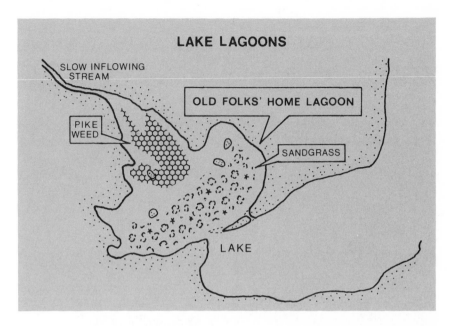

such as Old Folks' Home are typical spring spawning areas sought by northern pike. At such times these areas will receive a number of huge pike.

8) Lake Islands. A hotspot that has produced twenty-one pike of 30 inches or over for our party, Lake Islands has become our top island resort for both large walleyes and large northerns. The islands are tall and quite steep. At one end a rock formation projects outward into the lake to form a reef some 40 yards long by 20 yards wide. Water depths above the reef are 3 to 4 feet. Along the entire down-lake edge of the reef the water depth drops to 10 to 12 feet where a swath of large, irregular-shaped rocks make jigging somewhat difficult, yet rewarding. The bottom beyond this rocky depth is composed of silt from which patches of short-stemmed sandgrass grow in abundance. The water depth here is 15 to 18 feet. Although we will troll plugs along the island edge (starting from behind the reef and working to the far end) when action slows or weather hinders working the reef, the most productive spot is alongside the reef and its adjacent lake bottom. The boat is anchored to the reef, and jigs are cast beyond the rocky dropoff and slowly worked back to the boat. As the use of wire leaders with jigs results in poor action, we prefer to risk the chance of a breakoff by a northern with a direct tie to the line. If a northern is found to be present we will tie on a shallow-running crankbait and cover the reef's shallow water or work the dropoff rocks.

The following should serve as a guide to recognizing an island hotspot.

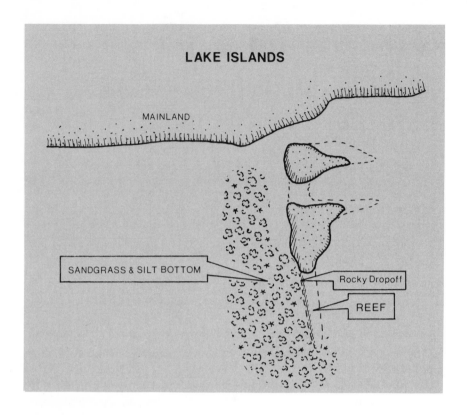

Islands of good height and offering a sharp incline to the water's surface usually mean deep water and fish. On the other hand, islands low in height with gradually sloping sides will generally lack the immediate shoreline depth and structure necessary for success.

Lake Outlet Areas. *Example*: Dinner Bucket. Dinner Bucket has produced seven pike of 30 inches or over. Lake outlets are generally of two types: a deep-lake basin or a shallow-lake flat at the head of an outflowing river channel. The Dinner Bucket is an outlet of the second type, possessing a wide, shallow flat which funnels into a shallow channel flanked by rocks. The bottom of the flat is sand silt (patched with sandgrass), and the channel is sand and rock covered with curly-leafed cabbage. The flat is a uniform 5 feet in depth. The main channel is 6 feet deep at its center. During the early-morning hours northerns will generally be located along or near the rocky edge of the current rather than in midstream. These pike will wait among the weeds near the rocky edge to strike from ambush. During the early-evening hours the pike will generally be found on the flats where walleyes and fallfish move in to feed. I feel that, because of the current

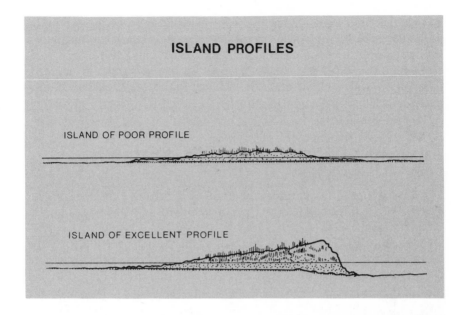

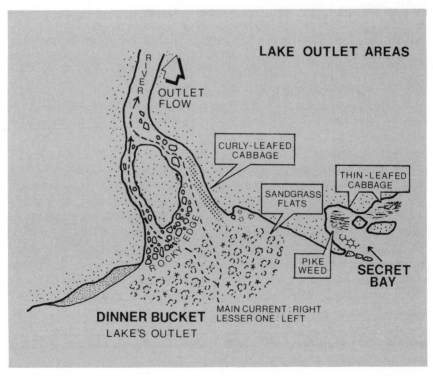

and lack of good water depth, the fish will spend most of the day in the deeper lake waters. However, during the evening and early-morning hours they will move into the area to feed. Adjacent bays and deep-water structure within ¼-mile or less of a river outlet should always be investigated, especially during midday when the shallow outlet area becomes unproductive.

Favorable Conditions for Action

Although I have taken northerns at all times of day (not at night) regardless of weather conditions, there are definite periods which tend to prompt action.

Early Morning. The first two hours of daylight are a prime time for the taking of most freshwater game fish. This certainly is my favorite time of day when fishing for trophy northern pike. At such times both pike and their prey are most apt to be found near shallow shoreline areas. Especially good early-morning locations are weedy lake lagoons and bays, river coves, lake outlets, and river narrows. Generally speaking, weather conditions are calm from dawn to mid-morning and thus afford the angler favorable surface visibility. Moving in under a shroud of slowly rising fog to fish a glassy-surfaced bay of thick pike weed, with the eerie cry of a distant loon heard in the stillness of early morn, can send a chill of anticipation coursing through the frame of any fisherman.

Midday. I cannot say why, but it seems that trophy northerns will often feed between the hours of 10 AM and 2 PM during the summer and early-autumn months. I have taken a number of adult pike at such times over the years providing the day was not clear and calm. The areas which I prefer between mid-morning and late afternoon are the deeper lake and river areas and certain weedy bays or coves if choppy or rough waters prevail.

Late Afternoon/Early Evening. When the sun approaches the horizon in its descent, big northerns tend to move into the same areas as during the early-morning hours. Casting is much preferred to trolling at such times, as the pike tend to cruise the shallower waters in search of a meal. Trophy walleyes, largemouth bass, brown trout, and certain other species of freshwater game fish can be considered nocturnal feeders, but not northern pike. Therefore once darkness begins to set in, an angler can forget about them.

Days of Overcast Skies with Calm Waters. Schools of walleyes will feed during overcast days in calm or choppy waters and thus will offer the possibility of there being a feeding northern nearby or in their midst. Consequently areas frequented by walleyes during the day (particularly deep waters with nearby shoreline cover) are always a wise choice. Also, weedy areas (bays, lagoons, and coves) will remain productive longer into the day. Either casting to surface weed areas or trolling deeper water areas can be expected to provide good results.

Days of Choppy Waters. As previously mentioned, choppy waters can often spell success when it comes to trophy pike fishing, as the big ones will often cruise about near the surface and at moderate depths in search of food. I have observed fallfish of 10 to 12 inches in length skipping 10 or 12 feet across the surface of a bay during choppy-water conditions. Although no surface sign betrayed the pursuing northern's presence, it was obvious that the chase was on. Another sign of near-surface pike is the aerial shower of minnows as the school scatters in fright. This may be accompanied by either a surface wake or a surface swirl of the attacking northern. If in range and ready for a presentation, the angler should immediately cast to 5 or 6 feet of where the minnows landed in their flight, allowing the lure, preferably a spoon or spinner, to sink for about two seconds while maintaining a taut line, and retrieve with an alternate fast and let-back return. Such antics do not always spell success for the angler. I have been in the presence of numerous trophy pike involved in stirring up the minnows of a weedy bay and yet have been unable to coax one to take an artificial. It can be one of the most frustrating situations to be encountered by a pike fisherman. Another visible sign of a pike's presence is either a surface-breaking swirl or a deep, lingering surface boil. However, the angler must remember that such signs do not necessarily mean that the fish is feeding near the surface. While playing trophy northerns I have observed that a quick power turn executed at a depth of 5 or 6 feet will produce a delayed surface boil that seems to continue for a few moments. Therefore in casting to a surface disturbance, one should govern the depth of retrieve according to the type of swirl or boil. If the fish breaks water, retrieve shallow, and if it does not break water, retrieve at a moderate (4- or 5 feet) depth. Remember that often a trophy northern will follow at a deep or moderate level and will be provoked into an attack as it observes the lure beginning to travel upward (toward the boat) as if attempting to escape to the surface. A strike at the boat, although spectacular, is the least desirable location for hooking a big fish, since the angler is usually startled, and the reduced stretch factor in the monofilament line makes a break-off likely; yet it is a common occurrence when fishing pike country. The final sign to heed in observing the presence and location of trophy northerns is a movement or parting of surface weeds or submerged brush which breaks the surface. Such movement is a tipoff of a pike on the prowl.

Rough Water and/or Stormy Weather. Rough weather conditions often result in active feeding by large pike, as small baitfish are forced into shallower and more sheltered waters: bays, lagoons, coves, lake and island shorelines where the waves are beating in over rocks and boulders. Within the limits of safety, such times, although not easy or overly enjoyable fishing, can bring results for the pike fisherman. It may mean that one person handles the boat while the other fishes and that trolling is the preferred method rather than drift or anchored-boat casting.

Concentration of Birds. I have used Arctic terns as indicators when fishing for lake trout shortly after ice-out in Lac Waconichi, Quebec. As they would group to circle lower and lower we would quickly motor to the spot, knowing the terns had observed a school of baitfish and/or lakers. As the bait was driven to the surface, the terns would drop to about 10 feet from the water and, once the lakers began their feeding frenzy, which literally boiled the surface, would swoop to pick up crippled bait-fish, sometimes even alighting upon the exposed back of a laker to pick at the cripples. Gulls also have excellent eyesight and are able to spot crippled fish from the air. Occasionally they will congregate and circle over a particular area of water where northerns are feeding. It is not a common occurrence, but now and then it will happen, and the angler should be aware of its meaning.

Outfitting for Trophy Northern Pike

Successful northern-pike fishing begins with a boat. The angler who attempts to fish for northerns from shore limits his range drastically and, at the same time, limits the chance of landing any trophy pike hooked. I know of seven trophy fish, including my largest to date, which could not be checked in their first run of over 100 yards.

I prefer to fish from my Fish Hawk No. 2, a 17-foot Grumman square-stern aluminum canoe. It is dark green, sound-dampened by removable floor mats of 1-inch-thick polyurethane, and powered by a 9½ H.P. Evinrude motor. While a total of sixty-one northern pike of 10 pounds and over have been taken by myself and others while fishing from this canoe, I readily acknowledge the limitations of fishing and traveling rough waters with such a boat. Therefore, I feel that the safest, yet most versatile, way to go is as follows:

A 16-foot aluminum boat weighing no more than 300 pounds with either an 18- or 20-H.P. motor is my recommendation for maximum boat and motor size. I would recommend a minimum length of 14 feet (wide beam) with a 9½-H.P. motor. A foot-operated electric motor is a worthwhile accessory for maintaining the correct line of drift while casting. However, when frequent battery recharging is unattainable it is useless. Through the use of such an outfit the angler can safely travel and fish large bodies of water and yet be able to portage or line the boat when size and weight become a factor in traversing rapids.

Selection of the proper rod, reel, and line are generally governed by personal preference. The rod should possess a stiff backbone for setting the hook in a pike's tightly closed mouth. The reel should possess an easily adjusted and smooth-running drag system. The line should be at least 100 yards in length. I have always been a bait-casting, rather than a spin-casting, angler (when I'm not fly-fishing for trout). I prefer to carry two casting rods rigged to meet the demands of the particular area being fished at the moment. One is a 5½-foot Fenwick HMG Graphite (GFC554/moderate action) and the other (my favorite) an old 5-foot solid triangular glass Shakespeare with stiff backbone and an extra-fast 18-inch tip. My reel choice is the Garcia Abu Ambassadeur in models 5600 C or 5000. My line choice is either Squidding (flat braided nylon) or Cortland braided nylon; either line in 15 pounds test. For those wishing to use a spinning rod and reel, I would suggest open-faced rather than closed-face reels be employed, as the drag system of most open-faced reels is smoother than those of the closed-face models.

I would suggest the following lures.

Lures (Spoons):

Eppinger Dardevlet: in gold, copper, or pearl scale colors.

Marathon (sometimes called a Rattle Spoon): in hammer-scale finish; either gold or copper in color and of 3 inches length.

Aqua Spoon or Flash Bait 166 (Dardevlet imitation but lighter in weight; manufactured in Minneapolis): in either hammer-scale finish or plain and in either gold or copper.

Weedless Dardevlet with single weedless trailer hook in copper.

Kush Spoon: 3½ inches length; with silver belly, red and yellow divided back.

Johnson Spoon: either in silver or black and rigged with either a fish belly, Mister Twister tail, or plastic worm.

Williams Wobbler: 6-inch length with gold and silver back and belly.

Lures (Plugs):

Cisco Kid: in orange-dog, yellow, or perch colors.

Cisco Kid Junior: in yellow or perch colors.

Canadian Wiggler: solid silver color.

Musky Flatfish: orange with black spots.

Heddon Bomber: (for trolling) in yellow or perch colors.

Norman 3000-DR: rainbow trout finish.

Lures (Spinners):

Mepps Spinner/plastic minnow: large size.

Mepps Giant Killer: pearl scale blade and yellow tail; for trolling in deep-water areas.

Shannon Spinnerbait: large size in chartreuse or white.

Zorro Spinnerbait: safety-pin large size in chartreuse.

Abu Spinner: large size in silver blade and red or yellow tail.

Lures (Jigs):

Walleye jigs: ¼-and ½-ounce sizes with yellow, white, or black hair tails (either bucktail, polar bear, or black bear).

Ball-head jigs: ¼-and ½-ounce sizes; same colors as walleye jigs.

Essential Tacklebox Accessories:

Wire leaders: I prefer plastic-covered, braided-wire leaders of from 15 to 18 pounds test in the 6-inch length; leaders with ball-bearing swivels and size 10 standard-clip snaps. I have lost very few pike because the leader was too short and have found longer leaders prevent ease in casting.

Chatillion scales: Each of our party carries a pair of Chatillions to either 30 pounds or 60 pounds maximum for weighing all northerns measuring 30 inches or longer. Although not a necessity, such scales take up little room within a tacklebox and provide accurate weights for the sake of interest or research.

Long-nose pliers and jaw spreaders: These two items are essential safety tools for aiding in the removal of hooks from within the mouth of a pike, whether such fish be of adult or immature size.

Retractable tape measure: Although either a portable measuring board (to the nearest ¼ inch) or steel tape attached to the boat bottom is best for quick, easy, and accurate measuring, a retractable metal tape of 6 feet length is a good companion for the Chatillion scales.

Personal emergency items: Any tacklebox should contain certain health and safety items for emergency use. The most important among these are bandaids, aspirin, sunburn prevention cream or salve, insect repellent, antacid tablets, a lighter or matches, and a small flashlight. Those items which may be damaged or destroyed by water should be stored in a water-proof container or wrap.

The final item to be included in outfitting for trophy northern-pike fishing is a large landing net. Each of our party's boats contains a net measuring 36 inches across the opening, a deep heavy-duty nylon-mesh bag and a handle with end grip. When the net is not in use, it can be quickly adjusted to half its overall length. An angler works long and hard to hook up with a big fish. An extra-large net may look unnecessary but might well save the angler a trophy northern pike.

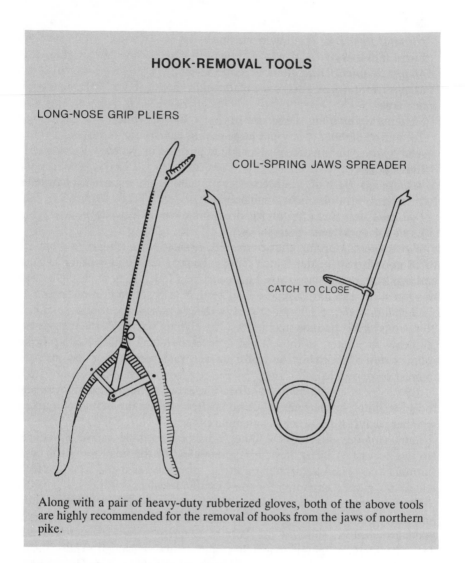

HOOK-REMOVAL TOOLS

LONG-NOSE GRIP PLIERS

COIL-SPRING JAWS SPREADER

CATCH TO CLOSE

Along with a pair of heavy-duty rubberized gloves, both of the above tools are highly recommended for the removal of hooks from the jaws of northern pike.

Fishing Methods and Techniques

Northerns may be taken by live-bait fishing, trolling, spin casting, bait casting and, during winter months, ice fishing. However, for the purpose of this chapter I will stick to my favorite method, bait casting.

Any fishing requires a high degree of concentration. Many fine fish have been lost on the strike because of a momentary lapse of attention. In executing and retrieving a cast the angler must 1) properly read sign and cover, 2) select an appropriate choice of lure, 3) present an accurately directed cast to the appropriate location, and 4) work a retrieve which will provoke an attack.

Slow and Steady Retrieve. I feel too many anglers fail to connect because they tend to retrieve too fast. Immature pike love to chase a fast-moving lure, but not the old mossbacks. The same applies in regards to trolling speed. Casting or trolling, most of the time they like it slow and steady.

Fast and Steady Retrieve. This sometimes brings results, either when working a deep-running crankbait along the bottom or in a skittering top-water retrieve of a weedless spoon over the top of thick surface weeds.

Alternate Fast and Slow Retrieve. This technique is best employed when using a crankbait rather than a spoon.

At-Boat Drop-back. Muskies are notorious for following right up to the boat to strike or reject the lure. Northerns are, too. The wise angler will always complete a retrieve with this in mind and will hesitate before lifting for the next cast. If a missed strike results as the lure is lifted, it should be quickly flipped 6 to 8 feet from the boat and allowed to sink on a taut line to a depth of 4 or 5 feet before slowly retrieving.

Retrieving a Weeded Lure. In heavily fished waters a lure that has fouled weeds dragging from it will result only in a rejection by pike and other fish. However, in the unfished areas we fish in Canada, I have taken more than one pike at the boat while my lure was trailing a small amount of weeds. Once I was reaching for a weeded spoon as I lifted it from the water in a fast retrieve only to have a large pike miss the spoon (and my hand) by inches. In fact the largest northern taken by a member of our party was taken by casting an Abu Spinner into thick river weeds. The lure was allowed to sink until hung in the weeds, where it was merely worked by alternate rod pulls and let-backs. In so doing the spinner would flutter back after each pull. Suddenly, the huge northern loomed up to strip the Abu free of the weeds. When landed, the trophy pike measured 48 inches and tipped the scales at just over 30 pounds.

Hooking and Playing Trophy Northerns

Hooking the Fish

Contrary to general opinion, a feeding adult northern pike will often follow or attack from a considerable distance. I once observed an old mossback attack a skittered lure from some 20 yards distant. As the spoon

Bill Ware with a 48-inch northern of just over 30 pounds that fell victim to an Abu spinner fished over a river weedbed.

splashed its way across one weed patch, there appeared a wake from an adjacent patch which closed rapidly, much like a torpedo headed for an unsuspecting ship. Once within about 10 feet of the lure, the pike's bill broke the surface as the mouth opened and remained so until the strike. It was an awesome sight and but one of numerous observed attacks initiated from a distance. Thus you may draw a fish even though your presentation is a bit off. Once a trophy northern hits, however, there are three essentials for success: proper techniques in hooking, playing, and landing the fish.

Usually when the lure is taken, the northern's jaws shut so rapidly and firmly that the fish is momentarily unaware of what it is holding. Once the pike halts or slows its run, it generally will relax the jaws slightly. At this time I prefer to drive the hook home with two or three firm and forceful up and to the side thrusts of the rod tip. At such times the angler must be careful to keep a taut line between each hooking thrust. Many times the jaws are so tightly closed over the lure that the hook barbs do not penetrate the flesh until the jaws relax. At this moment the hooks must be driven home.

The two most risky times in a strike are when a trophy northern strikes at the boat and when a fish hits from a distance and immediately runs directly toward the boat. In the first instance I prefer to let the rod tip absorb the force and weight of the fish by easing the tip down in the direction of the pike's run, even if it means lowering the tip beneath the surface. At the same time the arms extend and the body leans forward to ease the stress upon the shortened line. Totally different is the situation involving an onrushing northern. Here the line must be rapidly reeled in to pick up the resulting slack. At such time the rod tip and arms should be kept high in readiness to absorb the force and weight of the pike. As slack line is taken up the angler should observe the direction of the pike's run. Then, at the first pressure, the rod tip and arms should absorb the force by lowering to the direction of the run in order to prevent a breakoff.

After a trophy pike is hooked there remain the essential skills of playing and landing the fish before the hurrahs of success can be carried across the waters. First and foremost, enjoy the ensuing thrill of battle, for battle it will be. The angler must remember not to attempt a match of brute strength. Certainly such a fish is strong, and certainly you, as angler, are stronger. Nevertheless, the connecting links (the rod, line, leader, and hooks) are of lesser mettle.

Playing Tips

Get away from cover and obstacles. Nine times out of ten a large northern hooked while fishing within a weedbed will immediately attempt to move out of the weeds in trade for the sanctuary of deep water. This is his first major mistake in the battle, a mistake on which the wise angler will capitalize. The angler's partner should paddle the boat at a quiet, steady pace as soon as possible. The angler should merely attempt to follow the pike, while maintaining only a holding pressure with the reel drag setting, and should not attempt to gain ground on the fish. Once outside the weedbed the boat should continue toward the deepest, obstacle-free water in sight until well away from the weedbed's outside edge. At this point the northern will generally have slowed to rest, either along or near the bottom. The boat should be positioned broadside to the pike and with the fish between the boat and the weedbed as it is worked slowly up toward the surface. Once the fish surfaces and gets a good look at the boat and/or angler he will realize his dilemma. Again the angler must be ready to bend to the will of his opponent as the pike generally turns to run for the cover of the weedbed or other obstacles.

Adjust drag tension if needed during the contest. Proper reel-drag tension should have been checked before ever making the first cast of the day. Still, there are times during the playing of a large fish when a readjustment may be called for. Therefore, the angler should check at first sight of the fish to see how well it is hooked and, if it appears poorly hooked, lessen the reel's drag setting. The same applies to raising a fish or slowing its run. However, as far as possible such readjustments should not be attempted during a power surge. One of the main reasons I outfit my rods with Abu Ambassadeur series 5000 reels is because of the smoothness of the star drag and the ease of adjustment while playing a large fish. If need be, during a power run the spool can be lightly thumbed to exert more restraint on the reel than is being produced by the drag.

Proper Landing of Pike

If landed by beaching, the fish should be well played out before heading ashore. This method is excellent where the angler wishes to either keep or release the fish and where the trophy pike is too large for easy netting. Such landing should be made at a shallow, non-obstructed shoreline area. Upon beaching the boat, the partner should immediately wade out to about knee depth to grasp the fish with both hands from behind the gill covers; one hand from behind the neck and the other from ahead of the belly. The fish can thus be either slid ashore or lifted and carried ashore. An adult pike should never be dragged ashore by the line.

If landed by net, the fish should be well played out before any attempt is made. By far, netting is the most desirable method of landing a fish which is to be released. If and when the fish is ready, the net is directed from the side forward into the path of the pike. At the same time the angler eases pressure, allowing the northern to move forward into the net. Extreme care must be executed where a set of hooks are exposed in order to prevent such hooks from becoming snagged in the net as it enters. The follow-through is forward and a turning of the frame to a face-up position as it nears the tail of the fish.

Handling and Releasing

As previously mentioned, an adult northern pike will fight to near exhaustion and therefore will require care in handling and releasing if it is to survive the ordeal. The following are some suggestions for the handling and release of adult pike.

1) Avoid letting the fish thrash about before its release.

2) Avoid damaging the eyes or gills while removing hooks or while photographing prior to its release. A broken gill is a very serious injury to a fish, as the gills are its breathing apparatus. I have taken two or three pike which have survived a broken gill, as evidenced by its healing scar tissue, but generally such injury will result in the fish's death.

3) When removing hooks and weighing, measuring, and photographing a trophy northern, it should be allowed to rest and breathe within the net.

4) Extreme care, both in regard to the angler's safety and in regard to the pike's well-being, should be exercised during the hook-removal process. A lure hooked in the gills is often best removed from behind the gill; pulling the lure through the gills, unsnapping the lure, resnapping the leader clasp and pulling the leader back out through the mouth. Where there is difficulty in removing the hook from tough inner or outer tissue it is often best to cut the hook free rather than to rip it free. Long-nose pliers are essential for removal of a hook deeply embedded in the gullet or back of the mouth. Often a live-bait fisherman who takes a pike to be released will snip the leader with a pair of wire cutters because the baited hook is out of sight within the esophagus.

5) The proper method of reviving a northern pike during its release is to gently support it just beneath the surface. This is done by holding the fish at the neck, and at the belly with the palm of the hand. Then, with a gentle alternating forward and backward movement of the fish, water is allowed to pass through the gills. After a few moments, check the pike's stability by releasing it. If there seems to be difficulty in its remaining upright the process is repeated. However, if the fish remains in good balance and the gills, fins, and tail are actively functioning, stimulate its desire to escape by squeezing the base of the tail. No healthy fish can tolerate this act.

Hook Removal from an Angler

Probably the least obvious cause for concern in regard to angling safety, especially when removing hooks from the mouth of a northern pike, are the hooks themselves. Particularly dangerous are those lures possessing more than one set of hooks. A slip of the hand while a fish thrashes about can result in a hooked fisherman. We have experienced one incident in which one of our party became hooked by a thrashing pike. It was an especially painful experience as both were attached to the same lure. The assistance of the angler's partner was necessary first to subdue and unhook the pike and then to remove the hook from the angler.

HOOK REMOVAL

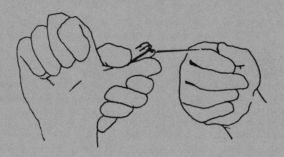

Three hands are needed for this operation: cut a section of line and loop it around the hook bend. Press the hook eye firmly against the skin and pull the loop of line. The hook should pop out.

If and when emergency treatment is called for in the removal of a hook from a fisherman, there are two methods from which to choose. The more painful of the two calls for the hook to be cut in two at its shank bend (about ½ inch from the point of penetration). It is then forced until the point and barb reappear through the skin, where it is pulled on out.

The second method is the newest and best recommended technique which, surprisingly, is nearly painless. It requires assistance and is accomplished as follows:

1) Cut a 10-inch length of heavy line or monofilament.

2) Run the 10-inch line section behind the curve of the embedded hook so as to form a loop around the hook bend.

3) Grasp the looped line and, with a finger of the opposite hand,

4) Push the hook eye down against the skin with firm pressure.

5) Give the loop line a quick, firmly grasped yank while the hook eye is held against the skin.

Through this technique the hook's barb is allowed to follow the entry channel back out without catching the skin. It works like a charm and is a technique every fisherman should be acquainted with.

Poor Man's Lobster

Northern pike, like its cousins the pickerel and the muskellunge, are noted for being a bony fish. Therefore, despite its fine texture and taste, it is often not used for eating. However, there is little chance of missing the forked bones found within a large adult northern, and there is meat enough to feed the multitude. One of my favorite recipes for serving such fish is Poor Man's Lobster, which is prepared in the following manner:

1) Cut the loin strips from each side of the backbone.

2) Place 2 quarts of water in a large boiler and add 1½ tablespoons salt.

3) Bring salted water to a boil while placing the pike loins in a large piece of cheesecloth and tie off to form a mesh bag of fish.

4) Add the mesh bag of fish to the boiling water and cover.

5) Allow to cook for 5 minutes after water resumes boiling.

6) Melt 8 ounces of either butter or margarine; if using margarine, add ½ teaspoon imitation butter flavoring after the margarine has melted and stir a few seconds.

7) Remove the mesh bag of fish from boiling water and allow to drain while placing melted butter or margarine into individual cups.

8) Remove fish from cheesecloth and serve in equal portions.

To eat, the meat is flaked apart and each flake is dipped in melted butter/margarine to be eaten. The taste is very much like that of butter-dipped lobster and will be relished by anyone who enjoys seafood.

5/Garpin' for Carp

by Todd Swainbank

P ity the poor carp, whose introduction into this country is regarded as a fisheries-management fiasco. Derisively called bugle-mouth bass, shot with arrows, speared, stoned, blamed for fouling waterways and eating game-fish eggs, caught and often thrown on the bank to rot, carp get no respect. Since we're stuck with them anyway, let's take a closer look at these powerful, widely distributed, and much-maligned fish. With many of our natural waterways succumbing to years of pollution and degradation, anglers may well reverse their negative feeling about rough fish species and gladly pursue these breeds.

Life History and Growth Rates

(According to McClane's *New Standard Fishing Encyclopedia*)*

Carp were brought to this country from Germany in 1876, and because of their wide adaptability, tremendous reproductive potential, and tolerance of many bottom types, they have established themselves in virtually every major waterway.

These fish spawn between April and July depending on latitude. When water temperatures warm to 60 to 65 degrees, shallow-water migrations occur, especially in weedy areas. Tremendous splashing and thrashing accompanies spawning, and often overly inspired breeders beach themselves.

Eggs are broadcast over wide areas and stick in masses to plants and bottom debris. The eggs are then deserted and hatch in about a week. Carp are very prolific: an average of 150,000 eggs per pound of body weight is not unusual. A large fish may deposit as many as 2 million eggs.

Carp gain an average of 1 pound of weight each year, with gains of 3

*A. J. McClane, *1974 New Standard Fishing Encyclopedia,* (New York: Holt, Rinehart and Winston), p. 197.

pounds yearly in exceptionally fertile waters. It is this rapid growth potential that attracted underdeveloped countries to the carp as a cheap food source. The fast growth results from one of the most efficient food-to-flesh conversions in the animal kingdom. The omnivorous carp expends very little energy while moving slowly over the bottom, sucking up just about anything tasty with their vacuum-cleaner mouths.

The rod-and-reel record for this country is a mammoth 55 pounds, 5 ounces for a carp caught in Clearwater Lake, Minnesota. The heaviest carp on record is an 83-pound, 8-ounce lunker netted in South Africa.

Carp are long-lived (twenty to twenty-five years in the wild), tolerant of high and low temperatures, able to utilize atmospheric oxygen (and so are the last to die in polluted waters), and above all, smart.

What Would a Good Public Relations Campaign Say About Carp?

Carp have reputations for eating game-fish eggs. According to a five-year study conducted by the New York State Department of Conservation in which over six hundred stomach analyses were done, however, not a single fish egg was found. Compared to that egg-eating, nest-raiding pirate, the popular blue gill sunfish, the carp is an innocent. It might pick up an egg on occasion, because carp are wide-ranging bottom feeders, but it would be a rare occurrence.

Carp are very powerful fighters. Their thick bodies and broad tails enable them to fight long and hard, even if not as spectacularly as some more popular species. When hooked in shallow mudflat areas they will streak with surprising speed and power for deep water in a straight-line, high-speed surge.

Carp are among the "smartest" fish in fresh water. Different species of game fish were put in separate ponds, then each fish was caught using a variety of techniques. Researchers wanted to learn how long it took to catch the same fish twice using the same technique. When the results were in, it took longer to fool the same carp twice than any other test species.

Carp are highly esteemed for both food and sport in Europe and Asia. In Europe many fishing tournaments are geared toward rough fish, and light-action rods up to 20 feet long are used to provide maximum sport. Everywhere carp are found they can easily be caught using a wide array of tackle and can almost always be caught from shore.

Carp are tasty if prepared properly. It is important to skin them and trim off the dark flesh. They are excellent when smoked, and the roe is edible and often sold in canned form. The flesh is an important ingredient in making gefilte fish.

Now, does that sound like a fish that should be thrown on the bank to rot?

How to Go Garpin' for Carp

We usually go garpin' for carp in late May. Big carp are spawning then and can be found in shallow canals, rivers, and bays. No garpin' for carp excursion is complete without a chilled twelve-pack of beer, munchies, a radio, and a comfortable seat, in addition to rod and reel.

Nightcrawlers and canned corn are excellent baits; I've even caught carp on flies, jigs, and crankbaits. The ultimate carp bait is, however, the corn-meal doughball!

Boil water in a small pot, add Karo syrup and cornmeal, remove from heat and stir. The perfect doughball will have the consistency of Playdoh and can actually be bounced. If a rolled doughball is thrown at a wall and it bounces off without breaking apart, it is perfect and will stay on the hook for many casts.

A medium-action spinning rod and open-faced spinning reel filled with 8- to 10-pound-test monofilament line is fine for garpin' for carp. No sinkers should be used if they can be avoided. Carp are very cautious feeders, and if sinkers have to be used they should be slip sinkers, so no excess weight is detected as the carp moves off with the bait.

Cover a single hook between size 4 and size 8 with a pear-shaped dough-ball, and fling it out gently. Put your rod in a Y-crotched stick, turn on the radio, open a beer, and relax. But be ready! When carp are in shallow the action can be unbelievably fast. If action is slow try "chumming"—tossing extra bait into the water to attract fish—with canned corn or dough-ball bits. Baiting areas with stale bread and cakes can keep carp in the same spot for weeks.

Garpin' for Carp: Glossary of Terms

Inspired garping carpers have come up with their own vocabulary to describe common events when carp fishing.

Express bite: When a carp picks up your doughball and streaks off at full speed, you have just had an "express bite." More rods are pulled off the bank and into the water by carp than probably any other fish.

Taking it straight out: When a carp picks up your doughball, let him run all the slack out of your line, and just before your rod tip starts bouncing, set the hook as hard as your tackle allows. "Cross his eyes," as Texas bass anglers say. The carp when hooked will streak off, and if your timing is right and your reel drag is set right you can pull yourself right to your feet, ready for further combat.

Reverse bite: There is no guarantee that a biting carp will move away from you with the bait. He might move directly toward you. You will notice slack line building up every few seconds. Reel in the slack gently, but don't over-reel or the carp will feel the rod pressure and drop the bait. Set the hook.

A 50-pounder: When a large carp is hooked (over 20 pounds) start yelling, "It's a 50-pounder!" This brings people running in a hurry and may also cause traffic jams.

Song-and-dance bite: Wise old carp sometimes take their sweet time about streaking off with the doughball. They take it out an inch at a time, drop it, pick it up and drop it, again and again. Patience, garping carpers, these fish are often 50-pounders. Wait until they take it straight out.

Eric Seidler with a nice carp taken on doughbait with a light-action downrigger rod.

6/Introduction to Fly-fishing

Flies called dry float
  Boats with sails of feather
Wet flies sink when in the drink
  They're best in lousy weather
Nymphs, the young of the dry fly dun
  Wingless river daughters
Streamers fin into the dim
  deep dark underwaters

E. Seidler

Any freshwater fish that can be taken on an artificial lure can be caught on a fly, and the basic techniques necessary to catch any fish with a fly will, by and large, work on all. These include 1) getting the fly in the water (the cast), 2) controlling it while it is there (the drift or retrieve), and 3) hooking and landing the fish (the thrill). *All* further refinements are dictated by the species of fish and the particular bodies of water in which you fish for them.

First Things First

Do you have a rod? Can you cast it? If not and you are completely new to fly-fishing, honestly answer the question, "Where will I do the majority of my fishing?" The following categories should get you closer to a choice of rod, reel, and line that will be comfortable. To start I recommend floating, weight-forward lines, balanced by line weight with the corresponding rod (Figure 1).

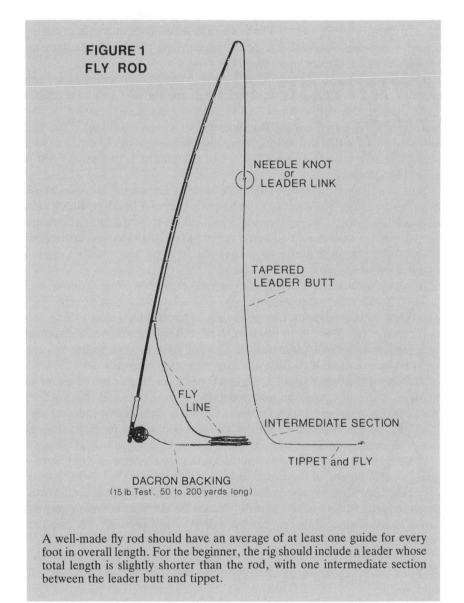

**FIGURE 1
FLY ROD**

NEEDLE KNOT
or
LEADER LINK

TAPERED
LEADER BUTT

FLY
LINE

INTERMEDIATE SECTION

TIPPET and FLY

DACRON BACKING
(15 lb Test, 50 to 200 yards long)

A well-made fly rod should have an average of at least one guide for every foot in overall length. For the beginner, the rig should include a leader whose total length is slightly shorter than the rod, with one intermediate section between the leader butt and tippet.

Small, brush-lined trout streams, meadow brooks, small panfish ponds . . . . Tiny water of all kinds can be comfortably fished with short casts (10- to 25 feet) and small flies (Number 12 and smaller). Therefore, short, light rods and lines (7 to 8½ feet, 4 to 5 weight) are appropriate.

Long rods are cumbersome in the brush, and heavy ones make short casting a trial. I recommend a leader 6 inches shorter than the rod length, tapered to a 2- or 3-pound-test tippet 18 inches long.

Medium-sized trout or smallmouth-bass streams and ponds that are relatively clear of weed growth, sunken timber, and the like, can be managed quite comfortably with rods of 8 to 9½ feet in length and 5, 6 or 7 in line weight. The increased casting distances (25 to 45 feet) and larger flies (up to Number 4, perhaps) justify longer and heavier gear. Again, a leader slightly shorter than the rod with a tippet strength of 3- to 8-pound test is probably sufficient.

Bass or northern-pike ponds and lakes with heavy weeds, lily pads, brush piles, and accumulated timber take heavy tackle and big flies. Beefy rods of 8 to 9½ feet for 7-, 8- or 9-weight lines with short, 5 to 6 foot, 12-pound-test leaders are necessary to fight the snags and salad and to deliver Number 4/0 deerhair bugs and 8-inch streamers the 30 to 50 feet usually required in this kind of fishing.

Big lakes and rivers, and big trout, smallmouth bass, shad, salmon, and steelhead, *etc.*, often require long casts with a large range of fly sizes and, occasionally, split shot or weighted flies. This is demanding fishing, requiring long rods of 8½ to 10 feet with 7- to 10-weight lines and (frequently) long leaders of up to 15 feet overall. Casting a large, air-resistant fly on a long leader for distance is difficult. Don't be undergunned.

The era of the really sweet fiberglass rods at reasonable prices seems to be over. The most common material today is graphite, and that's where the deals are. Expect to spend at least $75 for a nice, mass-produced rod. They will be much easier to find in the middle weights (6, 7, 8) than at either extreme.

"Level lines" (i.e., with uniform thickness) are obsolete—avoid them—and "double tapers" do not cast quite as easily as "weight forward" lines. "Sinking lines" are for special purposes and are a real hassle for novices. A good quality line will last several years with minimal attention and will cost $20-30. A cheap line that does not float or cast properly will convince you to take up tennis.

Any fly reel that holds all of the fly line plus 50 yards of dacron backing will be suitable for most of the fishing the majority of anglers is likely to undertake.

Now that you have the tackle, acquire the cast. Ask a friend to help, or emulate any stranger you are privileged to observe whose fly spends more time in the water than in the air or in the trees. Go to the library and take out any casting manual or instructional video by Joan Salvato Wulff or Lefty Kreh. You may even choose to attend one of the many fine fly-fishing schools that have opened up shop in various parts of the country.

Casting

The sole object of fly casting is to get the fly in the water. This may seem obvious, but as with any other human activity, those who excel set the standards for the rest of us. The bow hunter must practice until the target is centered, or the result afield is wounded game; the wing shot must internalize a set of highly sophisticated reflexes, or the bird will keep flying. Urgent, practical reasons exist for the ultimate refinement of these skills, and a high degree of precision should be attained before a novice even begins to put them into practice.

Fly-fishing is much friendlier in this sense. The beginner can go fishing with one basic cast and learn the refinements over time, at need.

I have watched too many people spend their fishing time trying to keep an extra few feet of line in the air while attempting to reach a target they have chosen on the basis of challenging their casting skills. These people are fishing to cast, not casting to fish. They are so distracted by the business in the air that they don't concentrate on the water, where the fish are. Ultimately the most important skills that are acquired through fly-fishing are getting close to fish without disturbing them, and putting a fly in the water with due regard to controlling its behavior once it is there. If you pick your casts on the basis of where the fish are and put yourself where a short, controlled cast will reach them, you will not only catch many more fish, you will be able to figure out what went wrong when you didn't. If you get too close and spook the fish, try a different angle of approach next time. Try putting a tongue of broken water between you and the fish and wade tenderly. Be aware of the silt stream dislodged by your boots. Get down on your knees to get your shadow off the water. Almost anything will work better than backing up and attempting a longer cast. Perhaps the problem is with a conflicting current that carries your fly away from the fish so they never even see it. From a distance you can only guess. Even if you guess correctly you will have much more difficulty making the necessary adjustments if you are a long way off than you would have had with less line on the water. Over the years as you fish to specific, fishy targets your casting will improve by itself. The experience of finding fish and watching their behavior in the presence of your fly will make casting what it should be—a necessary interruption in fishing the fly, to be performed as efficiently as possible so that the fly may fish again. If you are going salmon fishing, steelheading, bonefishing, or big-water trout fishing, by all means learn to throw an entire line. But the vast majority of fishing opportunities available to the vast majority of people require casts of 50 feet or less, executed without undue hazard to bystanders, and made to land gently on the water.

Assuming that you have never handled a fly rod before, here's what you should do to learn to cast.

On a windless day go to an open stretch of stream that is free of overhead obstacles with a slow to moderate current, where *nobody* is fishing or likely to want to fish anytime soon. Tie on a fly, say a Number 10 with the hook point clipped off. (Always practice with a fly. Always evaluate a rod's potential with both leader and fly tied on. As tackle dealers all know, a rod casts bare line much more easily than it does with line, leader, and flyrigged.)

Wade out to midstream and face downstream so that you can be sure there is nothing to hang up your backcast. Now point your rod downstream, parallel to the water's surface, and strip out four rod-lengths of line, including leader (which should be, for most fly-fishing purposes, a few inches shorter than the rod itself). With the index finger of your rod hand, anchor the fly line against the rod grip (right- or left-handed, it doesn't matter), and put your line hand in your pocket.

Feel the current tugging on the line. Slowly lift the rod and notice the bend that is put there by the pull of the current on the line. The degree of bend represents energy being stored in the rod, and as it bends, the rod is said to be *loading*. Most of the energy required for the rod to throw the line into a *backcast* is stored (loaded) in the rod during the first fraction of a second of the cast. This is called the *pickup* (Figure 2).

Once the rod is loaded and the backcast is in progress, the caster's attention should be given to the timing of the *forward cast*. The forward cast should begin when the line's rearward momentum re-loads the rod with sufficient energy to (with a very little bit of help) throw the line forward again. If you lift the rod more sharply you will notice (along with a greater degree of loading) that at a certain point enough energy is imparted to the line so that the surface tension of the water is overcome. The line suddenly jumps into the air, comes sailing back at you, and lands wrapped around your rod, neck, and shoulders. (This is why we clipped off the hook point.) You have made a good start. You have begun to learn the *pickup* and *power stroke*.

Allow the line to drift back downstream and repeat the pickup motion until you can predict the moment at which the line will become airborne. Continue the repetition until you can *control* the moment at which it leaves the water, either early or late in the power stroke. The object is *not* to rip the line directly off of the water (which would happen if you were using a broom handle), but to quickly and smoothly store sufficient energy in the bending rod (by loading against the resistance of the line in the water) so that, a split second after the rod loads, it slides the line out of the water and into the air. If you are tearing great rents in the water surface, you

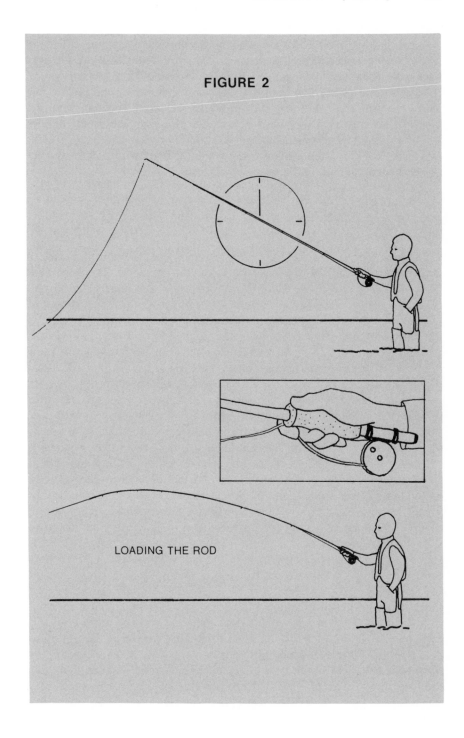

FIGURE 2

LOADING THE ROD

are applying too much force too quickly. If your line is bogging down and not achieving sufficient altitude to clear both you and your rod on its way back over your shoulder, you are applying too little force too late.

Now take your line hand out of your pocket and grasp the fly line just above the rod grip, releasing it from under the index finger of your rod hand. Make your next pickup as before, but this time accompany it with a short, smooth, downward pull on the line with your line hand. This is called the *line haul*, and it allows you to load the rod with a much shorter power stroke than would be required otherwise.

The Backcast

The best piece of advice I got as a beginner was, "If you take care of your backcast, your forward cast will take care of itself." This is so near the truth that I pass it on. The first consideration that must be addressed concerning your backcast is, "Where do I want it to go?" The answer is, "Over the rod and rising until it straightens out behind you." Any arc in the path your rod hand takes from the beginning of your power stroke through the moment your backcast straightens out behind you will allow the backcast to drop and hit the water. This will rob your forward cast of power and accuracy. If you hold your casting arm, bent at the elbow, with your hand at shoulder height and the rod at roughly 10 o'clock to the water surface (the baseline), and then bring your rod hand back even with your ear in a straight line that *rises* from the baseline at an angle of about 25 to 30 degrees, your rod tip, fly line, leader, and fly will follow a parallel, ascending path. To make certain that it does so, your line hand should always follow the rod hand, lagging behind just enough to keep tension on the line. This is crucial. Should the line hand overtake the rod hand as it goes up and back at any time during the power stroke, the cast will collapse. You can prove this to yourself by letting go of the line just after it leaves the water.

Let's try once more. Begin to load the rod with a pickup. Move your hand firmly but smoothly from 10 o'clock back to your ear in a *straight* line, rising from the baseline at a 20- to 30-degree angle (depending on wind, length of line, rod action and obstacles to the rear) and stop when your hand gets to your ear—that's right, stop the rod and allow your rod hand to drift up and slightly backward with the weight of the unfurling line. If all has gone well a loop of line is now traveling up and to your rear (turn your head and watch it) at the same angle to the baseline that your rod hand (and therefore your rod tip) described during the power stroke (Figure 3).

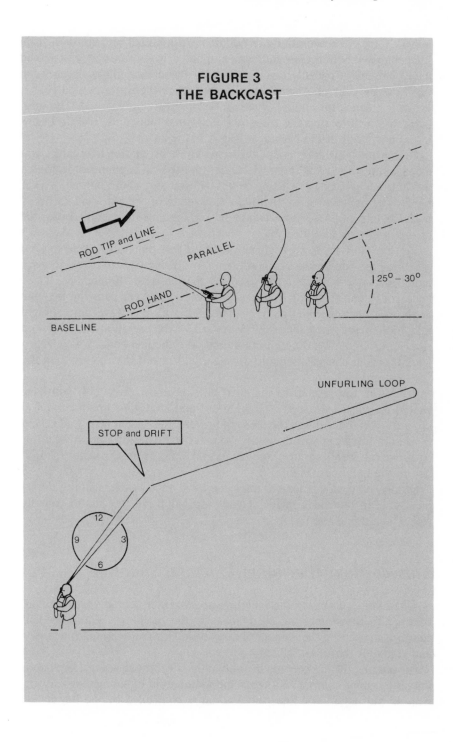

FIGURE 3
THE BACKCAST

Now let's leave everything in midair for a moment and consider what happens next. When your rod hand stopped at your ear, your rod should have been left at roughly 1 or 2 o'clock on a clockface; if it went back too far it outran your line, which sagged and struck the water behind you. If it didn't go back far enough, the cast collapsed right overhead. The ideal point at which to stop the rod is the point just before the rod tip begins to arc down out of the path on which it has been.

No matter how short your power stroke is, no matter how much arm extension or wrist rotation or whatever you use—all elements of form that are hotly debated in fly-casting circles—if you stop there and allow your hand to be pulled ever so slightly by the weight of the unfurling backcast, until the line and leader are completely straightened out behind you, the picture will look like Figure 4.

You are now ready to begin the forward cast that will re-load the rod and bring the line forward for a presentation. Bring your rod hand forward along the same path that you used for the backcast. Remember, if you keep your hand traveling in a straight line and prevent your rod tip from arcing out of its parallel path, your fly line will also travel in a straight line, both up into the backcast and forward for the presentation. To ensure sufficient rod loading during the forward cast, the line hand, which lagged behind on the backcast, should be slightly ahead of the rod hand on the way forward and down.

When the rod returns to the 10 o'clock position, stop it. If you have waited for the backcast to straighten out and kept your line hand ahead of your rod hand through the forward power stroke, your line, leader, and fly should travel, at speed, toward your target. Aim for a point a foot or so above the water surface, and try to make the fly hit the water (gently) before the line does (Figure 5).

Finally, no cast is complete until you have once again anchored the fly line between the index finger of your rod hand and the grip of your fly rod. Make this a habit.

Falsecasting: Extending Line and Shooting

When you are able to pick the line up, throw it behind you, and then return it to the water, you are halfway to the basic cast. The other half concerns measuring the amount of line needed for the fly to reach a target, and getting it there.

Falsecasting means keeping the line in the air through several back-and-forward-casting motions. By using the momentum of succeeding forward casts to pull additional line (the amount is controlled by the line hand)

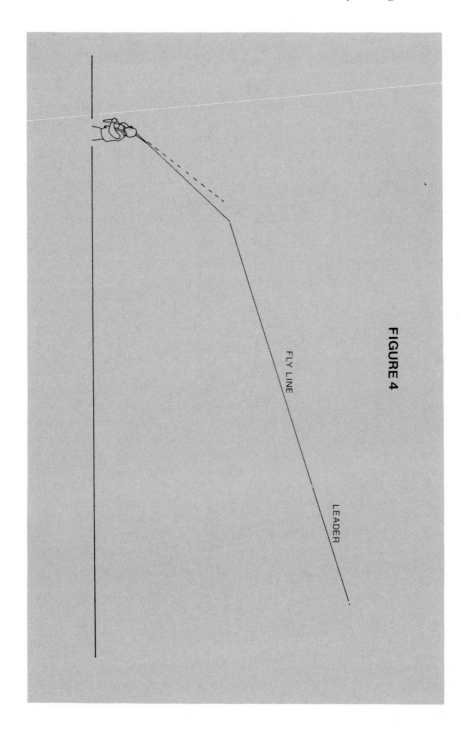

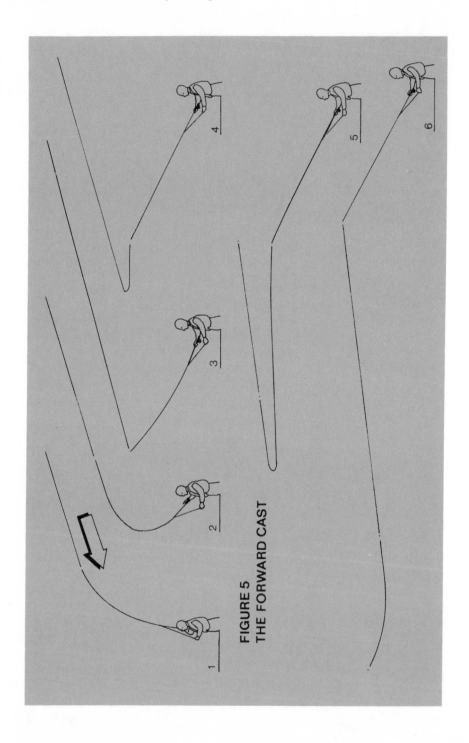

FIGURE 5
THE FORWARD CAST

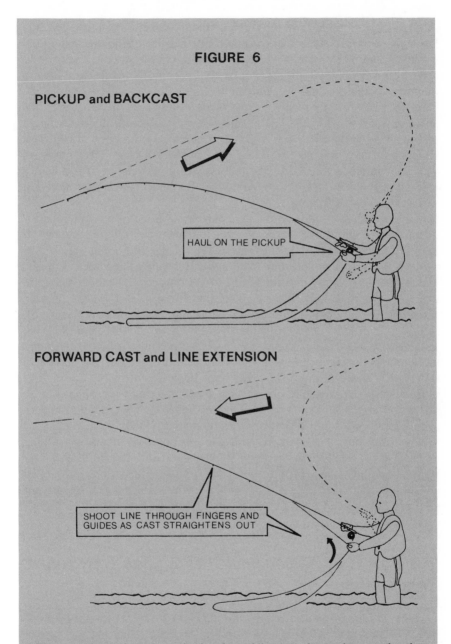

FIGURE 6

PICKUP and BACKCAST

HAUL ON THE PICKUP

FORWARD CAST and LINE EXTENSION

SHOOT LINE THROUGH FINGERS AND
GUIDES AS CAST STRAIGHTENS OUT

The caster may either extend a few feet of line on a forward cast and make another backcast, or shoot all of the remaining line toward the target.

through the rod guides and into the air, the fly caster can, in two or three falsecasts, extend upwards of 60 feet of line before setting it down on the water. If a longer cast is needed, the final forward cast can be made to carry as much as 30 additional feet of line through the guides and toward the target. This is called *shooting the line*.

Begin, as before, by facing downstream, trailing four rod lengths of line in the current. Anchor the line against your rod grip with the index finger of your rod hand and strip 6 to 8 feet of additional line out of your reel so that it forms a loop between your rod hand and the reel. Reach forward with your line hand and take the line out from between your rod hand's index finger and the rod grip, holding it in readiness for the *line haul* that will accompany the pickup.

Make a backcast followed by a forward cast aimed at a point approximately 4 feet above the water. As the forward cast straightens out, but before it loses momentum, allow a few feet of the additional line to flow through the fingers of your line hand and out through the guides. Stop the line in your line hand before it begins to fall towards the water, haul, and make another backcast. Repeat. The final forward cast can be used to shoot all the remaining additional line you may wish to throw (Figure 6). With a little practice, two falsecasts and a shoot will double your distance. Endeavor to use as few falsecasts as possible; not only will your fly spend more time in the water, but you will avoid the loss of control that inevitably sets in after three or more falsecasts have been executed.

At some point you may observe fly casters making what appear to be dozens of falsecasts without extending any line. Don't be fooled: they are simply air-drying waterlogged dry flies so that they will float again.

Now you *could* tie on a fly with a hook point on it and go fishing *downstream* (an excellent direction in which to fish), but before you get smug and self-satisfied, turn around and try casting upstream. Can't even get started, can you? That nice, friendly downstream tug that let you get your rod half-loaded for a pickup is all behind you now.

The Roll Cast, Compound Pickup, and Upstream Presentation

To avoid *lining*—spooking fish with your line—no cast should be made directly upstream. Select a target up and across stream and face across current, perpendicular to the flow, with your casting shoulder downstream. Let out the usual four rod lengths of line. Then, with elbow bent, point your rod up and slightly back. A sag will develop in the line between the

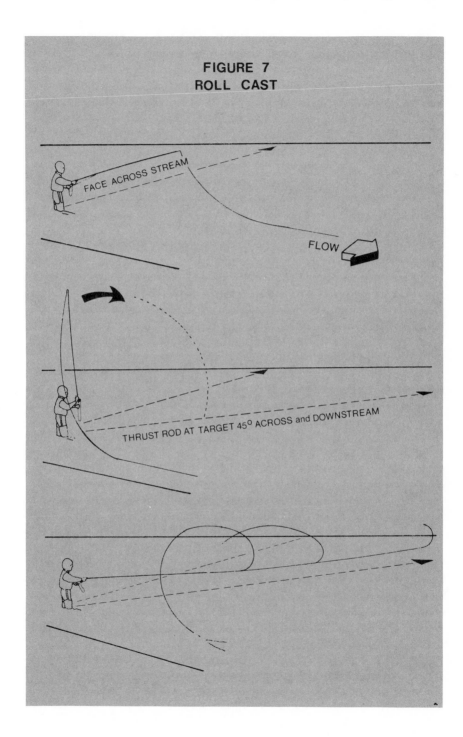

**FIGURE 7
ROLL CAST**

FACE ACROSS STREAM

FLOW

THRUST ROD AT TARGET 45° ACROSS and DOWNSTREAM

rod and water surface, a sag which will prove very useful. Pick a target that is 45 degrees across and downstream, and vigorously thrust your rod down and out until it points directly at the target. This motion will create a loop or wave in the line that will pick the line up and roll it in the direction your rod is pointing. You can now use the momentum of the loop, while it's still in the air and before it loses speed, to load the rod for a backcast (Figure 7). As your backcast straightens out, turn your upper body to face up- and across stream, and throw your forward cast in this direction. Because of wind or obstructions, it will sometimes be necessary to change direction in stages with a few falsecasts. On extremely rare occasions when there are obstructions behind you, you may need to use a reverse cast. It is made by facing 180 degrees from your target and using your second backcast for the presentation.

Far more frequently you will find yourself with no room at all for a backcast. At these times a well-planned roll cast is your best chance.

If, once you have made your initial up- and across-stream presentation, you don't want to wait for the line to travel all the way downstream before you make your next cast, you can make a roll cast-compound pickup (see bottom of Figure 7) directly across stream, or you can help the rod load by exaggerating the line haul (with your line hand) so that even though the current is bringing the line toward you, between your line hand and the power stroke you will be able to overtake the current, straighten out the line, and sufficiently load the rod to get back into action.

If after a few practice sessions you are still unable to do business with your fly tackle, seek help. You may be doing something wrong, or you may be the victim of a tackle imbalance. Even top-shelf rods are sometimes rated for line weights according to the peculiar casting styles of their designers. For my own style of casting, I find that a lot of rods are rated too light—6-weight rods that, in my opinion, perform better with 7- or 8- weight lines—but even so, most rods can be made to throw lines of one weight increment up or down from their ratings. All things being equal, minor imbalances should not affect your ability to learn to cast (as they are imperceptible to the beginner), but major ones can sink you like a stone. Leaders that are too long, or flies that are too big, are common, correctable, imbalances that can frustrate a novice. What is too long or too big? Ultimately, as you gain experience, that is for you to decide. There are many charts and rules of thumb concerning tippet diameter, leader length, line weight, and fly size that have been very effective in convincing beginners that a whole range of rods and lines must be purchased to cover various fishing conditions. It just ain't so. It's true that no one rod will do it all. It's equally true that two rods, say a 5-weight and an 8-weight, will do almost all of it. As a novice you should be primarily concerned with making an adequate presentation with the tackle you own. If you are popping off flies (either on your backcast or in fish), go to a heavier tippet, and watch your backcast to be certain it straightens out before you begin the forward cast or presentation. If you're having a miserable time casting, shorten your leader (try 6-inch to start with), tie on a smaller fly, re-examine your cast—does your line hand keep tension on the line *throughout* the cast, does your rod hand travel in a straight line? *etc.* Only when you have examined your own equipment and methods should you buy something, like a heavier or (possibly) lighter fly line.

Unavoidable Fuss

Leaders must be tapered, for two reasons: first, to turn over the fly, and second, so that if your fly breaks off you will only lose a portion of the last section (the tippet), which is the easiest to replace.

I use Cortland Line Co. 444 tapered leader butts. They have the least "memory" (which means that I can straighten them out by pulling at either end) and are the most durable of any factory-tapered leaders on the market. I frequently get an entire year's fishing out of one. Attach your leader to your fly line with a needle knot or a leader link (see Figure 8).

For the intermediate sections of the leader I use Maxima Chameleon for the same reasons as above, and because I feel that it has superior knot strength. There are currently a lot of new and highly touted brands of fine-diameter leader material on the market. I have tried them all and found them all to be wretched in terms of knot strength, durability, and memory. Intermediate leader sections and tippets should be joined by blood knots or double surgeon knots. Try to avoid mating two sections of monofilament that are more than .003-inch different in diameter. The fly should be attached to the tippet with a double-improved clinch knot (Figure 8). For a tighter set, all knots should be lubricated with saliva before being drawn tight.

Always carry a hook hone. Always sharpen your hooks (Figure 9). Check the hook point after *every* missed fish. This may be the most important paragraph in this book!

The Flies

A fly is an imitation of an organism of interest to fish *or* a handmade lure that may or may not imitate an organism of interest to fish and that

FIGURE 8

LEADER LINK  Flyline to leader connection

NEEDLE or TUBE KNOT Same. A tube, needle, or nail can be used to guide the leader through the coils.

BLOOD KNOT Mating monofilament leader sections

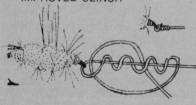

DOUBLE SURGEON Same

IMPROVED CLINCH For small flies and light tippets

DOUBLE IMPROVED CLINCH For larger flies and heavier tippets

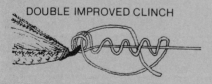

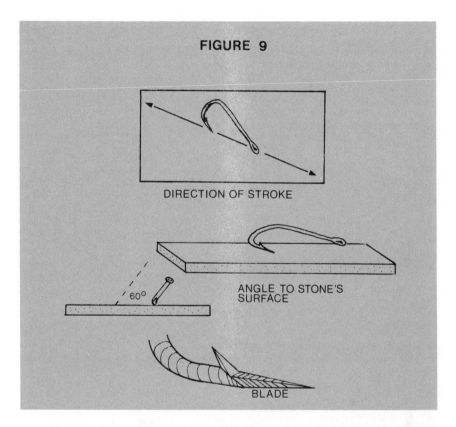

is too light to cast by any means other than fly casting. These organisms include insects, crustaceans, minnows, etc.

Dry Flies imitate or suggest aquatic winged adult insects that float, at a life stage just after emergence (metamorphosis) from the nymph stage, or upon their return to the water to lay eggs and die. These include mayflies, stoneflies, caddis and midges, and also "terrestrials" such as ants, hoppers, beetles, etc., that enter the water by mischance in sufficient numbers to make their imitations effective lures.

Wet Flies sink. They include nymphs, streamers, traditional wet flies, emergers, and stillborns.

Nymphs are the sub-aquatic larval life stage of winged airborne insects. The term also refers to any wingless wet fly including (but not limited to) stoneflies, mayflies, crane flies, mosquitoes, dobson flies, caddis, and dragonfly larva. The term nymph is also used to describe egg flies ("salmon nymphs") and any other wet fly that is fished dead drift. In some parts of the country imitations of scuds, crayfish, and other crustaceans are referred to as nymphs.

FIGURE 10
FLIES
DRAWN TO SCALE

DRY FLY

"HENDRICKSON"

Mayfly Dun

WET FLIES

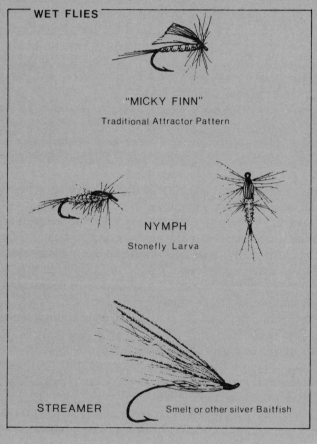

"MICKY FINN"

Traditional Attractor Pattern

NYMPH

Stonefly Larva

STREAMER   Smelt or other silver Baitfish

Streamers imitate or suggest small fish, leeches, and crustaceans.

Traditional wet flies are non-imitative winged and hackled sub-surface lures that are usually swung or retrieved rather than dead drifted in the current.

Emergers and Stillborns imitate insects in transition from the nymph to the adult phase and those that die in the process.

By all means tie flies yourself. Poul Jorgenson's *Modern Fly Dressings for the Practical Angler* (1976, Winchester Press) will go far to get you started and may perhaps be the only fly-tying book you will ever need. However, there are many other good ones, both general and specialized, waiting to suit the requirements you develop in your fishing. If dry fly-fishing for trout catches you, you will never see the end of it. The waters are so well charted, from the anatomy of the tiniest relevant aquatic insects to emergence charts for virtually every major watershed in which they and trout occur, that dry fly-fishing has become a sort of *samadhi* today in the U.S. People leave careers and family in search of the perfect paralepto-phlebia imitation and pass out of all knowing.

Fly Selection

Fly talk is endless and arcane. The literature is likewise profuse. For our purposes (getting you on the water with as little preliminary fuss as possible) only a short discussion is in order.

Dry Flies and Other Flies that Float

These fall into two categories:

1) Insect imitations that are immobile as they are borne along by the current and are therefore allowed to drift "dead" (mayflies and midges).

2) Flies that are manipulated by the angler, who, by imparting movement to the fly, imitates more mobile creatures (stoneflies, some mayflies, caddis, hoppers, *etc.*)

This dichotomy applies equally to nymphs.

If your home waters are trout streams and rivers, a good initial assortment from Category 1 should include Adamses, Hendricksons, March Browns, Humpies, Light Cahills, White Caddis, and Dark Caddis in sizes Number 12 to 18.

From Category 2 your fly selection is *the same.* That's right: any fly that can be dead drifted can also be twitched, skittered, dapped, or retrieved in a variety of interesting ways that elicit a variety of interesting responses from fish, ranging from immediate strikes to abject terror and panicked flight. Try everything.

Other flies that float are floating nymphs (see Michael Kimball's chapters) and the various bugs, poppers, mice, bombers, and hoppers used for bass, pike, and (under some circumstances) huge trout and salmon. All (except floating nymphs) are big —Number 10 to 4/0—and all are meant to be manipulated by the angler. Most are constructed of deerhair or cork with feathers and are made to move a lot of water when retrieved. A 4/0 weedless deerhair moth, frog, or mouse will catch largemouth bass and pike as well as any other top-water stick, plug, or popper-type bait. Smaller ones—Number 4 to 2/0—are excellent for smallmouth bass, pickerel, brown trout at night, and (I'm told) Alaskan rainbow trout. In smaller sizes of Number 8 to 4 these flies will take Atlantic (and landlocked Atlantic) salmon and steelhead. The smallest deerhair bugs (Number 10, 8, or 6) are perfect for panfish. All floating flies need to be dressed with floatant. Floatants come in many forms—waxes, pastes, liquids, ointments. All seem to work equally well.

Flies that Sink

Sinking flies consistently catch the most and the biggest. From just under the surface to scraping the bottom, nymphs (see Chapters 9 and 10), streamers (see Chapter 8), emergers, wets, egg patterns, crayfish, scuds, and leeches put the lie to any pretense that fly-fishing is an innocent pastime.

Largemouth bass and pike like huge streamers (up to Number 4/0, 6 to 12 inches long) about as well as plastic worms, crankbaits, and spoons. Weedless patterns can be fished in the trash, and weighted streamers, bucktails, and marabous can be just as effective as jigs over a clean bottom.

Smallmouth bass in lakes or streams (and walleyes, for that matter) are excellent fly-rod fish. They get enthusiastic over any midsized streamer (1½ to 3 inches), and a big wet fly or nymph fished deeply will take as many stream or river bass as *anything* else.

The three chapters following deal in depth with subsurface flies and techniques for trout and salmon, so I won't anticipate them here. Instead let's turn briefly to the fly's behavior on or in the water, and what we can do to control it.

Moving Water

In this country—it means something else in Britain—to *dead drift* a fly means to take pains that it move with the flow of water as if helpless and unimpeded, unable to swim if submerged, and unable to walk, fly or skitter if floating. Trout, for whom a dead drift is an important technique, will generally elect to follow the feeding strategy that requires the least expenditure of energy. A helpless, drifting insect is the easiest to catch.

The fly caster's task is to manage the cast and drift in such a way that the line and leader are not put under tension by the current, thereby dragging the fly out of the path that the fish *knows* it would take if it were unimpeded. The fish has deliberately put itself directly in, under, or to one side of that path—the tongue of current that will bear the most and the easiest to identify and capture prey organisms within taking range of itself. They are very good at this game; playing it makes up the bulk of their existence. At those times when there is a significant population of non-swimming or weak-swimming organisms in drift, fish will tend to forgo active prey that they would at other times chase. In rivers with good insect populations these circumstances prevail much of the time. This feeding strategy is often referred to as *selectivity,* and the fish themselves as *selective trout.* The process of *matching the hatch* is one of eliminating the possible alternatives and so identifying a given group of hatching insects through study of the insect populations in a given stream, and then trying various flies on a given day so as to arrive at the best possible imitation of that species and its life-cycle stage (nymph? emerger? dun? spinner?, *etc.*). Then you must fish the fly you select in such a manner that the fish, in full confidence, will take it to be the genuine article.

To learn to fish acceptably to these selective fish, go to the stream. Tie on the biggest, most visible dry fly you own and throw it across a fast current into a slow current so that your line lands in the swift one. Watch as your line is dragged downstream, dragging your fly *out* of the path it would take if it were freely drifting. Next, move to an area where the opposite current combination occurs, and throw your fly into the fast (farther) current while allowing your line to hang in the intervening slow water. Notice that your fly is again dragged out of what would be its natural path. This is *drag,* and the only way to overcome it is by 1) planning your cast so that the line lands on the water with slack curves that compensate for the current it lands on, and 2) by mending the line.

Mending the Line

Even if you never learn to cast more than 50 feet, you are fishing with the best if you understand curve or slack casting and line mending (Figure 11). Go back to the first location of current combinations described above, and again place your fly in the slow water. Before the intervening fast current begins to drag the fly toward you and down flow, throw a curve of line—like swinging one end of a jumprope—upstream. Next, try to do it without moving the fly. If you were lucky and mended enough line at the right time, the fly moved no differently from any other piece of floating

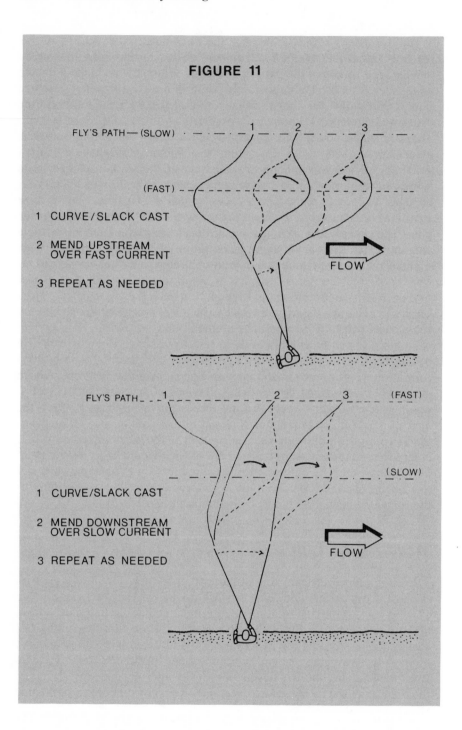

FIGURE 11

debris in its immediate vicinity. If you were late, or threw too little or too much of a loop upstream, you saw the fly drag, or jump and then drag. If you were born lucky, a fish took it no matter what you did. When you can get your dry fly to move downstream at a speed of zero relative to the current it's in, you have arrived, and should then try the same trick with a nymph.

Having learned to overcome drag, you should then learn to use it. There are many times and places when trout, for one reason or another (a paucity of prey altogether, or a preponderance of strong-swimming organisms), will chase after food. Stream bass virtually always will. Allowing or making a fly drag across stream or upstream at various speeds and depths (or on the surface) will take many fish. So will allowing it to hang motionless in the current. Drawing a nymph, streamer, or wet fly from downstream and on the bottom slightly up- and across stream and toward the surface may be the all-around-any-species ultimate riff in fly-fishing moving water.

Still Water

Trout in beaver ponds may be the most difficult fish of all. Extremely light tackle, very long, fine leaders, generally tiny flies, and rough going in dense brush with or without a float tube, fishing over extremely spooky fish in silt-bottomed, snag-filled, God-forsaken backwaters . . . . well, let's just say I ain't going back there. If you get good at that game you will be the only one on your block.

In the big lakes, streamers take trout any time they are within reach of the fly caster.

Warm-Water Species

Where I have fished for them, any technique that works for one will work interchangeably for largemouth bass, pickerel, pike, smallmouth bass, and bluegill (bearing in mind the necessity for smaller flies for the last two). The most fun can be had from these fish when they are taking on top. For largemouth, pike, and pickerel, tie or buy any deerhair bug about the size of a ¾ ounce Johnson silver minnow on a Number 4/0 hook (with a weedguard). If you wish, add a trailer of black marabou (to imitate a twister tail) and walk it over the lily pads, let it sit motionless in openings, and chug it through clear water. You won't win any tournaments, but you'll take plenty of fish.

Striking and Playing

If your hooking reflexes have been developed through the use of bait and hardware tackle, you will quickly realize that hooking fish on fly tackle requires different timing and a lighter touch overall. Long rods, light leaders, and the tendency of novices to jerk the line with their line hands while striking too quickly and with too much force result in many fish swimming around with flies in their mouths and many more that never felt the hook.

If your fly is downstream of you and your line is under tension from the pull of the current when a fish hits, it is only necessary to hold steady and allow the rod to load while slowly raising it above your shoulder. If it is a good fish, it only needs a little help to hook itself. If you are fishing over small fish or fish that peck and turn without taking solidly, you may hurry things along by raising your rod more quickly; but even a small fish downstream of you in a heavy current can tear off your fly if you add more force. If you strike too quickly you will jerk the fly out of the fish's mouth before it is ever really in it far enough to hook up.

Striking fish that take a fly upstream or across stream of you while your line is not under tension from the pull of the current (as in dead drifting) is a different matter entirely. Here you are on your own; the fish will not help you hook up. If you are fishing dry and can see the take, you must get into action quickly, but, as with the downstream fly, there is always the danger of setting the hook too hard and/or too soon. This danger can be avoided by understanding that while hook setting with bait or lure tackle is a straightforward matter of pulling a hook home, hook setting with fly tackle (assuming a floating line) has two components. The first is getting the line moving, breaking the surface tension (the fly line is in the meniscus) and straightening out the slack that inevitably (and correctly) accumulates in the course of a well-managed dead drift. This takes considerably more speed and force than the second component, which is driving the hook into the fish's mouth. The idea is to raise the rod (moving the line) and, when the line is straight and the fish's weight is felt, hold steady, exerting a constant pressure on the fish in anticipation of the first run. The pull of the current on the straight line under tension and the weight of the line itself are sufficient to load the rod and set the hook. Avoid any excessive follow-through. Relax!

Up- or across-stream dead drifting sunken flies (generally nymphs) brings an added difficulty to the task of hooking up, namely strike detection, which is dealt with fully in Michael Kimball's chapter on subsurface nymphing.

Playing

Get the fish on the reel. Throughout the drift or retrieve you have been accumulating line in your line hand; if you have been careless, you have been dropping it at your feet where it has found its way into and around every stick, stone, and crevice—in fact, you are almost certainly standing on it. You must, as soon as a fish is hooked, clear the decks. Get all of the line not immediately taken by the fish on its first run back on the reel so that you can move with your fish and give it line unhindered. Get into the habit of playing all but the smallest fish from the reel. I have seen many upland trout anglers come to grief by attempting to play salmon, steelhead, and big trout by stripping line back through the guides and dropping it on the ground or on the water without (apparently) any intuition that the fish may wish to take it back again. Get in the habit; it only takes one 10-pounder to pay you back. You will be halfway there if you fish out every cast by collecting retrieved line in neat loops that are held in your line hand in readiness for your next cast and that are easily handled in the event of a hookup. My own method is to strip once and drop the loop, strip again and hold the loop. If I were to hold every loop stripped back in I would have to hold twice as many loops in my line hand with twice the potential for tangling.

Due to the weight and water resistance of fly line compared to monofilament, the drag on your fly reel should be set much more lightly than the drag on your spinning or casting gear. In most situations it is sufficient to set it at the tension necessary to prevent overwind from occurring. Most good fly reels are designed with a palming rim on the handle side of the spool which enables you to apply additional manual pressure if needed.

Play your fish with a high rod, nod when it jumps, and pump it toward you smoothly. Old hands learn the perfect pressure. Yours will, too.

7/Streamer Seasons

by Eric Seidler

When the ice goes out of the large northeastern lakes and surface temperatures begin to climb, trout and salmon begin hunting the shorelines and tributaries for smelt, alewives, and a host of other less abundant baitfish that come close to shore seeking the spring warmth. This annual event puts the big lake migrators within reach of the flyfisher, and presents a unique opportunity to experience streamer fishing at its best.

In the Finger Lakes of central New York, where I do most of my fishing, the rainbow trout ascend the tributary streams to spawn in the early spring. Shortly thereafter the smelt do the same, bringing with them hunting landlocks and browns that sweep in and out of the lower stretches of the streams and up and down the lake shores in waves that are betrayed by the heavy rolls of feeding predators and the frantic shoals of fleeing prey. These are highly mobile fish; finding bait and staying with it is the key to success.

Open Water

Finding baitfish in open water can be accomplished in two ways: let the game fish find them for you, or let the birds do it. If you see gulls, game fish, or baitfish breaking the surface, go there by chest wader (the limitations are obvious), belly boat, or canoe.

Wind Fishing

Get *up*wind of the spot you're going to fish—the harder it's blowing, the better. Use a floating double-taper line, 5-weight or lighter, and a 15-foot leader tapered to a four-pound test tippet. Do not cast. Instead, hold your rod high and pay out line, allowing the wind and waves to bring your fly to the action. Keep your rod extended at arm's length, and move the line with the rod tip to take advantage of any gust or freshet that may occur. Between the wind and waves your streamer will dance, dart, leap out of the water, and sizzle across the surface, all without leaving the bait boil. One presentation can be fished in this manner for five or ten minutes. Surprisingly light winds can suffice if you lengthen your leader, tie on a lighter fly, and get closer to the fish.

Often a fish will strike several times (especially lakers and landlocks), seemingly in an effort to wound or tire the fly before taking solidly. Try not to remove the fly from the area by attempting to set the hook prematurely, and do not retrieve it unless you are becalmed, drift out of position, or the bait moves off. Of course, even if you have fish following a retrieved fly in open water, at some point you have to take it out of the water to make another presentation. I have seen too many fish turn away at this point that might have taken if the streamer could have kept fishing.

Momentary calms on open water serve you by allowing the streamer to pause and settle. This moment is a magic one, and the one following when the stalled fly comes to life again is equally special, as they are the times

A Finger Lakes landlock caught on a 3½-inch smelt streamer.

when solid strikes most frequently occur. At the strike quickly get in contact with the fish by rapidly reeling in the belly of line that the wind has taken and raising your rod. Only after you have felt the fish's weight should you set the hook. Setting the hook too hard and too soon will take your fly away93from the fish and convince it that your streamer *can't* be caught today.

In a stiff wind I use unweighted streamers tied on heavy hooks (Number 2/0 Mustad, Number 36890 salmon hooks), with mylar bodies, silver doll's-hair wings, and peacock hurl toppings. Any 2- to 4-inch silvery baitfish imitation will do as long as it is heavy enough to stay in the water and light enough for the wind to move it. On relatively calm days I use the same fly tied on a regular streamer hook. I fish from a 17-foot canoe with an electric trolling motor, and when I can't find bait I fish blind by slowly moving across and slightly upwind while allowing my streamer to work downwind, generally no more than 50 feet from the boat. If the wind dies I troll home and hit the streams.

Stream Fishing

Holding lies that draw spawning-run rainbows (and therefore the hordes of early-season anglers) may only hold hunting fish for short periods of time as they transit an area in search of prey or rest during those times when the bite is off. These obvious holding lies are just that—obvious— and it is often impossible to get a fly in edgewise. Due to the mobility of these fish, however, the bite, when it comes, is just as likely to occur in areas of the stream that do not draw holding fish under normal circumstances and therefore are usually free of other anglers. In the often sluggish, silty downstream areas of tributaries where the bottom is of uniform depth and catfishing seems more plausible than fly-fishing for salmonids, bait and game are passing through constantly. Either walk the banks until you see fish breaking water, or get in and wade very slowly downstream, fishing blind, until you encounter a group of fish. Try to keep to the middle of the waterway. Hunting fish will have to pass you and may do so on either side. If you move slowly you needn't worry about spooking fish. Migrating fish are much more tolerant than resident fish; I have often had them hold in my wake and have had takes a dozen or so feet directly downstream of me.

Make your casts to alternate banks, quartering downstream (see Chapter 6, Figure 7) and across, and allow each cast to fish for as long as possible. As the streamer fly swings toward midstream, impart a slight flickering motion to it with your rod tip, but don't overdo it. If you jerk your fly with the rod or strip it in with your line hand you are almost certain to be out of balance if a fish hits, unable to stop yourself from taking the fly away from the fish, or worse, breaking off at the strike. Keep your rod tip high and hold a "shock loop" in your line hand so that you can give with the fish at the first surge of the strike (see "The Soft Retrieve" in the chapter Landlocks in a Nutshell). When the fly stalls directly downstream of you, let it hang and flutter in the current, draw it forward, let it flow back, then begin a slow hand-twist retrieve (see Figure 5, Chapter 10) as a final persuader to any following fish that has not quite made up its mind to take. Blind fishing in this way accounts for many incidental takes but is really just a pastime compared to the main event.

The Bite

Ignore nothing. Wear polarized glasses, turn up your hearing aid. Any disturbance that troubles the waters should galvanize you into action. Proceed with flawless efficiency. The first indication that enough salmon or trout have encountered enough smelt or other bait to precipitate a feeding period may be no more than a bulge of water as a fish rolls or an unexplained wake. When the bite really gets going, however, bait will be jumping, and the hunters will be crashing around with the abandon of bluefish. Throw your fly at any disturbance, no matter how slight. If the smelt are breaking water put your streamer in the area as quickly as you can. I have found (by watching bait jump out of the path of fish I have hooked) that jumping smelt are generally around 10 to 15 feet ahead of their pursuers. The faster you can get your imitation into the area, the more likely it is to be the only available victim when the pursuit arrives. Always try to keep your fly in the hotspot for as long as possible. It is much more productive to work a lively fly through an area slowly than it is to repeatedly cast and retrieve a streamer that appears to the fish for only a moment and then leaves the area. Endeavor to make your streamer the most disoriented, oblivious, easily captured baitfish in an otherwise rapidly departing school. Keep your streamer near the surface; a deep fly is relatively unproductive in sluggish water. I tie mine unweighted and fish the top foot or so of the water column.

Moving Upstream

In search of hunting salmonids, we encounter the stretches of broken water (pools alternating with runs and rapids, waterfall basins, *etc.*) commonly associated with trout and salmon fishing. If migratory baitfish are present, ignore the classic-looking trout cover and find them. Everybody else on the stream will be whipping the obvious pools to a froth; the fish that are holding in them will be seeing literally thousands of casts a day. It's true that marauding groups of hunters must move through these pools on the way up- or downstream, and some are caught when they do. ("Dammit, we stood here all day and all caught fish within minutes of each other," is a common tune from the bridge-abutment and pool patrol.) You will do much better by discovering the shoals of bait that use the gravel runs and pockets in between the "club water," and the best way to do that is to walk the creek with polarized glasses until you find them. They will be using a host of (to the casual observer) unlikely looking places, endeavoring (in as much as a witless school of sprats may be said to endeavor) to stay 1) together, and 2) apart from the predator fish.

The predators will be, largely, single fish competing with each other for limited areas of concealment to either side or downstream of bait concentrations. By concealment I don't mean undercuts, brush, or obstructions, necessarily. I mean fast water adjoining slow water, broken, often white water adjoining less-broken water, midriver braids bordered by counter currents on either side. Haystacks that would make a kayaker shout can hold these fish if any possibility exists that an individual of a shoal of bait may, in a bad moment, become weakened or disoriented, tumble out of the more-or- less organized school it is with, and enter, alone, the current tongue (generally just to the side and downstream of the bait) that the hunter is using against just this eventuality.

I know a place between two bridges: channelized, rip-rapped, dug, ditched, scoured, and graveled in an effort to prevent flooding in (of course) a flood plain (see figure). The stream flows (30 yards wide) down a 5% grade over highway department rubble, gravel, and silt. Due to the gradient, every spring there are at least one or two dining-room-sized "plateaus" of gravel (heaped up by the ice and then sorted by the runoff) that are unbroken by larger rocks (sometimes there's a shopping cart, but no matter) that provide smelt with a place to school. Together they mill around in a circle all day, waiting for nightfall or falling water or the voice of the river to move them (if the smelters don't) upriver. These plateaus are (depending on the height of the water) 6 inches to several feet deep, and the channels to either side and downstream are considerably deeper and faster. If, on any given day, the smelt are using them (and they will even in very low water), the trout and salmon *will* be using the associated fast-water channels for concealment and convenience. Even on days when the velocity of the water that is diverted by these midstream channels appears to be too great for any fish to hold in comfort, they are there. In hundreds of hours of fishing and observing smelt on these plateaus, I have never seen a predator

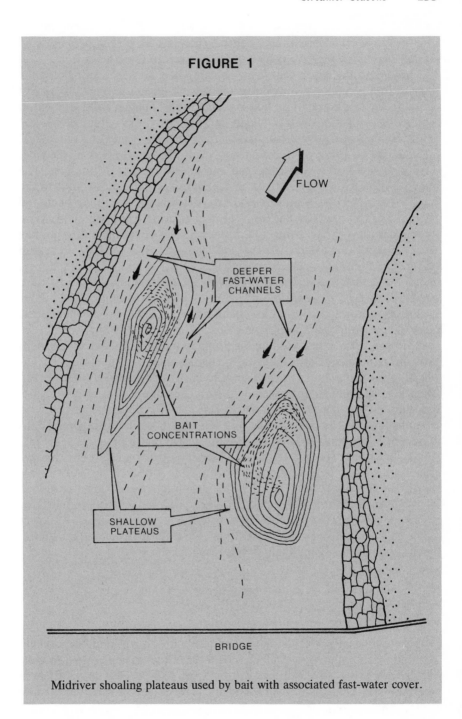

FIGURE 1

FLOW

DEEPER
FAST-WATER
CHANNELS

BAIT
CONCENTRATIONS

SHALLOW
PLATEAUS

BRIDGE

Midriver shoaling plateaus used by bait with associated fast-water cover.

fish invade one and break up a school, though I have seen people do it. It may happen at night, but by day the game is in the ditches.

Sometimes, the areas that draw shoaling bait are right up against the banks of the stream, with the covering current not more than 5 to 10 feet offshore. Wherever you find bait shoaling in this manner (and you will, if you look) you have found a golden opportunity, a real setup. Get in the water 20 to 30 feet upstream of the bait and throw your fly into the middle of it. If the covering current that you suspect holds game is to the side, lead your line into it with your rod and let the current do the rest. The flow will drag your streamer out of the school of bait and swing it to the surface out over the waiting predator. Allow your fly to play back and forth in the covering current for as long as your patience will allow. Give the predator every opportunity. Let the streamer cover the entire holding area by letting it drift downstream and then—slowly—working it back up again. If the masking current is below the bait, sweep your rod, slowly, back and forth across its breadth so that your fly traverses all of it. Picture the covering current as a wall and paint it with your streamer. The hunter you're after will choose its own moment to attack; as with fall-run landlocks, your chances improve the longer you stay with an individual fish. Lake-run browns, post-spawn rainbows feeding up on the way back to the lake, and spring landlocks are, far from being spooked by repeated presentations, really just waiting for you to put your streamer exactly where they want it. You have to push their buttons. They don't want to risk a miss any more than other predators. Keep your own manipulation of the fly to a minimum—let the current play with it—lead it around with your rod tip in search of the spot. Moving the streamer quickly will put your game off. If you make your fly appear unable to escape or oblivious to any danger, you stand a much better chance of encouraging a take. If, as a last resort (after you have lost confidence that there's a fish to be had) you introduce a little panic to your fly's behavior by quickly ripping it across the surface, you may get a predator to show itself by taking a lunge at it. This will almost always be a missed fish, but if you have avoided stinging it with the hook it will probably hit again if you resume fishing slowly.

Close Encounters

Often, especially with landlocks but also with browns and occasionally with rainbows, your first contact with a taker will be a very gentle pull, almost a sucking on the fly. It can feel just like picking up a leaf or a drifting weed. This fish is almost yours. You found its spot, and it will probably take at the next opportunity you give it. Sometimes it will pull lightly in this way on several subsequent presentations and then go down for awhile. Rest it. A half hour is more than enough, ten or fifteen minutes is usually all that is required for the fish to forget. As always when fishing a downstream fly, *don't* set the hook, let the fish do it. A 5-pounder going one way while a hook is yanked the other way is a small tragedy that I see played out over and over again on my home waters. Everybody gets jumpy when the next fish might go 10 pounds, but if you give in to the temptation to let 'em have it, you will probably lose your fly and maybe hook one fish in ten.

On Smaller Streams

Even when shoaling baitfish are not present—during the late-spring or fall runs of migratory salmonids, or on upland streams at any time of year—a streamer fly is often the best choice. As a searching pattern on unfamiliar water, a streamer can allow you to get to know a new stream, by covering a lot of water quickly, to a degree of intimacy that is not obtainable by just walking its banks. Streamers make things happen when nothing else seems to be going on.

On most of the nation's streams and rivers extensive, dependable hatches of insects are not present. Even if an isolated hatch does occur, however, large trout and bass often react by exploiting the availability of small fish, young-of-the-year fry, chubs, dace, darters, shiners—in short, "minnows"—that are drawn to the surface, or at any rate out of concealment, by the appearance of relatively large numbers of insects in drift. Lake and pond bass, pike and pickerel, all turn on when the bugs get the bait moving. The same is true of trout and river bass. At times when the insect or other invertebrate activity that gets it all going is insufficient for the larger predators to bother with, smaller fish (and large predatory invertebrates such as helgramites and crayfish) move around and make mistakes. Dawn is a peak period of invertebrate activity. Nymph migrations from nighttime feeding areas to daytime hiding areas leave a considerable number of both nymphs and predatory invertebrates caught in the open. Often they are torn from the stream bed by the current and carried helplessly, in drift, until they are eaten. Sculpins, darters, and crayfish will be spending this period of activity searching the stream bed and rock crevices for strays. Muddler minnows, sculpins, or any other brown-gray, mottled streamer fly will draw strikes from waiting predators.

Streamer Selection and Presentation

Though exact imitation is never necessary when streamer fishing, size and color can be important. I tie my streamers to correspond with the smallest *prevalent* size of baitfish or crayfish present. (Even when I tie smelt flies I match the 3- to 4-inch fish, even though individuals of 7 to 11 inches are present.) Any time this is shorter than 1 inch I use a nymph. As the season progresses, I use larger and larger flies, up to about 4 inches in length for trout and smallmouth, and up to 10 inches for bass and pike.

To suggest bottom-dwelling species I use the colors of the crayfish in my local streams when they are in the soft- shelled phase. (This differs with locality.) To suggest shiners, trout fry, and other silvery baitfish I use the same dressing that I described earlier for smelt, although often in much smaller sizes.

Behavior is the key to streamer fishing; that of the big fish and that of the little fish are inextricably bound together. A trout or stream bass, in all but the slowest currents, will always seek a place of concealment from which it can attack up or across stream. A baitfish streaking downstream, head first (over short distances they can really go) is too fast a target and can quickly negotiate shallow areas and rock crevices that would ground or otherwise thwart a larger pursuer. Plug yourself into the system. The old saws about imitating wounded or fleeing baitfish with streamer, crank-bait, spinner, or whatever, only work when the individual that is fleeing is *definitely* catchable by the predator. The fundamental principle of falconry that can be applied to fishing is, if a hawk in training is flown at quarry with every advantage in terms of wind direction and speed, cover and timing, it will learn that it *can* catch departing prey. If the falconer is remiss in providing these advantages, the hawk will quickly lose confidence and refuse the chase. A fish has been in training all its life; your job is to exploit its powers of discretion and push the fish brain button that is marked "I'll have that, whatever it is,"—streamer, wet, dry, jig, plug, rag, or worm gob—"no problem!" A streamer racing head first downstream may draw a strike, but it will usually be a miss, and you will have functioned merely as one more agent in the education of a fish that could have been caught if you'd made your fly easier to catch.

In moderate to fast flows, make your streamer presentations down and across, drifting downstream broadside to the current, or dead downstream, tail first, slowly inching in drops and pauses into a likely ambush. By gently pulsing it with your rod and/or a slow, uneven hand-twist retrieve, provide the fly with life, *but* don't jerk it, strip it quickly, or in any way provide it with the appearance that it is aware of pursuit or capable of evading it. A well-tied streamer is made to "breathe" of itself. If it has flexible materials in the dressing, for instance marabou, ostrich and peacock hurl, bucktail, bear hair (brown or polar), craft-shop doll's hair, *etc.*, the fly playing in the current will suggest the small movements of unconcerned prey fish. Released from the necessity of continually retrieving the fly (as with a spoon or spinner), the angler can concentrate on using the current to swim it into areas of predator concealment such as undercut banks, deadfalls, overhangs, brushpiles, and around boulders, and keeping it there. Inch by inch, allow your streamer to find trouble.

In slow water where less current is available to do the work, you'll have to do more of it. But even here a slow retrieve that fits and starts in inches, rather than jerks in feet, will bring the payoff. Watch baitfish. You will seldom see one that has not been frightened make a sustained run for any appreciable distance. They bob and dart and fool around, roughly maintaining position over short periods of time but covering plenty of water all the same. Gradually they enter new currents and then leave them again. They don't traverse open areas in deliberate 2-foot bursts of speed, which is exactly how most people fish a streamer fly. If you see a minnow fleeing, it has already escaped, and you will very rarely see what *was* chasing it.

When fishing the bottom I use a buoyant, muddler-type fly and add lead 20 inches or so up the line; this minimizes hangups. When fishing on top I use the smelt dressing tied on a hook that is heavy enough to keep the fly just inches under the surface. In really fast flows I add a BB to the leader to prevent its breaking the surface. In slow waters I use the most flexible, breathable wing materials I can find (marabou, doll's hair). In fast water I use stiffer materials (bucktail, bear hair). that will resist current instead of just being plastered back against the fly body. For dark fly bodies I use a dirty-cream yarn ribbed with copper wire, and for bright ones I use pearly mylar tubing. The patterns are unimportant—it's where you put them and what they do when they get there that counts.

8/Nymph Fishing to Non-Surface-Feeding Trout

by J. Michael Kimball

The nature of nymph fishing to non-rising trout on the stream bottom is entirely different from nymph fishing to visible feeders on the surface. Tackle, technique, and philosophy are at opposing ends of the fishing spectrum. The specific information needed and even the angler's attitude will require refocusing. Nymph fishing to non-surface feeders has its own group of converts who thrive on its unique challenges.

One of the major distinctions is the size of the fish. Nonrising fish, usually invisible to the angler, include not only resident stream fish, but also migratory lake fish returning to their spawning beds. These spawners offer the fisherman an opportunity to cast over formidable fish—far larger than their stream-bred relatives. The fisherman must know the spawner's habitat as well as its behavior.

Tackle

Rods

There are unique tackle considerations for non-rising fish, dependent primarily on stream conditions but also on whether the angling is focused on spawners or resident fish in holding position. Both breeders and holders

This over-12-pound steelhead (rainbow) was taken by the author on a stonefly nymph in New York State.

are oriented to the stream bottom rather than the surface. When neither fish is actively feeding they will frequently not move any significant distance to capture food. Consequently, it is imperative for the angler to reach the bottom with his nymph. A rod of at least 8 feet is recommended, and an even longer rod in the 8½- to 10-foot category may be more serviceable. The value of the longer rod lies in the angler's need to continually mend the line in order to keep the fly on the stream bed. Longer, heavier rods facilitate the use of heavy lines and weighted flies, often so necessary for this type of nymph fishing. Casting weighted lines and flies can be an unsatisfying ordeal to some when contrasted with the delicate casting so often associated with rising fish. However, for many, this lack of finesse is a fair trade for the capture of these outsized fish.

Lines

Most major line companies now produce a high-density sinking-tip line to get the fly to the bottom quickly. I like to use a sinking-tip line where the first 10 to 30 feet of the line sinks and the remainder floats. For most conditions, the 10-foot sinking tip is preferable. The longer floating portions of this line permit easier mending and optimum line control.

For extremely deep, fast waters like Montana's Missouri River, it is sometimes advantageous to use a lead-core shooting head. Sunset Line and Twine Company makes a lead shooting head called The Cannonball, which gets to the bottom exceptionally well. In very still waters, where mending the line is less critical for maintaining a drag-free float, a straight high-density sinking line is my choice. Cortland Line Company's Number-4 sinking line and Scientific Angler's Hi-Speed Hi-Density lines are excellent choices for searching the bottom of lakes and quiet pools.

Leaders

In choosing the appropriate leader, the prime consideration is to keep the fly on the stream bottom. One of the most frequently repeated mistakes is selecting too long a leader. The conventional leader lengths of 7½ to 12 feet have a tendency to plane the fly toward the surface. A maximum leader length of 6 feet, and optimally 3 to 4 feet will suffice. Under extremely heavy water conditions, when fishing to spawning fish, I have shortened my leader to as little as 2 feet to eliminate the tendency of longer leaders to ride to the surface. Another means of keeping line on the bottom is to attach a 1- to 3-foot section of lead-core trolling line to the butt section of the leader, then tie a 2- to 3-foot tippet onto the end of the trolling line. Lead core can be a misery to cast, but its rewards can be more than ample compensation.

The single most effective means of keeping the fly where the fish are is to use split shot, on a dropper, positioned 1 to 2 feet from the end of the leader. A good way to attach the split shot is to tie the tippet to the rest of the leader with a blood knot. Then, rather than clipping one end of the blood knot, let that extra line extend down approximately 1 to 2 inches, forming an anchor line, and clamp the split shot to that extension. Although this method may be aesthetically lacking to some, it will successfully keep the fly on the bottom when all else fails. During spring runoff conditions in New York's Finger Lakes region, I've found no better way to catch spawning rainbows with a nymph.

One further word of advice regarding split shot: I strongly suggest a side-arm horizontal cast to avoid snagging one's face or body. Author Charles Brooks has called casting with weighted flies "a form of Russian roulette with the eyes and ears as the stakes."

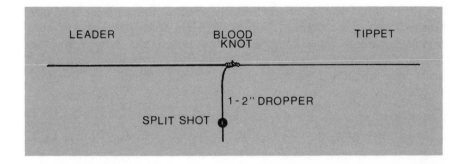

Nymph Patterns

When there are no visible rises, no hatch, and often invisible fish, the angler must rely on other sources for determining what food is available to the fish. A wire-mesh seine is a vital tool for collecting underwater insect life. By kicking up some stones and bottom turf, the angler, or his partner, can position a net downstream to intercept drifting specimens. If a seine is unavailable, a few moments devoted to upturning rocks and examining them should reveal the type of nymphal life in the stream. It is often useful to take some collected specimens back to the fly-tying vise to assist in duplicating the exact nymph patterns in a particular water. A good collecting formula for temporarily preserving the specimens is a mixture of 80% rubbing alcohol and 20% water with a few drops of formalin added as a color preserver. There is no substitute for personally collecting and observing the nymphal life of a stream; however, when firsthand information is unavailable, Ernest Schwiebert's *Nymphs* (Winchester Press, 1983) is an excellent source book for investigating the types of nymph life that inhabit different types of rivers.

In the absence of other alternatives, exploring the water with an attractor nymph pattern (i.e., which attracts by a flash of bright color rather than by imitating specific prey) can be successful. Attractors are generally tied in sizes 2 to 12, with emphasis on the larger sizes. I usually tie them to simulate the ubiquitous stonefly. Most good trout rivers in the United States support at least a small population of various stoneflies, and fish seem to exhibit an affinity for these nymphs wherever they appear in their natural form. The stonefly genus *Pteronarcys* can be found on streams from the Adirondacks to the waters of Northern California, and its abundance makes it a consistently effective attractor pattern throughout the states. Another stonefly of particular significance in the Finger Lakes region and Catskills is the genus *Perla,* an excellent choice when in need of an attractor fly.

Weighted *Perla* nymphs are particularly effective for tempting the large browns of New York's Mongaup River. When in need of a mayfly attractor nymph, I use a Number 12 impressionistic nymph tied to represent the common *Ephemerella* genus. The following is a description of how to tie these three attractor nymphs.

Pteronarcys Nymph

Hook	Size 4-8, Mustad 9672, 3X long
Nylon	Olive 6/0
Tails	Grey quill fibers
Body	Grey dubbing mixed with hare's mask and ribbed with colorless, transparent swannundaze. Fine lead wire tied laterally along hook shank
Thorax	Grey dubbing mixed with hare's mask
Wing Cases	Brownish-grey quill fibers, should equal roughly half of insect
Legs	Grey partridge blended with thorax materials and "picked out" with a dubbing needle

This is a fly that I originated to represent the large *Pteronarcys* flies of New York's Delaware River.

Perla Nymph

Hook	Size 6-10, Mustad 9672, 3X long
Nylon	Amber 6/0
Tails	Woodchuck
Body	Amber, Australian possum blended with hare's mask and ribbed with fine gold wire. Fine lead wire tied laterally along hook shank
Thorax	Same as body, omit gold wire
Wing Cases	Amber mottled turkey quill, should equal roughly half of insect
Legs	Lemon wood-duck flank feathers mixed with hare's mask and "picked out" with a dubbing needle

Well-known Adirondack fly tier and fisherman, Francis Betters, created this fly to imitate the *Perla capita* stonefly of his native Au Sable River. His skillful use of this nymph has produced an enviable number of exceptional fish from these waters.

Ephemerella **Nymph**	
Hook	Size 10-12, Mustad 3906
Nylon	Amber 6/0
Tails	Partridge fibers
Body	Hare's mask. Fine lead wire tied laterally along hook shank
Thorax	Hare's mask
Wing Cases	Mottled brownish turkey quill
Legs	Light partridge hackle blended with thorax materials and "picked out" with a dubbing needle

I frequently tie attractor stoneflies as wiggle-nymphs such as were first described in *Selective Trout,* by Douglas Swisher and Carl Richards (Nick Lyons Books, 1983). Personal experience has fashioned an adaptation which improves the effectiveness of these nymphs. When the abdomen is attached to the loop on the shank of the hook it is important that the loop be tied so that the opening is vertical. This is accomplished by lashing the loop onto the dorsal side of the hook shank, which causes the abdomen when hinged onto this loop to flutter vertically, mimicking the natural vertical undulations of nymph movement. If the loop opening is horizontally tied, so that the ends of the loop lie on the lateral sides of the hook shank, the abdomen will wag from side to side unnaturally. However, this horizontal loop *is* a superior device for designing jointed streamers, since this horizontal action strongly suggests the horizontal movement of a minnow's tail.

Technique

Big fish that are not actively feeding typically seek protective cover. These hiding places are provided either by the sheer depth of hollowed-out pools and stream channels, or by natural stream impediments such as logs, boulders, and undercut banks. Whatever form their cover takes, the fish tend to be on the bottom. Consequently, not only nymph equipment, but nymphing techniques must be designed to present the fly in a natural manner on the bottom of the river bed.

Charles Brooks, in his *Nymph Fishing for Larger Trout* (Nick Lyons

A slight hesitation in striking a downstream fish will result in proper corner of jaw hooking.

Books, 1976) describes a number of useful nymphing techniques for a wide variety of stream conditions. When fishing to bottom-holding fish my preference is Brooks's own method, which basically entails casting upstream to allow the fly to float dead drift along the bottom to a fish holding downstream from the fisherman. This method is well adapted to the deep waters of Fall Creek in Ithaca, New York, as well as to Western rivers like the Roaring Fork in Aspen, Colorado, where noted guide Chuck Fothergill uses a slight modification of this method and succinctly describes it as his "upstream, dead-drift, tight-line, high-rod, weighted-nymph" technique. Regardless of the chosen method, success demands not only that the fly remain on the stream bottom but also that the fly move along at a rate not in excess of the speed of the current. Any nymph moving more swiftly than the current will be easily perceived as a fraud. Exception, of course, is taken to this rule when the angler deliberately imparts action to a fly.

Fishermen generally find one of the most taxing features of nymph fishing is learning when and how to strike a taking fish. The difficulty of detecting the strike relates to the fact that a fish will often take and reject the fly before a telltale pause in the progress of the line can be perceived. Thus, the object is to strike whenever there is an interruption in the natural drift of the line. In some cases the fly will simply be snagged in the rock bottom, resulting in the loss of many flies. However, this is unavoidable. The angler who loses no flies is fishing the technique incorrectly. A good aid in learning this technique is to use a strike indicator, such as a different colored line section. Often the hesitation in the line is so imperceptible that the angler doesn't realize a fish has taken the fly. The best remedy for deciphering this enigma is the development of that sixth sense so many nymph fishermen talk about, and that only comes with practice.

A secondary problem arises, especially for the Brooks method advocate, when the angler sets the hook on a downstream fish: the fly is literally pulled out of the fish's mouth. To counter this action, the angler must develop a slight hesitation in his strike to allow the fish time to take and turn on the fly. This is the same hesitation required of the Atlantic salmon fisherman and is also acquired through hours of trial and error. When a downstream fish is hooked in the front half of either the upper or lower jaw, the strike has probably been premature. If the fish is hooked in the corners of the jaw or in the rear portion of the mouth, then the hesitation hooking technique has probably been performed correctly. The reverse of this statement is true when striking a fish that is lying upstream from the fisherman.

There is a small variation of the Brooks method which I use when fishing specifically for spawning trout. Instead of casting directly upstream, I prefer to throw an upstream curve in the line by means of a reach cast, as described by Douglas Swisher and Carl Richards in their *Fly Fishing Strategy* (Nick Lyons Books, 1975). The upstream curve not only permits a deeper drift of the fly, but also allows for a more natural, drag-free float of the nymph.

Spawning Fish

One of the greatest challenges when fishing to inactive fish is locating them. Frequently when large fish are migrating from the lakes into the streams, there is a concurrent influx of hordes of anglers. Consequently, on popular rivers where the spawning season is brief, crowds of fishermen invariably chase the fish off the redds and into the deep holding waters of the stream. The only practical defense against this situation is to either arrive at the stream very early in the morning before the fish have been spooked off the redds, or to be well familiarized with the holding water and resting places of spawning fish for that specific river. In working strange waters, a guide or friend who knows the nature of the stream is indispensable. I have found the "chuck-and-chance-it" method relatively ineffective when fishing to spawning trout on unfamiliar water. Immediately after the height of the spawning season, the crowds begin to wane, enabling a resourceful angler to capitalize on a few weeks of relative solitude while fishing to some lunkers who have not yet returned to the lake.

Again the Charles Brooks method is the best approach when nymphing for spawners. The refusal of spawning trout to move great distances to take a nymph requires precise casting and bottom-bumping drifts. If the spawning fish are sizable enough to warrant the time, the typical number of casts presented to rising fish will not suffice with spawners. The angler's patience will be brought to bear by the necessity of passing the nymph in front of the fish for as long as his or her endurance will permit. In fishing to surface feeders during a hatch, frequently the first cast is the best opportunity, and every succeeding cast loses its impact. In fishing to spawners the first is still the best, but it may require two-hundred-plus casts to produce results. Changing angles to ensure a proper drift sometimes seems to be a deciding factor in a long-awaited take.

Although arduously passing a fly over the same large fish can be frustrating in the extreme, the satisfaction of netting a fish measured in pounds rather than inches is more than commensurate with the efforts required. The excitement for the stream fisherman lies in the lure of lake-bred fish of such great proportions. Once having captured a spawner, the excitement quickly becomes an annual addiction, explaining the ever-increasing popularity of this eastern sport.

9/Nymph Fishing to Surface-Feeding Trout

by J. Michael Kimball

Although trout-fishing literature has existed for five hundred years, it is remarkable that until the turn of this century only cursory mention was made of nymphs or nymph fishing. Moreover no comprehensive source book on the subject could be found prior to this decade. As early as 1600 John Taverner made mention of immature underwater insects in his scientific publication on *Certaine Experiments Concerning Fish and Fruite.* During the 1700's and 1800's, contributions were added to the foundation of nymph fishing by such writers as Richard and Charles Borulker, who dominated eighteenth-century fly-fishing with *The Art of Angling,* Alfred Ronald, who wrote the 1836 classic *Fly Fishers Entomology,* John Younger with the 1840 *River Angling,* W. C. Stewart, who promoted upstream wet-fly technique in his 1857 *The Practical Angler,* and T. E. Pritt, who in 1885 wrote of soft-hackle wet flies in his *Yorkshire Trout Flies.*

But it wasn't until the early 1900's, when the Englishman George M. Skues broke with tradition and jolted the fishing world with his famous "Halford debates," that nymph fishing as we know it today was permitted its first recognition. Skues supported his experimental use of nymphs as a viable alternative to F. M. Halford's purist dry-fly methods. His studies of nymph fishing, *Minor Tactics of the Chalk Stream* in 1910, *The Way of a Trout with a Fly* in 1921, and *Nymph Fishing for Chalk Stream Trout* in 1939, remain required reading for the serious nymph fisherman.

For all the controversy he aroused, it's apparent from his writings that Skues and his followers had acquired only a superficial understanding of the nymph. Its habitat and individual characteristics as related to fishing technique eluded him. However, once the idea of nymph fishing had been introduced, several writers carried the flag throughout the twentieth century, each building on the scant information at hand. Edward R. Hewitt is considered to be the first from the United States to write of nymph fishing. Although his works of the 1920's, 1930's and 1940's are at times contradictory, vestiges of his methods still are practiced today. Other authors like James Leisenring (*Art of Tying the Wet Fly,* 1941), Alvin Grove *(The Lure and Lore of Trout Fishing,* 1951), Sid Gordon *(How to Fish from Top to Bottom,* 1955), and Poly Rosborough *(Fishing and Tying the Fuzzy Nymphs,* 1969) all anticipated the explosion of present-day enthusiasm for nymph fishing.

The 1970's ushered in the first fisherman-author who attempted to write exclusively about nymphs in the same manner that had for centuries been reserved for dry flies. Ernest Schwiebert's monumental book, *Nymphs,* published in 1973, was the first work of its kind. Prior to its release, fishing literature had not yet comprehensively explored the ecology of the underwater insect. In *Nymphs* Schweibert bridged the literary gap from the general to the specific. During the first part of this century many fishermen and some anecdotal writers subscribed to the commonly held theory, "When all else fails, try a nymph." The corollary spoken by an experienced dry fly-fisherman would be unthinkable: "Try a mayfly."

The concept of the *right* nymph was a long time in evolving. Schwiebert's book attempted to answer the question of what kind of nymph—even, perhaps, before it occurred to many fishermen to ask. Fishes' selectivity to specific nymphs had not often been considered a major factor, and transitions in habits are hard fought.

Although Schwiebert touched on how to fish the nymph, it was Charles Brooks in *Nymph Fishing for Larger Trout* who compiled under one cover the earlier works on nymphs and nymph-fishing techniques. Brooks's book summarizes fishing the nymph, while Schwiebert's book focuses more on identifying the specific attributes of important nymph species and how they can be represented at the vise.

Generally speaking, there are two kinds of nymph fishing, each offering its own challenges and each requiring its own specialized equipment. The two categories are directly related to the diverse feeding behavior of surface-feeding fish and non-surface feeding fish.

Nymphing for Surface-Feeding Fish

Although Skues and others have written very literate studies on nymph fishing England's chalk streams, their works never attained the sophistication demanded of the nymph fisherman today. Nymphing for rising fish feeding visibly on the surface requires the angler to identify the types of nymphal life found in the stream. Once the dun (i.e., the mature fly) of a given species is recognized on the water, the fisherman must associate not only the physical appearance of the nymph but also the correct behavior and motions for that particular species. Armed with this information the angler will be more likely to choose the appropriate fly and to discern what technique should be applied to its presentation.

The Latin names of each insect species are by no means a prerequisite to skillful fishing, but it is essential to have a clear concept of size, shape, general coloration, and emergence habits of the various orders of nymphs. For instance certain mayfly nymphs such as *Isonychia sadleri* will emerge by crowding onto rocks protruding above the water's surface, whereas *Ephemerella dorothea* will emerge midstream. Consequently the informed angler would surmise that during an *Isonychia* hatch, fish would tend to congregate in the shallows in order to intercept nymphs migrating to the rocks to hatch. If fishing to a *dorothea* hatch, the concentration might be best directed to areas where the stream creates food channels for feeding fish.

There are four main orders of nymphs that are of significance to the fisherman: 1) *Ephemeroptera* (mayflies), 2) *Trichoptera* (caddis), 3) *Plecoptera* (stoneflies), and 4) *Diptera* (midges). There are also other categories such as *Odonata* and *Neuroptera* and the class *Crustacea* which contain flies that may be of local interest to regional fishermen. Of the big three, *Ephemeropterans* tend to be recognized as the most numerous and consequently the most important to the nymph fisherman. Though less renowned, *Dipteran* pupae of the family *Chironomidae* are a highly underrated food source deserving of greater angler attention, as I have found. The following is a very brief summarization of some relevant details of important *Ephemeropteran* nymphs and their behavioral characteristics in the United States. For the more serious student, a more detailed format can be found in many of the recent volumes on nymph fishing.

Tackle for Surface Feeders

Rods

The tools in a fisherman's arsenal can fluctuate greatly depending on his game. When nymph fishing to surface feeders, special equipment is needed for the task. My choice is a medium- to fast-action rod of 8½ feet for a

Summary of Some Important *Ephemeroptera* North American Nymphs and Their Characteristics[a]

Nymph	Common Name	Size (mm)	Location[b]	Water Type[c]	Hatching Time[d]	General Coloration
Gen. *Ephemerella*						
Sp. *subvaria*	Hendrickson	9-13	E, M	F-Md	A	mottled brown
Sp. *rotunda*	Sulfur	7-9	E, M	Md-F	A, E	mottled brown
Sp. *dorothea*	Sulfur	6-9	E, M	S-F	A, E	mottled brown
Sp. *infrequens*	Pale Morning Dun	7-9	W	F-Md	A	brown
Sp. *inermis*	Pale Morning Dun	5-9	W	S-F	A	olive brown
Sp. *grandis*	Western Green Drake	14-17	W	S-Md		brown
Sp. *falvilinea*	Slate-Wing Olive	8-10	W	Md-F	A-E	brown
Gen. *Ephemera*						
Sp. *guttulata*	Eastern Green Drake	18-22	E	S-F	A-E	pale olive
Sp. *simulans*	Brown Drake	10-15	E, M, W	S-F	E	mottled brown
Gen. *Pseudocloeon*						
Sp. *anoka*	Blue-Wing Olive	4-5	M	S-Md	A-E	olive
Sp. *edmundsi*	Blue-Wing Olive	4-5	W	S-Md	A-E	olive
Gen. *Epeorus*						
Sp. *pleuralis*	Quill Gordon	9-11	E	F	A	grayish-brown
Gen. *Tricorythodes*						
Sp. *stygiatus*	Trico	3-4	E, M	S	Mo	brown
Sp. *minutus*	Trico	3-5	W	S	Mo	medium brown

Gen. *Paraleptophlebia*						
Sp. *adoptive*	Red Quill	6-8	E, M	Md-F	A	brown
Sp. *heteronea*	Slate-Wing Monogany Dun	7-9	W	S-F	Mo	brown
Sp. *debilis*	Dark Blue Quill	7-9	E, M, W	Md-F	A	brown
Gen. *Baetis*						
Sp. *vagas*	Blue-Wing Olive	6-8	E, M	S-Md	A	olive brown
Sp. *tricaudatus*	Blue-Wing Olive	6-7	W	S-F	A	olive brown
Gen. *Stenonema*						
Sp. *fuscum*	Grey Fox	9-12	E, M	Md-F	A-E	amber brown
Sp. *vicarium*	March Brown	10-16	E, M	S-F	E	amber brown
Sp. *ithaca*	Light Cahill	10-12	E, M	Md-F	A-E	amber brown
Sp. *canadense*	Light Cahill	10-12	E, M	Md-F	A-E	amber brown
Gen. *Isonychia*						
Sp. *sadleri*	Leadwing Coachman	12-15	E, M	F	A-E	dark brown
Gen. *Callibaetis*						
Sp. *coloradensis*	Speckled-Wing Dun	9-12	W	S	Mo	greyish-brown
Gen. *Potamanthus*						
Sp. *distinctus*	Paulinskill	13-16	E, M	S	E	brown
Gen. *Hexagenia*						
Sp. *limbata*	Giant Michigan Caddis	16-35	M, W	S	E	amber brown

[a] A more complete list of nymphs and their characteristics can be found in Al Caucci, Bob Nastasi, *Hatches* (Comparahatch, Ltd., 1975) and Doug Swisher, Carl Richards, *Selective Trout* (Nick Lyons Books, 1983).

[b] E = East   W = West   [c]Md = Medium   [d]Mo = Morning
M = Midwest   S = South   F = Fast   A = Afternoon
     S = Slow   E = Evening

A stomach pump proves conclusively what trout are feeding on. The next step is to imitate those insects.

5- or 6-weight line, but most rods of dry-fly action are a good choice. This personal endorsement for dry-fly tools is not the typical selection for nymph-fishing equipment, however, and may require some further background discussion.

The consensus of current opinion agrees with the axiom that fish feed on nymphs before a hatch, then as the hatch progresses, they switch their affinity to the duns. Thus we have been told that preceding a hatch we must scrape the stream bottom with the appropriate nymph pattern and after the hatch moves into full swing, we must switch to a dry-fly pattern representing the dun of that species.

In my experience I have encountered the opposite of that axiom more frequently than its rule. Trout, and most particularly good trout, will feed on nymphs right up to the last insect inhaled, therein violating the "before the hatch only" limitation on the nymph. It wasn't until the recent pop-ularization of the stomach pump (used to extract the contents of fish stom-achs) that many fishermen began to realize trout feed on nymphs not only before the hatch but also right through the hatch, *and* that many trophy fish will select nymphs exclusively through even the heaviest hatch of duns.

I have witnessed this event many times in my fishing life. I recall a mild afternoon in early August while fishing the Henry's Fork of Idaho's Snake River, when *Ephemerella inermis* had first started to appear. This hatch is one of the better ones on this prolific river, and large fish began rising all over the flats. One especially large trout was rising not 6 inches from the bank, making the unmistakable dense boil of an outsized fish. A hatch of pale-sulfur duns now blanketed the water around me, but repeated casts with a Number-18 *inermis* dun were consistently refused. To my right was an island fringed with some exposed grass which formed a natural collecting spot for floating debris. A close inspection revealed a relatively large quan-tity of empty *inermis* nymphal shucks.

My fish's rise form was not the bulgy type normally associated with nymph feeding but was instead the classic head-and-tail rise of a surface feeder. Nevertheless, with so many nymphs on that nest of grass beside me, I switched to an *inermis* nymph. Fifteen minutes later the pumped

This 23-inch rainbow was taken on Henry's Fork of Idaho's Snake River and fell victim to a nymph fished in the surface film.

stomach of a 23-inch rainbow revealed a capacity crowd of nymphs. This nymphing phenomenon has repeated itself innumerable times on innumerable rivers. As a result, during most hatches, my first choice is a nymph fished in the surface film for the duration of the hatch.

The discovery that good fish often feed exclusively to nymphs through the duration of a hatch should put to rest some of the conventional equipment dictates for nymph fishing. For years we have been told to use slow-action rods to keep our nymphs soaking wet during casting and to allow us to feel a taking fish's gulp right down to the butt of the rod. However, the slow-action rod lacks the accuracy and power of a classic dry-fly rod. On western water, too, where wind is an everyday foe, the medium- to fast-action rod better enables the angler to deliver the fly to the narrow feeding lanes so often frequented by rising fish.

Lines

Similarly, nymph fishing of this type should be done with a floating line. When fishing crystal-clear, smooth-current spring creeks where conditions require exact and subtle presentations, it is generally difficult to use larger than Number-6 weight line, and lines of 4 and 5 weight are preferable. Larger lines have a tendency to create disturbances during the pickup and setdown of a cast. These wakes on the water's surface can put sophisticated fish on streams like Pennsylvania's Letort down for the day.

Cortland Line Company has recently come out with a new line called a Nymph Tip with a strike indicator built into the tip of the line. For the beginning nymph fisherman, the fluorescent indicator is a great asset in detecting a fish's take. However, I prefer to stay with conventional lines which force the angler to use greater concentration. When the fisherman's eye is on an indicator, his attention is diverted from the true target. As a result, important stream data are lost, such as subtle leader drag, type and frequency of the rise form, and the general behavior of the fish. For this reason, I don't recommend a strike indicator for nymph fishing to rising fish, but it can be an indispensable aid when fishing nymphs to fish that are not visibly feeding.

Leaders and Tippets

Much research has been dedicated to the design of leaders and leader tapers. There is a never-ending quest to design a small-diameter leader with large-diameter strength.

Most manufactured leaders do not come with a tippet point longer than 2 feet. For fooling difficult fish I prefer a tippet length of approximately 4 feet. By using a 4-foot tippet, what is sacrificed in accuracy is regained in a more natural presentation. The longer tippet allows the nymph to drop lightly on the water, trailing corkscrew coils of extra tippet which uncurl as the fly floats downstream to the holding position of the fish. This technique allows for a longer inspection by the trout before drag sets in.

Fly Patterns

When selecting or tying nymphs to be used for rising trout a premium should be placed on the following essentials: 1) lifelike materials which match natural colors, 2) appropriate size of the imitation, and 3) appropriate shape of the fly. The primary attribute of an effective nymph is that it will act naturally in the water. An impressionistic representation which doesn't adhere strictly to each insect feature but moves pliantly when immersed will likely produce more consistently than a rigid counterpart. Ostrich and peacock herl, marabou, rabbit, and other soft materials lend themselves to a less static appearance and should be employed whenever possible. These, blended with antron dubbing for sparkle and translucency, literally breathe when placed in water and offer the angler very lifelike imitations.

It is common practice to use partridge flank feathers as the legs on nymphs since the mottled partridge represents the coloration of so many nymphs, but this material, when used to construct legs for *small* flies, appears brittle and static. The tapered ends of partridge do not retain the flexibility of the longer length hackle and cause the short leg projections of smaller nymphs to look like tiny metal needles when wet. The soft, webby fibers of dyed ostrich herl are far superior for constructing nymphs of sizes 18 and smaller. Partridge can be most successfully used to construct large insects' legs, since the longer fibers retain their pliability and offer less resistance to water currents.

One can't mention fly tying without Poul Jorgensen's name coming to mind. He has popularized an extremely lifelike pattern for larger nymphs which combines a fur underbody with an outer shell of dyed latex. Picking out the fur along the abdominal and thoracic segments gives the fly a very "buggy," realistic appearance. Latex is well adapted to the construction of the larger caddis and stonefly nymphs, which are time-tested big fish takers. Poul's imitation of a *Pteronarcys* stonefly recently lured a handsome 6-pound brown from the headwaters of Montana's Madison River. Their specific construction is well defined in his *Modern Flydressings for the Practical Angler* (Winchester Press, 1976).

When choosing fly-tying material, I prefer to give first priority to their lifelike properties and second place to exact coloration. Often both can be combined with successful dying. Although precision color coding is not vital to me in constructing flies, it is notable that water will darken most tying materials. A knowledgeable tier can compensate accordingly. I generally carry a selection of colored waterproof pens as a streamside aid for on-the-spot color coding when flies need to more closely match the hatch.

Size

When trout are selectively feeding, size of nymphs fished becomes an exacting criterion in matching the hatch. As Swisher and Richards point out in *Selective Trout,* size is most critical when fishing to midges. The percentage difference of fly size when comparing a size 22 to size 24 is far greater than the percentage change going from size 8 to size 10. The first example represents roughly 22% difference in overall size, whereas in the other case the difference is approximately 13%. Consequently, a miscalculation in the midge classification will be much more evident to the fish than a comparable error in the large stonefly category.

Shape

An often-overlooked feature in selecting or tying imitations is the form or shape of the fly. A final trim job at the fly-tying vise can significantly alter a well-tied pattern for better or for worse. Nymphs, depending on their species, can vary from flat, linear shapes to rounded, cylindrical ones. The angler must have a working knowledge of the stream habitat and the shape of the nymphs it engenders. The inverse of the rule regarding size applies to the importance of shape; that is, as the fly becomes larger, the appropriate shape is more crucial. A case in point is the stonefly, *Pteronarcys dorsata,* which has a flat, linear body. The angular configuration is well suited to the rock-bottom, fast-water stream in which this insect typically thrives. Fishing a fly of the same size and pattern but with a rounded shape will not likely be as effective for fooling the sophisticated fish of today's hard-fished waters.

On the other hand the Brown Drake, *Ephemera simulans,* has a convex, cylindrical body designed for burrowing into the sand and gravel of slower-moving streams. Its rounded anatomy is well adapted to its stream behavior. Selective fish seem to have no difficulty perceiving a misshapen substitute. Fortunately, flies of the midge category, such as tiny *Pseudocloeon* nymphs (4 to 5 milimeters) offer the fly tier some artistic leeway in refining their shape, since the importance of exact configuration diminishes somewhat with pattern size. However, the discerning fisherman would be wise to attempt to duplicate exacting shapes even in the smaller sizes.

Wiggle-Nymphs

In 1971 Swisher and Richards's *Selective Trout* popularized a new design of nymphs called the wiggle-nymph. The wiggle-nymph is a jointed-body nymph which allows the abdominal section to swing freely in the water imparting a very lifelike action to the fly. I have fished the wiggle-nymph extensively and have found this fly to be best for fishing large imitations in slow currents. In fast water such as Ithaca, New York's Fall Creek (below the falls), the force of the water tends to negate the jointed effect since the heavy current straightens the fly out. This pattern is especially effective when fished in deep, quiet pools or lakes, since the still water allows the wiggle-nymph's abdominal section to flex and float freely in the water. A jiggling action imparted in the angler's retrieve will cause the jointed section to undulate in an enticing motion. When the wiggle-nymph is fished dead

The wiggle nymph can be deadly, especially in deep pools.

drift, the slower currents will induce a similar motion. This pattern is an excellent choice when used for the larger burrowing flies, like *Ephemera simulans* and *Ephemera gluttalata,* or when fishing the outsized *Hexagenia limbata* hatches, for which Michigan's Au Sable River is so famous. I have fished the smaller jointed flies representing nymphs of *Tricorythodes, Baetis* and *Pseudocloeon* tied as small as Number 24, but I have not found them to be more effective than conventionally tied nymphs. However, when fished to the Brown and Green Drakes or the larger *Hexagenia* hatches, the wiggle-nymph has my strongest personal endorsement.

Emergers

One popular group of flies today is the emerger. This is the transitory state between the nymph and the dun, and for many has practically rendered traditional wet flies obsolete. Many emerger patterns are tied as floating extensions of wet flies, but for most hatches I feel the emerger should be tied to look more like a nymph than a wet fly. Specifically, the concept of the nymph-like emerger pattern is to imitate that phase of development in which the nymph's wing case splits and the adult wing begins to emerge along the dorsal side of the nymphal shuck. Since the wings have not *fully* emerged, they should be much shorter than the wings on conventional wet-fly patterns.

Many emergers are tied with quill wings. However, these appear rigid and quite unlike the fluid, membranous wings of a natural fly. Many flexible materials such as marabou, dyed silk stockings, rabbit (applied by the spinning-loop method), longer strands of partridge hackle, and the soft downy fibers at the base of many hackle stems can be used for designing the partially emerged wings of this important hatching stage. Furthermore, since emergers represent a surface developmental stage, this pattern should be tied with buoyant materials and fished in the surface film.

In many cases the emerger pattern is superior to the real nymph, particularly in species that are characterized by a prolonged emergence period. This is a great advantage to the fisherman since the longer the time interval needed for the adult insect to break through the nymphal shuck, the greater success an angler can anticipate from that pattern. Many insects of the genera *Ephemerella* and *Stenonema* have this character, and emergers tied to imitate these flies can be superior fish takers.

Mike Lawson, talented fly tier and proprietor of Idaho's Henry's Fork, Inc., and Fred Arbona, author of *Mayflies, the Angler and the Trout* (Winchester Press, 1980) showed me an emerger they developed for two of Henry's Fork's more well-known *Ephemerella* hatches, *Ephemerella gran-*

dis (Green Drake) and *Ephemerella inermis* (Pale Morning Dun). I was told that the fly, tied with a few turns of grizzly hackle (swept back and kept short) and a body of pale olive-yellow Fly-Rite, was a "winner" when fished nymph-like in the surface film to the Ph.D.'s of the river. I tied a similar pattern, with a slightly darker body, for the *Ephemerella subvaria* (Henrickson), of New York's West Branch of the Delaware River. Five browns in eight casts, between 1 and 2½ pounds, has me more than a little interested in the future of the "Lawson-Arbona emerger." The fly reminds me of the popular soft-hackle, emerger-like flies found in Sylvester Nemes's *The Soft Hackled Fly* (Chatham Press, 1975).

Poul Jorgensen has also created some excellent emerger patterns to represent the sulfurs, *Ephemerella dorothea* and *Ephemerella rotunda,* so prevalent on the limestone streams of Pennsylvania's Cumberland Valley. He uses the spinning-loop method to apply a soft, natural-fur wing to represent this developmental stage. This is a highly successful pattern for fishing the sulfur hatches of Pennsylvania's Big Spring, Letort, and Falling Spring Run.

Brilliant writer Art Lee, an editor of *Fly Fisherman* magazine, has also developed a series of midge emergers. These are tied in sizes 22 to 24 with short strands of mallard shoulder fibers. They are Art's ace in the hole for the August days on the Willowemoc which borders the backyard of his cottage in Roscoe, New York.

Stillborns

Another fly increasing in popularity today is an imitation of a stillborn insect. Stillborns are flies that die or become crippled in the process of attempting to crack the nymphal shell. They can be seen floating awash in the surface film often still trailing their nymphal shuck. The innovative researchers Doug Swisher and Carl Richards introduced this fly in their 1975 edition of *Fly Fishing Strategy*, but most of their patterns were geared to dry-fly imitations. Their style is to tie the insects as dry flies with a spray of hen hackle at the tail to simulate the trailing shell. Whenever stillborns appear in reasonable numbers, trout seem to be more selective to this stage of the nymph. This preference may be explained in part through fishes' need to conserve energy. In order for trout to stay alive, the energy received from their food must exceed the energy expended in its capture. The stillborn's struggle to be free of its shuck must broadcast its vulnerable condition, and the energy used in its capture is rarely wasted, for the chase generally results in a guaranteed meal.

I prefer a slight variation of Swisher and Richards's stillborn dry-fly representation. I have found it most effective to tie these flies as floating nymphs with an adult insect emerging from the partially empty shuck. Using a Mustad 95831, 2X long hook, I tie an imitation of the actual nymphal shell onto the rear of the hook shank. In most cases the abdominal section of the shell should be tied with transparent materials such as dyed microweb to represent a shuck that no longer fully contains a nymph. I have also tied this shell as a wiggle-nymph to simulate the soft, flexible nature of the paper-thin, half-empty nymphal container. Then to the front section of the hook, a no-hackle dry fly is tied in the usual way except that one or both of the wing tips are trapped by the nymphal wing case. This differs from the typical Swisher and Richards pattern, which has a nymphal case only suggested by clumping trailing hackle and slightly protruding adult wings. In my "trailing-nymph" variation, the adult is exposed to emulate a phase of development in which the front half of the dun has emerged but is still trailing its nymphal shell. This fly is tied with buoyant materials and fished in the surface film in much the same way an emerger is fished.

I've found this stillborn variant to be more effective in the orders of *Diptera* and *Trichoptera* than in the *Ephemeropterans*. During a midge hatch there is no better fly than this pattern to represent the *dipteran* stillborns of Montana's spring creeks. I have used this pattern with consistent success from the East to the West Coast, particularly during heavy hatches, and would expect that further research on stillborns will prove them to be more universally effective than is now claimed.

Technique

Hatches

When an angler is confronted with the complexities of a hatch, the first task is to identify the insect on the water. For the nymph fisherman the next procedure is to differentiate the developmental stage the fish are selecting for—nymphs, stillborns, or emergers. After observing the dun, a knowledge of entomology can be used to deduce the nymph of the same species. Nymphs, or their shells, that may be floating on the water often provide useful clues for solving the puzzle of the right nymph.

The angler's challenge is heightened during a multiple hatch in which two or more species of insects are hatching concurrently. The problem becomes further compounded when various developmental stages of these insects occur simultaneously. When the information at hand is conflicting, observing the rise form can help in decoding the appropriate fly. Angling literature is replete with attempts to categorize the relationships between the rise form and the type of fly being taken. For instance, a trout's back bulging through the water generally indicates he is taking a nymph. A sipping rise suggests an immobile fly—often a spinner off the surface film. Typically, a slash rise is associated with an active insect like a caddis. A head-and-tail rise is usually to a dun.

Unfortunately, I have witnessed repeated violations of this categorical analysis, but most commonly I find exceptions to the last view. Often I have encountered textbook-perfect head-and-tail risers whose stomach contents were not full of duns but rather were packed almost exclusively with nymphs. As noted above, the understanding that fish surface feeding during a hatch are more apt to be nymphing than sipping drys is long overdue. Traditional doctrine had undoubtedly stymied this discovery, but knowledgeable anglers are beginning to capitalize on this behavior of nymphing fish.

A variation of the multiple hatch that can be very deceiving is a masking hatch. This is a situation in which there are two different insect species simultaneously on the water, a small fly coupled with the presence of a usually more numerous larger fly. The angler's eye first perceives the larger fly, so that the fish's habitual preference for the smaller fly is concealed. Masking hatches are often the cause of fishless days. I recall a classic example of a masking hatch which occurred a few years ago on a small Wyoming spring creek. Two flies, *Ephemerella inermis* and *Centroptilum elsa*, were concurrently hatching on a frosty, late-September day. The large *E. inermis* had been hatching since August in this area, and a Number 18 *Ephemerella* nymph had been a sure bet to fish to the *inermis* hatch. Even though I had recognized *C. elsa* on the water for at least a week, habit and previous success with the *inermis* nymph had obscured their presence. This day, however, brought a change of pace—it wasn't until the hatch was almost over that one of the less-educated fish finally accepted the *inermis* nymph. The stomach pump revealed his preference for the tiny *Centroptilum* nymphs. I've witnessed numerous comparable masking hatches around my home waters of Ithaca, New York, which have disguised fishes' preference for *Paraleptophlebia adoptiva* in the presence of the larger *Ephemerella subvaria* (Hendricksons).

One of the least-understood aspects of multiple hatches is the individuality of fish. It is commonly believed that once a fly raises a few fish, this fly will be successful for the remainder of the hatch. But there is no guarantee that all fish in the river are feeding on the same fly. When two or more distinct species of insects are hatching, it is sometimes possible to observe some fish along the same stretch of water, and sometimes even in the same pool, feeding on not only different insect species but also on different stages of the same insect. This phenomenon further demonstrates the indispensable nature of the stomach pump in solving the food enigma. In addition a monocular can assist in disclosing surface activity; and the rise form, though not a foolproof clue, can provide some missing links.

Casting Approach

The manner in which a nymph is presented is dependent in part on the character of the stream. Charles Brooks in *Nymph Fishing for Larger Trout* has extensively covered the delivery of the fly as related to a broad spectrum of stream conditions. This long-overdue methodology is an excellent reference for the nymph fisherman. No one method is ever adequate all of the time. A thorough understanding of each approach as described by Brooks is fundamental to fishing a large number of streams and can provide practical alternatives even on one familiar stream.

Fly-fishing doctrine has dictated that something approximating a three-quarters upstream cast is the most effective means of achieving a drag-free float—a float in which the fly is not restrained or pulled off its natural course by the current. However, unless a three-quarters upstream cast is accompanied with either a very wide upstream curve or lots of slack line, the nymph fisherman is faced with only short intervals of dragless drifts. Also, nymph fishermen that use roll casts as part of their delivery frequently find it difficult to consistently throw good upstream curves, especially when faced with windy conditions. This is another case where tradition has hindered the development of flyfishing technique. It has been my experience that best results can be achieved by varying the appropriate casting position from any point directly above to directly across from a feeding fish. It is much easier to throw wide reach curves (both positive and negative) when quartering downstream than when adhering to upstream tradition. (See Chapter 6, Figures 7 and 11.) Roll casting, when accompanied with a reach curve and a mend as soon as the fly meets the water, achieves a much more natural float than its upstream counterpart.

The downstream dead-drift method is a technique born of necessity on the western spring creeks and the limestone streams of the East. These waters contain fish that do not recognize hatchery pellets and the sign on the bank reads "No-Kill." The fish are generally large and sophisticated, and angling success often requires breaking the rules. For some, downstream dead-drift fishing does break with tradition, but I suspect its success will someday make it the rule rather than the exception. Very simply, under most conditions, when properly executed, the three-quarters downstream cast can achieve longer, more natural drag-free floats than conventional upstream casts.

There are advantages of downstream casting other than long dragless drifts. With the help of a downstream mend, the fly can easily be made to arrive at the holding position of a feeding fish before the arrival of the leader. Also, once the nymph has passed over the fishes' station, the angler, being above the fish, can often induce a take by very gently twitching the nymph in the vicinity of the fish.

Downstream dead-drift nymphing is not without its disadvantages, and an understanding of these shortcomings can help you perfect the technique. In order to achieve a natural drift over a downstream fish, the fly should be cast approximately 2 feet ahead of the fish with enough slack and curves in the line and leader to allow the nymph not only to reach the fish but to pass at least 3 feet beyond its feeding position. A fly cast with too little slack in the line and leader will drag too close to the fish and may put it down for the day. But casting slack lines has its problems. Setting the hook while attempting to take the slack out of the line can be difficult. A long rod, held high overhead, can help remedy the problem of cumbersome slack in the leader. Occasionally, however, the fish's take occurs immediately upon the fly's reaching the water, and a rod held high overhead becomes of little use for striking in the conventional manner. In this case the best hook-setting method is not to attempt to raise the rod even higher, but rather to thrust the rod tip forward in much the same way a roll cast is accomplished. In extreme cases when a roll cast is not enough to remove all the loose coils from the leader, then a simultaneous downward pull on the line with the left hand (for a right-handed caster) will help to correct this situation. Assuming the fly is not instantly taken, a gradual lowering of the rod tip combined with continuous line mending should keep the nymph floating drag-free over the feeding station of the fish.

It is important to have placed enough slack in the line to allow the fly to pass well beyond the fish's suspected location, for as renowned author and limestone fisherman Vincent C. Marinaro points out in his *In the Ring of the Rise* (Nick Lyons Books, 1976), fish inspecting a fly will often drift back many feet before an actual rise occurs. Vince calls this feeding habit a complex rise, and it is thoroughly discussed in his innovative work. I have found this rise type to be a frequent occurrence on eastern and western spring creeks, and it is particularly important on Vince's home waters of Pennsylvania's Letort.

Another reason for ensuring a drift well beyond the fish is to minimize the effect of any surface disturbance during the pickup of the fly. As the fly continues past its original target, the rod tip should be moved laterally away from the fish. A sharp downward movement of the rod tip will initiate waves in the line that will cause the fly to literally jump from the water. A conventional pickup executed from a location above the rise form will frequently cause fish-frightening wakes on the water's surface and should be avoided whenever a snap pickup can be used. If the snap pickup cannot be applied, then a slow retrieve *under* the water's surface is far safer than risking a potential drag-causing pickup.

Occasionally an angler will be faced with a cast that is short of its target. This frequently happens when a fish changes his feeding position to a location below the original rising position or when the distance from the rise form is underestimated. The danger here arises in the potential for drag occurring directly in front of the fish. When this situation is recognized, a quick lowering of the rod tip and a mending motion while the fisherman simultaneously feeds line through the rod guides will generally get the fly past the fish without drag. This technique of mending and feeding line to downstream fish is a not-so-well-guarded secret of those who chase the wild rainbows of Northern California's Fall River.

If the short-line situation is recognized too late, then a very slight raising and lowering of the rod tip, causing a deliberate but controlled drag (*à la* Leonard M. Wright, Jr.) will often effect a quick strike. In fact this action, when properly executed, can be a deadly technique for fooling difficult fish. Leonard M. Wright, Jr.'s *Fishing the Dry Fly as a Living Insect* (Nick Lyons Books, 1972) explains this method in detail, and I have found it equally applicable to fishing nymphs for rising fish.

A major disadvantage of downstream dead-drift fishing is the lack of concealment of upstream objects. Practitioners of this technique should recognize the increased exposure of person and equipment and take appropriate corrective measures. Keeping a low silhouette, with clothes matching the backdrop of the particular river, will increase the angler's chance of success. On many of the West's famous trout streams, however, and notably on the Railroad Ranch of Henry's Fork, large areas are without prominent backdrops. When confronted with these conditions, hats and other clothing resembling the horizon or the sky color can facilitate the merging of angler and environment. The need for low profiles and camouflage clothing is particularly important on this country's spring creeks and absolutely critical for stalking such placid waters as the Letort.

Another factor to consider when determining a casting approach is the direction and the intensity of the wind. If there is a strong wind, then the angler must decide whether to cast into the wind or with the wind at his back. Many fishermen prefer the latter. However, experts like Phil Wright of Montana's Wise River contend that a good fisherman will cast better facing into the wind than *vice versa*. Wind is an almost everyday hindrance in the West and is often prevalent in the East during the blustery spring months of March, April, and May. Personally, I opt to first determine whether my imitation should float naturally on the water or whether it should be fished with a twitching retrieve. If I decide that a natural float is required, I cast against the wind, as its force will often cause the leader tippet to stack up on the water, and the gradual uncoiling will produce more drag-free float. Although this type of casting demands practice for an angler to hit his target, it is far preferable to casting with the wind at his back. Casting with the force of the wind ensures a more effortless delivery but will also straighten out the leader, rendering an almost simultaneous occurrence of the touchdown and drag of the fly.

Rhythm Feeding

Many anglers naturally assume that when a rising trout repeatedly ignores a well-placed fly, the refusal requires a change of pattern. I contend that a little observation and timing might provoke more favorable results than frequent pattern changing. It is important to recognize that a trout feeding during a heavy hatch won't consume every live insect which passes over him but will often rise in well-defined *rhythmic* patterns attuned, in part, to its assimilation rate of food. What I am suggesting is that the angler may often have chosen the right fly but be presenting it at the wrong time. To understand rhythm feeding, an important distinction must be drawn between a heavy and a light hatch. During the latter, rhythm feeding becomes secondary to survival. The flies drifting over the trout's feeding station are already intermittent enough to allow time for digestion, and fish will be inclined to capture a larger percentage of the insects that pass during times of sparse food supply. In a light-hatch situation, therefore, once a fish determines a preference for an insect, he is apt to take a major portion of the flies drifting over him. Under these circumstances, rhythm feeding ceases to be a factor, and changing patterns to match the naturals takes precedence as the more productive angling technique.

Most investigation of rhythm feeding has been of a very superficial nature. Only cursory allusions are made to its significance in today's fishing literature. Discussions typically take the posture, "It is important to cast the fly to coincide with the feeding rhythm of the fish." Little reference is made to the nature and complexity of the rhythm. A fish may alter its feeding pattern many times during a given feeding period. The rhythms can speed up and slow down periodically during any one feeding period, but nevertheless they often seem to maintain well-defined patterns. Rhythm changes during a hatch may depend upon the quality and quantity of food, the state of a fish's hunger, the competition with other fish, and many physiological and genetic factors which fishermen may never completely understand.

During periods of heavy feeding activity, customary in *Tricorythodes* hatches, the fisherman must determine the feeding rhythm of the fish at that particular point in time and deliver the fly at the appropriate moment. A very familiar feeding rhythm often noticed at Trico time is a rise, a few seconds' pause, and then two or three quick takes. Established rhythms change, frequently for no obvious reasons; however, the change is often to merely another set of feeding rhythms. The only method to combat this complexity is to time the intervals through observation.

One unique exception to varying rhythms occurred a few years ago on the Letort when I witnessed a small brown sipping *Diptera* according to a repeated time progression of 30 seconds, 12 seconds, 12 seconds, 50 seconds; 30-12-12-50; and so on. The fish fed as if cued by a bell; his progression was interrupted only three times in the course of 25 minutes! This little brown was the most consistent rhythm feeder I have ever witnessed. However, this is not surprising, since the Letort holds many "mosts" in my mind.

If your patience allows, and if the feeding intervals fall into a numerical sequence, a good understanding of rhythm feeding can suggest a good strategy. However, landing a cast on target at the split second of a fish's countdown is almost reward enough in itself, as anyone will discover once he tries to cast "on command." Although not a panacea for fishless days, an understanding of rhythm feeding has at times been an invaluable tool when sophisticated fish are exposed to heavy hatches.

10/Landlocks in a Nutshell

by Eric Seidler

L andlocked Atlantic salmon are being returned to the glacial lakes of New York, New England, and Canada. They are quickly regaining their status as the finest game fish native to the fresh waters of the Northeast, eclipsing in angler esteem the introduced species (rainbow trout, brown trout, and Pacific salmon) that have been mainstays of northeastern migratory game fishing for several generations. An early victim of damming, deforestation, and overfishing, the landlock had almost faded from memory in many areas, leaving traces of its former ubiquity only in the profusion of "Salmon Creeks" and "Salmon Rivers" entering lakes throughout its original range. At one time, Lake Ontario grew landlocks to 45 pounds, but by the turn of the century, paralleling the earlier destruction of the sea-runs, landlocked Atlantic stocks plummeted to a few isolated and overlooked populations in the Finger Lakes of New York, some Adirondack lakes, and a few basins scattered throughout the Northeast. Only in Maine and Canada did wild populations survive the hiatus in appreciable numbers.

Hard to handle in hatcheries, the vanishing native was replaced throughout most of its range by browns, rainbow trout, and Pacific salmon. Recent advances in hatchery techniques, however, have fostered a boom in landlocked Atlantic production. Lake Ontario has already returned fish of over 20 pounds; Champlain, fish of 18. Six- to 10-pounders are becoming common in the Finger Lakes. Many guides, charter captains, and anglers, realizing that landlocks belong, are asking fisheries services to curtail the stocking of competing Pacific species. Nursery streams on Lake Ontario have been closed to fishing throughout the spawning season to protect running Atlantics, which, unlike Pacific salmon, may survive to spawn several times.

Landlocks run twice yearly. In the spring they follow the spawning runs of smelt and are available for as long as smelt are in the streams. Spring salmon feed voraciously and are incidental to catches of trout wherever they occur. Most are caught on worms, egg sacks, glo-baits and hardware, because that's what most people fish with. A few of us manage to get a fly in edgewise, and we do extremely well (crowds permitting) with our streamers, nymphs, and wet flies.

It is the fall runs, however, that put the top few year classes of big fish in the rivers. Fall-run landlocks behave, within regional limits of variation, exactly like their oceanic counterparts. Their digestive functions cease entirely. The males grow extraordinary kypes (the hooking of the jaws in spawning condition) and use them on one another in breathtaking displays of aggression and territoriality. A pool full of spawning landlocks seethes with their antagonism. Nothing that swims is safe—minnows, crustacea, and swimming insects all bear their burden of salmon attacks—and herein lies a mystery. Although evolution has managed to prevent Atlantic salmon from utilizing any nutrition on the physiological level, the behaviors as-

Co-authors Todd and Eric hard at work. The smaller fish is a fresh-run female. The larger is a male in full spawning regalia.

sociated with feeding remain not only intact but are enhanced by the aggressiveness of fish in competition for dominance and territory.

A lone salmon may or may not attack a swimming object. Add a few more fish to a lie and *each* will start taking the initiative, as though the capture of that object gives the captor an added claim to the territory through which it passes. Thus they take a fly, or they may just as likely go tail up and settle into the rocks, appearing to ignore everything and each other until some further mystery triggers another period of pugnacity.

Their favorite places to hold are rockpiles, tail-outs, and in front of or to the sides of boulders (Figure 1), though on the whole they prefer the tail of a pool to its head. Depressions, ledge runs, and well-defined midriver braids draw them as well. They appear to prefer sunlight to shade and sand to gravel. Waterfall basins collect them, and impassible barriers are assaulted all season by landlocks trying to pass over.

Pursuers of rainbow trout, brown trout, and Pacific salmon have found themselves perplexed by the "new" fish, and generally have been unable to do more than chance onto the occasional Atlantic. Years of dead drifting nymphs, glo-baits, egg sacks, and the rest have persuaded most people who fish the runs that spawning salmonids have to be "fed" the hook, on the bottom, drag-free, with a high rod and a taut line. It is also felt that the hook set to spawning salmonids must be accomplished quickly (not all agree) at the slightest interruption of the bait's drift. Drift fishers have honed their skills into what has been described as a "sixth sense," a "knowing," without any overt visual or tactile cues that a fish has taken or even that one will take on a given drift.

This hair-trigger, hit-or-quit, now-or-never set of reflexes must be deliberately suppressed, or most of your experiences with landlocked Atlantic salmon will be unhappy. Drift fishing on the bottom results in infinitesimally few legitimate takes; rather, most fish contacted in this manner are snagged, snatched, or "lifted," lost and wounded. A quick hook set results in stung or "lipped" fish which are either never really hooked or, hooked poorly, tear off.

In short, there are a lot of ways to make a mess of landlocked salmon fishing. Fortunately, there are also a few ways to shine.

The Gear

You will want a fly rod 8 to 10 feet in length, Number 5 to Number 8 in line weight, and a single-action fly reel with a *reliable* drag, capacious enough to hold 100 to 150 yards of backing under your fly line. I prefer a

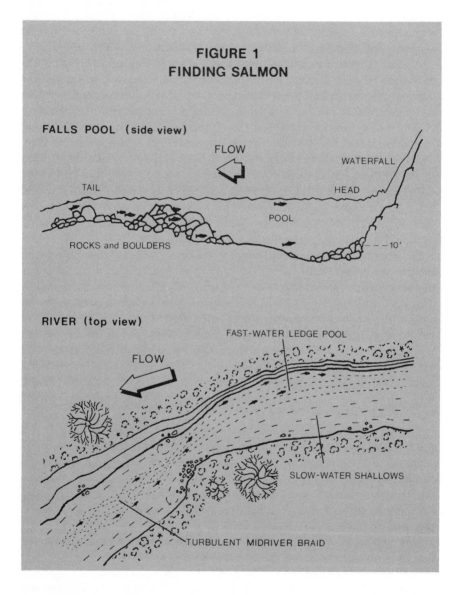

FIGURE 1
FINDING SALMON

FALLS POOL (side view)

FLOW

WATERFALL

TAIL

HEAD

POOL

ROCKS and BOULDERS

- - - 10'

RIVER (top view)

FAST-WATER LEDGE POOL

FLOW

SLOW-WATER SHALLOWS

TURBULENT MIDRIVER BRAID

large-diameter, narrow reel to wider, smaller-diameter reels because these fish run back at you much faster than you can take up line with the latter.

Shooting heads and other heroics are totally unnecessary on landlocked salmon streams, as they are generally no bigger than most eastern trout streams. Your line can be a double-taper or weight-forward floater of whatever weight you require to throw a Number 8 to Number 2/0 hook a comfortable 50 feet. Although they do require fewer falsecasts, a special touch is needed to mend a weight-forward line, so I do not recommend them unless you are already comfortable with one. Landlocked Atlantic salmon fishing is a game of control, *not* distance. Sinking lines have their place in early spring and late fall (and in very deep water at any time), but under most circumstances they can be dispensed with by the addition of *very* small shot or twist-ons to the leader. There is never a need to fish *on* the bottom, but in cold, turbid water over 6 to 8 feet deep it is often necessary to fish a fly two-thirds to three-quarters of the way down the water column. The deeper the water, the larger that fraction should be.

Leaders for floating lines should be 8 to 14 feet long and tapered to no less than 6-pound test. Eight-pound test is sufficiently light. Landlocks are *never* leader-shy unless they are inadvertently stroked by the vertical leaders of drift fishermen or deliberately harried by snaggers. The 8- to 14-foot leader lengths and .008- to .010-inch tippet diameters are for drift and depth control. Lighter tippets wear quickly and lose fish; heavier ones are too stiff for good fly action. A leader for a sunk line can be much shorter (5 to 6 feet), as the fly is almost invariably fished downstream to an upstream-facing fish, and a longer leader would eventually cause the fly to plane towards the surface.

Tie your leaders for strength and maximum casting comfort with a wide range of fly sizes. Perfect turnover of fly and tippet is not necessary and is often impossible due to the inevitable tackle imbalances (Number 2/0 fly, 5-weight line, 14-foot leader, 25-mph headwind, *etc.*) that occur. Boots, pliers, clippers, and a hook hone are the only other things you will need except the flies.

The Flies

Wets, dries, nymphs, streamers, tubes, shrimp, and leeches all catch salmon. For that matter they will hit maple leaves, carrot peels, cigar butts, and bare hooks. Barring absurdities, the only flies that will not catch Atlantic salmon are those which are not fished with confidence. Salmon will hit because it rains, clears, blows, or calms. They may take the first cast or the second, or they may watch a hundred casts go by, but, sooner or later, and with remarkable frequency, one will ghost out of the shadows, climb the water column, take, and turn. I don't believe that the specific fly has much to do with it, but some flies are better than others at certain times. Here are some basic guidelines.

Dry flies must be bushy and buoyant enough to float a considerable hook without being so heavily dressed that the hook gap is in any way obscured by the materials. They do not need to look like giant mayflies, and they may float flush with the surface. Upright wings and buzz hackles are unnecessary. Tie or buy Buck Bugs, Bombers, adult stoneflies, oversize deer-hair caddis, Renegades, Humpies—or make up your own patterns. Early fall, warm water, and clear shallows yield the best dry-fly fishing, and fresh, bright fish are the most likely to play.

In the spring, when landlocks come in chasing smelt, large streamers such as the Magog Smelt, Silver Doctor, or any of the mylar-and-hair patterns (the bigger the better) come into their own. Nymphs that catch landlocks include any appropriately sized (Number 8 to 2/0) fuzzy, buggy business (Isonychia, Hare's ear, stonefly) that you care to tie; however, the decidedly un-nymph-like way they must be fished renders them functionally equivalent to the staple of Atlantic salmon fishing worldwide—the wet fly (Figure 2).

The lore of salmon flies and their construction constitute pursuits in themselves. The range of exotic materials available to European tiers during the colonial era, combined with centuries of practical evolution in the eye of the salmon and in the hands of sports and poachers, have made the salmon wet into the beautifully balanced, intricate, and efficiently deadly tool that it has become. The vast array of successful variations on one theme is often intimidating to the newcomer; however, it is also an affirmation by both fish and anglers that they *all* work.

Whether you enjoy tying the classics or you purchase your flies, I suggest that you start with four to six patterns in a variety of sizes. Less than four will provide too few options for psychological comfort during a day's fishing, and more than five or six is an invitation to spend too much time agonizing over which pattern to use. I would have every confidence if I were restricted to the following flies: Green Highlander, Silver Doctor, Claret, Black Dose, Silver and Gray, and the Copper Killer. These six patterns have the twin virtues of long and illustrious service and sufficient color contrasts one with another, allowing the salmon angler to play a very productive game indeed.

Landlocked salmon are difficult to spook short of being stoned, snagged, or driven, and they are neither man-shy nor leader-shy. It is possible to get quite close and to put a lot of casts over them without decreasing (often, indeed, increasing) the likelihood of a take. They do, however, get pattern-shy, or, more accurately, bored and uninterested by repeated exposure, cast after cast, to the same fly. It is quite common to locate a group of fish in a lie and, using a predominantly green fly, say a Highlander, move 20 to 80% of the fish during the first dozen or two casts, each more often than once, only to have them sulk for the next half hour. At such times a

FIGURE 2
SALMON FLIES

"BOMBER" #4 hook

SMELT STREAMER #2 hook

STONEFLY NYMPH #2 hook
(weighted)

SALMON FLY #2/0 hook

change to a distinctly different-color fly, say a Claret, will frequently turn them all back on again as if they had never seen the first fly—even if one of them was caught on it. An argument could be made that the salmon would have started coming again without the color change, but I have proved it to myself time after time: radical color changes get results. On my home waters, as my friends and I fish various lies in rotation, we make it a practice to follow each other with different colors, without resting the fish. We have all had the same experience. No single color has emerged as significantly better than any other, although we each have our secret favorites. My box is full of one basic pattern in six basic color schemes; all are simple palmered-hackle-hair-wings, ribbed with pearl mylar and winged (sparsely) with bucktail. The bodies are dubbed or wrapped with chenille. The colors I favor are:

Body	Palmered Hackle	Bucktail Wing
Light Green to Chartreuse	Cree	Blue-Green
Light Blue	White	Blue
Claret	Furnace	Purple
Light Yellow to Yellow	Cree, White	Light Yellow
Black and Chartreuse	Furnace	Black and Green
Dark Brown	Black	Black

My flies preserve the silhouette of traditional salmon flies but use inexpensive, commonly available materials. They are easy to tie and take 80% of my salmon. The group of people I fish with have all rolled their own variations using the colors and techniques they favor, and we are all happy as clams with our flies. As landlocks are re-established in different areas, local tying traditions will probably contribute a new generation of classics to the canon.

Techniques for Landlocks

The only difference between landlocked Atlantic salmon fishing and sea-run Atlantic fishing is the size of the water. Landlocked streams are smaller than maritime rivers, providing frequent opportunities to fish for visible fish in water that is much easier to read and cover effectively with the fly. Big-water Atlantic salmon strategies are generally aimed at fishing over lies, often without any indication that they are currently holding fish. The angler fishing to unseen fish is always in danger of 1) leaving an active, potential taker too soon, or 2) having fish that may be holding run out and continue their journey upstream. Taking time out to change flies, rest fish, or whatever, can be the undoing of a whole afternoon's work, with the angler never the wiser. Big-water salmon fishers have learned that every

A 4¹/₂-pound, fly-caught landlock.

moment their fly is out of the water, Allah *does* subtract from their lives. Their average cast is an entire weight-forward line, and their average number of backcasts per delivery is one.

Landlocked streams are rarely so big that you can't see the fish if they are coming to your fly. Even though they all have sections where holding fish are not visible, finding fish is not time consuming, and once found they are much easier to fish over than sea-run salmon.

The first rule of landlock fishing is never to leave potential takers (or any group of fish) unless you have no other way of restoring your confidence or politeness requires that you move off the lie to give someone else a chance.

The second rule is always to follow a preceding fisher with a fly that is of a significantly different color from the one the fish have been seeing. Even if that fly has worked, it has probably lost its initial magic and put the rest of the fish in the holding area to sleep. You may wish to play around with fly sizes as well (this works for a lot of people); I stick with the big ones, sizes greater than or equal to Number 4.

The Cross-Current Draw

The third, final, and most important absolute necessity is that the angler learn to maximize any advantage afforded by wind, current, or casting position. Basically, salmon ignore a dead drift—they want to see a fly *live*. The most deadly course a fly can take in moderate to slow currents starts near the bottom and gently rises, smoothly and slowly coming as directly across the current as possible in the *cross-current draw*. The faster the flow, the further downstream of your casting position the fly will be forced to make its cross-stream swing. Mending is crucial and starts in the air. Ideally, you have put yourself in a position relative to wind and current which will allow you to throw the widest possible upstream loop in your line *before* it hits the water; this is called reach casting. Mending immediately to get the fly as deep as possible while keeping it down-flow of the leader, you await the moment when it is finally in position to be drawn across and (as

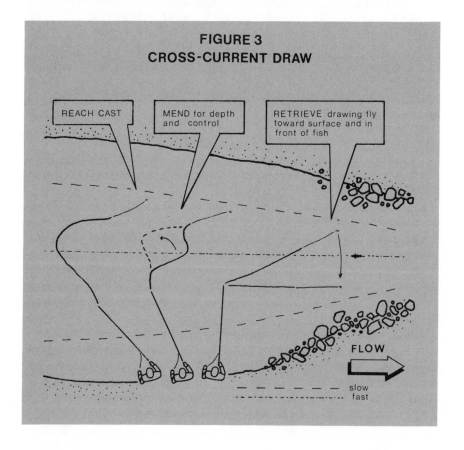

FIGURE 3
CROSS-CURRENT DRAW

current speeds dictate) back upstream. If you can see fish, try to draw the fly right in front of them at a right angle to the direction they are facing (Figure 3). My favorite retrieve starts with the fly at its deepest a few feet upflow of the salmon's far eye and rises roughly 1 foot in every 2 as it travels laterally across the fish's field of vision. This retrieve will take the lazy ones that won't chase a faster fly or one that swings nearer the surface. As the fly begins to rise, your breath will leave you as the fish tips up and also starts to rise while drifting slightly downstream. As the fly approaches the surface in front of the salmon's near eye, the fish will either settle back into its former position or rise, take, and turn away from you, intending to return to its lie (Figure 4).

The easiest thing to do at this point is to promptly take the fly away from the fish. If you have been fishing for trout, Pacific salmon, or steelhead, you are going to have trouble because *you have to let Atlantic salmon hook themselves.* Any attempt to set the hook before the fish has turned and started to *take line* back to where he came from will either miss completely, hook him poorly, or sting him. A short striker (one that nips or taps without taking solidly), left undisturbed by futile attempts to set the hook prematurely, may come to fifteen or more retrieves over several hours before finally taking solidly; a stung fish will be untouchable for the rest of the day.

If your salmon takes he will not spit the fly out until he has returned to his lie, and, during his turn prior to doing so, the hook will be dragged back into the near corner of his jaw where, if it is sharp enough and if you have slowly raised your rod and tightened your line, it will find bone and set so securely that pliers will be required to dislodge it. There is no place else on a salmon's mouth that holds a hook as well. If you learn to wait for solid strikes—and you will probably learn the hard way—you will go from nine out of ten missed or lost to five out of ten landed, and you won't put potential takers down.

Most days and most places, the opportunities for the perfect cross-current draw will be limited. While you make the inevitable compromises with water level, current speed, and so on, remember that a fly racing downstream (or, indeed, anywhere) will only draw a few crazy, overstimulated fish that will shatter your nerves by crashing violently into your fly and, for the most part, fail to hook up. In excessively deep, cold, or fast water where a smoothly rising cross-current swing can't be achieved (or won't draw the lazy ones when it is), the sparing use of small split shot and, in extreme cases, sinking lines may help unload the odds. Cold fish in water over 6 to 8 feet deep will rarely take toward the surface; they want flies fished at their level either across their line of sight or holding and dancing in front of them. Although I recommend a smooth retrieve when swinging

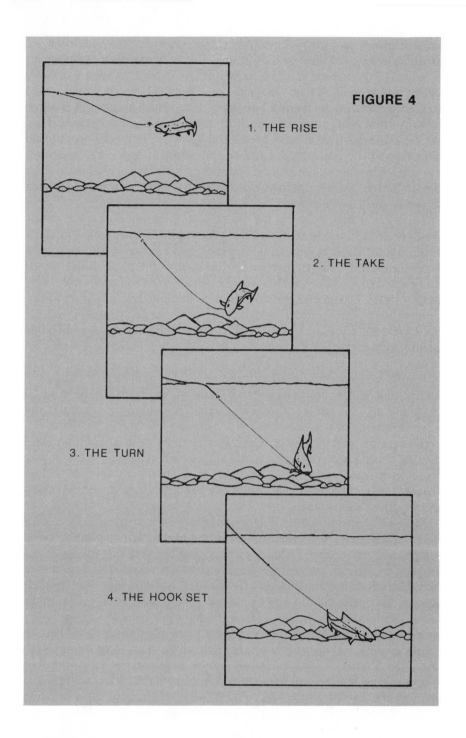

FIGURE 4

1. THE RISE

2. THE TAKE

3. THE TURN

4. THE HOOK SET

a fly across and up, various twitches, pulses, starts, and stops can increase the effectiveness of a deeply fished fly.

Regardless of depth, the most taking moment arrives when the fly stalls directly down-flow of the rod tip. Don't lift the fly out of the water until you have left time for a following fish to make up its mind. Give the fly a little twitch or two and keep your eyes on the general area to make sure that a refusing fish has turned away. If you haven't disturbed it by ripping your fly into the air, the same fish is more likely to play on a subsequent cast.

The Stalled-Fly Presentation

The "stalled fly," or "ambulatory trolling," is the best way to deal with fish that are holding in deep, narrow ledge pools or distinct braids in midriver. In these cold and generally fast-water situations it is important to get directly up-flow of the lie and just hold your fly in the current, on top or down deep, for what I can only describe as "long enough." Slowly and deliberately move your rod tip back and forth, allowing the fly to swing in short arcs below you, and again let it rest. If nothing happens, let out (or take in) a few more feet of line and repeat. On some rivers (for instance, the lower Saranac at Potsdam, New York) this is the prevailing and most practical technique. I once watched a man who made only five casts in an hour catch three fish. From my experience I can tell you that two of those casts were unnecessary. The stalled fly is the difference between a trouter and a salmon fisher; the latter never crosses a river without dangling a fly 30 feet or so downstream while doing so.

Dry-Fly Presentation

Let's go back to early autumn: 65-degree air, 65-degree water as clear as a bell and a little on the low side. Tie on a big, hairy dry and cast quartering upstream. Short drifts are the rule when dry-fly fishing for land-locks. If they don't see it land they don't usually take, preferring the maple leaf that lands directly overhead. If they don't take within 10 feet or so of drift, then cast again. Play with drag. Try everything from the slightest sideways pull up to and including skating your dry across stream (yes, like that maple leaf pushed by a cross-current wind). Try casting downstream and giving your dry a little tug—Leonard Wright's "sudden inch"—before it goes over the fish. Also try dapping (*i.e.*, casting so that just the leader and fly are on the water) downstream and downwind; this will work with wets, too. Dry-fly takes are sudden and dramatic—again, don't set the hook until the line jumps, or you will probably miss. Dry flies are wonderfully effective with landlocks, but only for a short stretch of the season. As winter approaches, the water rises, and the temperature drops, go under.

In the foregoing discussion I have made much of the necessity of waiting on landlocks and on not setting the hook prematurely. If you don't believe me, go miss a couple of dozen of them to persuade yourself. When you're done, come back and we will discuss the soft retrieve. . . .

The Soft Retrieve

The soft retrieve is merely a way of adding a shock absorber between the rod and fly sufficient to permit a salmon to take and turn, without the fly's being pulled out of its mouth or ripped off the line at the strike. It has two components. First, when retrieving across the flow, use a hand-twist retrieve (Figure 5) and keep your rod elevated so that the line can sag between rod tip and water. At the strike, *nod* the rod toward the fish to further decrease any tension on the line. Second, for acutely downstream presentations, use a low rod and keep an 18- to 24-inch shock loop of slack held loosely between your line hand and the reel so that a taking fish can turn and go without being pulled up short. Both soft-retrieve methods will increase your catch (Figure 6).

Playing Landlocks

Once a fish is hooked, clear the decks (that coil of line around your rod butt or under your foot) and get it on the reel. Let it go. You can't stop it—don't try. Keep your drag setting stiff enough to prevent overwind, and try to stay on the same side of the fish as the hook. Landlocks are faster and more aerial than Great Lakes steelhead or Pacifics. A friend of mine who came to town after a summer's guiding on Alaska's Nushigak River took a 12-pound landlock that he said compared favorably with much larger Alaskan silvers. The toughest ones are the ones that don't jump more than once or twice but burn way into your backing and then come at you so fast that you can't regain line quickly enough to stay in contact—and *then* jump 20 feet away from you while you still have 60 feet of slack

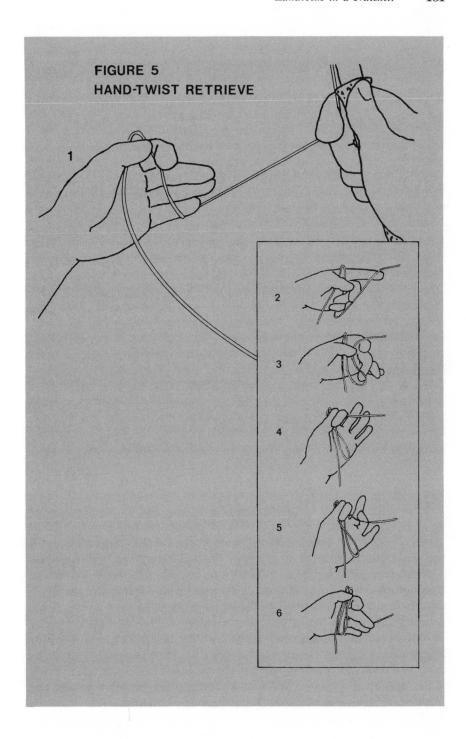

FIGURE 5
HAND-TWIST RETRIEVE

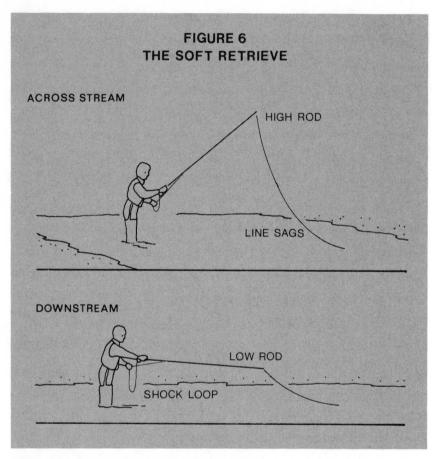

FIGURE 6
THE SOFT RETRIEVE

ACROSS STREAM

HIGH ROD

LINE SAGS

DOWNSTREAM

LOW ROD

SHOCK LOOP

line on the water. I repeat: if they are poorly hooked they will get off on a jump, a sudden run, or by rolling in the leader. If they are well hooked and you don't break them off, they stay hooked and will come in. When a salmon is played down, it turns on its side and is ready for landing. If the fish comes in rolled in your leader you will have to unroll it by slowly picking up your rod tip and slightly drawing back until the fish spins enough times (often four or five) to put you back in direct contact with the fly. If this is neglected and the fish bolts as you make in to land it, you risk a breakoff as the fish flexes against the turns of strained tippet. Having unrolled your fish, and if the bank is friendly, beach it; if not, and your fish is over 4 pounds or so (smaller ones being too slippery), make in, carefully reach down, and grasp it by the wrist just in front of the tail, pick it up, walk to shore, do a little dance, and grin like an idiot for the rest of the day—or, use a net, let it go, and smile like a saint.

Clear the decks, get it on the reel, and let go.

. . . twenty minutes later . . .

11/Deep-Water Trolling

by Capt. Ernie Lantiegne

The oars creaked at every stroke as the boy and the old man in the weathered old rowboat trolled slowly along the small Adirondack Lake. It was mid-July, and hot. The boy held the lead-core trolling line between his thumb and forefinger as the old man had shown him. He remembered every word he had been told. "These lake trout hang out right on the bottom in the summer, down where the water is cold. You have to troll enough line to keep your spoon just off bottom." The boy could feel the action of the spoon, telegraphed through the lead core.

The old man had ever so carefully placed the strip of sucker bait on the single hook of the spoon to make it work "just so." Stroke by stroke, the creaking of the oars was accompanied by the slow, rhythmic jerk of the lead core. Then it happened. As the spoon wobbled forward just off the bottom, it suddenly stopped. The line tightened, and the memory of the boy's first thrashing lake trout lasted forever.

The date was July 1952. The old man was my dad. I was eight years old. The technique was simple but oh, so effective. All it involved was a lead-core line wrapped on a piece of board, a single hook spoon-rigged "just so," and a lot of common sense and desire.

Deep-water trolling techniques and tackle have changed drastically since those days, but the basics are still the same. The fisherman can make it as complicated or as simple as he wants, but deep-water trolling does not *have to* be complicated. As a matter of fact, for the beginner or the pro, the secret to consistently catching fish in deep water is often just keeping things simple. The simpler the better. Add a generous portion of savvy, and mix in lots of desire, and you have a formula that will *catch fish!*

Trolling: The Whys and Wherefores

Trolling as a fishing technique is probably as old as the day when primitive man first learned to propel a water craft with a paddle. The reasons for fishing in those early days are a far cry from those of modern-day anglers, but the reasons for trolling are still the same. Trolling allows an angler to keep his lures in the water longer and to cover more water than any other fishing technique. Trolling also allows an angler to carefully control lure presentation, and to fine tune speed, depth, and lure action. Use of multiple lures at one time also gives the troller a tremendous advantage—the opportunity to fish a variety of sizes, colors, and shapes of spoons or plugs simultaneously. This improves the angler's chances of finding the "hot" lure for the day. Multiple-lure rigs can also put extra fish in the boat by creating the appearance of a school of bait.

Trolling is dragging a lure behind a moving boat in a manner that is appealing enough to entice a fish to strike. The fishing gear can be extremely simple. The only fly in the ointment is that the lure must be presented in the zone of water where the fish are located. This is especially important to the trout and salmon angler because salmonids generally prefer cold water. Fishermen capitalize on this fact in spring and fall by trolling the cooler surface waters. As surface temperatures warm with the approach of summer, however, the situation changes. Salmonids head for the deeper, cooler depths and deep-water trolling becomes the name of the game. That's not to say that trout and salmon do not inhabit deep water at times when surface temperatures are cold; they do. But, in summer deep-water trolling is a must if you want to catch trout and salmon.

Presenting a lure to a fish in deep water from a trolling boat is not quite as simple as surface trolling, simply because it involves placing and keeping a lure at a certain depth. One of the simplest and oldest techniques is to attach a large lead weight to a fishing line. This worked, but unless the angler was fishing right on the bottom he never really knew exactly how deep he was fishing. Also, heavy sinkers make it difficult to tell if you have a fish on, even one in the 5- to 10-pound class. Nevertheless, back in the 1940's and '50's this was the standard technique used by guides on Lake George in New York State to troll for lake trout with Christmas Tree spinners (i.e., several spinners in line simulating a school of bait fish) and a sewn bait. I talked to a sport once who had taken a 14-pound laker fishing this way. The guide had to tell him he had a fish on!

Times have changed, and today there are better ways to troll for trout and salmon in deep water. Perhaps the simplest and most effective way is

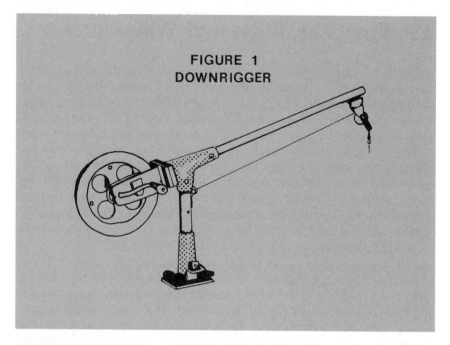

FIGURE 1
DOWNRIGGER

with the use of *downriggers* (see Figure 1). This technique and a few others, like wire-line fishing, diving planers, and sinkers used with releases, will be discussed in detail.

The Basics: Getting Started

So, you have never tried deep-water fishing and would like to. Or perhaps you have tried it but aren't having much luck. Or maybe you have been fishing deep water for years but would like to fine tune your technique a bit. In either case you have to consider some of these basics:

Fishing Waters

It may sound obvious, but you have to find good fishing waters, which harbor the species you want in numbers and sizes with which you are satisfied. As a fishery biologist with the New York State Department of Environmental Conservation for twenty-two years, I can tell you that fishing unproductive waters is one of the first mistakes that many anglers make.

For this angler, searching for good fishing waters paid off with a 40-pound chinook salmon.

There are hundreds of thousands of lakes and ponds on the North American continent, but they are not all good fishing waters. Don't waste your time trying to learn to fish deep water in a lake or pond where there are few or no fish. Do your homework. Talk to other fishermen. Stop in at sport shops. Read magazines. Best of all call the state natural-resources agency in your area and ask to speak to the fisheries-management unit. They should have the information you need.

Water, and How it Behaves. Scientists call this subject "limnology," but that is a word that could scare away even the meanest junkyard dog. We'll call it "water behavior," because that is what we are really talking about. It's simple but important to deep-water anglers. Water in a lake does not mix evenly like a good Tom Collins in a shaker. Instead it forms layers for a variety of reasons that we won't get into here. In spring we find colder water on the surface, and trout and salmon within easy reach. Later, as the sun warms an old fisherman's bones, it also warms the water. The result is still a layered effect, but now a warm layer is at the top and a cold layer at the bottom. The point where these two layers meet and the temperature drops quickly from warm to cold is called the *thermocline,* and in any lake it is one of the most productive fishing areas. The thermocline. Remember it, and it will help you catch fish!

Fish Behavior

This is the fun part if you really like to fish. It's fun to learn about fish behavior, and it's absolutely essential to the fisherman, particularly if you fish deep water. Fish behavior varies from species to species at different times and places. The *water temperature* preferred by each of the species of trout and salmon is *the most important behavioral characteristic* to the fisherman. If you don't know the water temperature preferred by a certain fish species, and you haven't found that water temperature in a lake, you will not catch fish consistently in deep water. Water temperature is so important that we'll talk about it in depth (no pun intended) later.

Another important behavioral difference among fish is *vertical distribution.* Some species, like lake trout, normally tend to locate near the bottom, often near *structure* (shoals, dropoffs, *etc.*), although they will suspend above the bottom, especially in some waters. Brown trout have a similar tendency to orient to the bottom and to stay inshore. Other species, like steelhead and cohos, are nomads and are almost always suspended off the bottom in the thermocline or near the surface if water temperatures are suitable.

Other important fish behavioral traits include forage preference, color preference (for example, steelhead love orange), speed (lake trout are slow compared to landlocked salmon), nocturnal behavior, *etc.*

Reading, talking with experienced anglers, and gaining your own experience are the best ways to learn about fish behavior. Some of the best sources of fishing information are fishing magazines.

The All-Purpose Trolling Boat: How to Rig It

Lake fishing requires a boat, and deep-water fishing often means the angler has to travel a bit farther offshore than other boat fishermen. Many, many books and magazine articles have been written about fishing boats, and many, many more will be written. Writers have recommended fishing craft ranging from the glorified inner tubes known as belly boats to $100,000 Bertrams. The fact is, however, that what an angler needs to get out on the water and back is a boat that is safe and serviceable and that fits his pocketbook. Fishing boats range from the smaller 12-foot and 14-foot aluminum car-top models to the fancy 20- and 30-foot offshore sportfishing boats used in the Great Lakes. Salt-water boats are even bigger and fancier.

You can rig almost any boat for deep-water trolling. You can install a couple of downriggers on a seaworthy 12-foot aluminum car-topper. There are many small, accessible trout and salmon waters where you can use a small boat.

Proper rigging and outfitting of a trolling boat, particularly one to be used for fishing deep water, may just be the most important step for the deep-water troller. Rig a boat properly, and the rest is easy. Rig a boat wrong, and you will never be as effective as you could be. Here is the gear you need and how to rig it:

Compasses

The importance of a compass cannot be stressed enough. This should be the first piece of equipment installed on an offshore trolling boat.

More than once while fishing on Lake Ontario I've seen a heavy fog bank move in unexpectedly, reducing visibility to less than 200 feet. In these conditions, the shore becomes but a memory. Several times in dense fog small boats with frightened anglers aboard have come alongside my boat with the question, "Which direction is shore?" When given a compass bearing to the nearest harbor they responded, "We don't have a compass!" Don't be like them.

Downriggers

"Controlled-depth trolling" is a phrase coined by the Riviera Co., the

This fishing boat is properly rigged, with downriggers mounted near the stern.

pioneer in development of commercially available downriggers. In a nut-shell this phrase describes the purpose of a downrigger. Proper placement of one or more downriggers on a boat is absolutely essential to effective operation and successful use of this piece of equipment. Tangled down-riggers, cables in the prop, broken fishing line, headaches, and alcoholism are but a few of the symptoms of improper installation.

Downriggers should be placed as far to the stern as possible while still allowing operation and rigging. The photo above shows a typical 20-foot inboard-outboard rigged with four downriggers. Note the short-arm down-riggers off the stern and the longer-arm riggers off the sides. Stern riggers are positioned to clear the propeller of the outdrive (or outboard), but are still easily accessible. The side riggers are set as far astern as possible to prevent tangling of downrigger cables and fishing lines on sharp turns. Side riggers must be mounted on swivel bases to allow them to swivel parallel to the boat for docking, trailering, and navigating. Side riggers should have at least 4-foot arms and should be rigged with a retrieving device similar to Cannon's Retro-ease. This is an ingenious but simple and inexpensive device that makes rigging lines on long-arm downriggers a snap. Be sure to mount side riggers far enough forward to clear the stern riggers when the side riggers are swiveled astern.

Downriggers should always be mounted as if you planned to haul a 1-ton weight around on them. If you wonder why, just imagine the force on a downrigger with a 200-pound test cable when a downrigger weight hangs up on bottom. Downriggers must be mounted with strong stainless-steel bolts and with reinforcement under the boat's gunnels. If you are in the market for a new or used trolling boat, look carefully for one with strong, wide gunnels that will allow easy but secure mounting of downriggers.

If you own a 14- or 16-foot aluminum boat with no gunnels, you can still install a couple of downriggers using a bit of old-fashioned horse sense. The best installations I have seen on boats like these usually involved a homemade mount attached to the rear seat next to the side of the boat.

Choice of electric or manual downriggers is up to the user. Most fishermen start off with manuals because of cost but in the end use electric models. It is almost impossible to effectively operate four downriggers on a boat unless they are electric. If you don't already own a downrigger and want to, I suggest you start by buying the best pair of electric models you can afford. If you can't afford electrics, buy a good pair of manuals.

If you install electric downriggers, do the extra step and install remote switches within easy reach of the captain's seat.

Downrigger Releases. A downrigger release works on the same principle as a clothes pin. The fishing line is clamped in the release tight enough to set the hook on a strike, but light enough to be released when a fish begins to fight. In the jargon of a downrigger fisherman, a "false release" is a missed strike when the line is pulled from the release without a hookup. One of the more common statements amidst the VHF radio chatter on the Great Lakes goes something like this. "Hey, Joe, how they bitin'?" "Not bad, Chuck. We've got three fish, and we've had eleven false releases."

Whoa! Eleven false releases? Something is dead wrong! No one would have that many false releases if his downrigger releases were working properly. Yet we hear of like cases all the time. Why? Because many fishermen either select poor releases, adjust release tension improperly, or leave too much slack in the line between the release and the rod. Once the line is set in the release and lowered to the proper depth, be sure to reel down, bending your rod tip in a good arc. When a fish hits you want the rod tip to snap upward sharply, helping to set the hook. If you've been having problems with false releases, tighten up the tension adjustment. If small fish aren't releasing it try to find a happy medium.

Downrigger releases are the critical link between you, your lure, and the fish. They are made in a great variety of shapes and sizes. The simplest, and my favorite, is a Number 12 rubber band. You simply loop the rubber band around your line twice and tighten it as shown in Figure 2. A touch of saliva added to the knot helps tighten it to prevent slippage. One loop

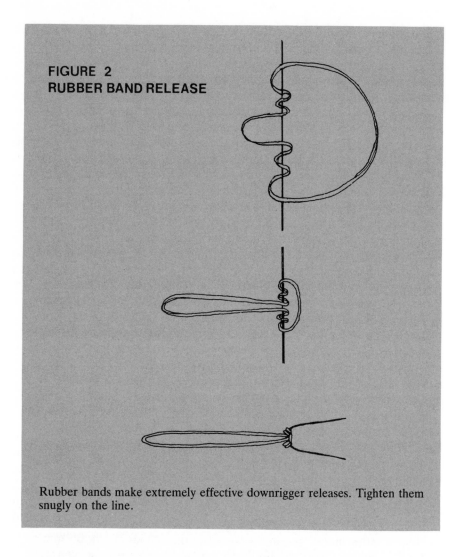

FIGURE 2
RUBBER BAND RELEASE

Rubber bands make extremely effective downrigger releases. Tighten them snugly on the line.

of the rubber band is not enough. The rubber band is strong enough to set the hook but breaks after the strike. Small trout generally will not break a Number 12 rubber band, but you can usually see the telltale shake of the rod tip when a small fish is on.

Downrigger Weights. Downrigger weights are made in a variety of shapes and sizes generally ranging from 8 to 10 pounds. Shapes vary from the standard spherical cannon ball to the streamlined, fish-shaped models. There is a definite difference in downrigger weights and how they track through the water, how they "bump" the bottom, how they visually attract fish, and, I think, how they sound to trout and salmon.

The cannon ball is probably the most commonly used weight. It tracks well through the water, tends to be relatively snag proof, and is easy to handle. When fish are spooky cannon balls may have an advantage in not scaring them, especially when you are fishing a lure close to the weight.

Another popular downrigger weight is the Herbie, a 10-pound, compact, fish-shaped weight with small angled fins on its sides. There is something special about a Herbie and the way it seems to attract trout and salmon better than most other weights. One word of caution, however: the Herbie hangs up on bottom worse than any other weight I have ever used.

The Super Salmon Tracker is a lean, fish-shaped 8- to 10-pound weight with the largest profile of any downrigger weight. Because of that it is a great attractor. It has a stainless-steel tail fin that can be bent slightly to the side to make the weight plane away from the boat to starboard and port. This keeps the weights spread apart, covers more water, and prevents tangling. The trackers' long, lean shape makes them virtually snag free. Under certain conditions my favorite weight is a chartreuse Salmon Tracker with a lure fished only 4 to 6 feet behind it.

Color does make a difference on downrigger weights. Chartreuse, fluorescent green, and black seem to be the most attractive to fish.

Thermistors

A thermistor is an electronic device capable of reading the water temperature at a given depth and relaying that information back to you in the boat. This is an essential piece of deep-water trolling equipment. Temperature is the key to finding fish, particularly active, feeding fish. If I had to choose only two pieces of electronic fishing gear for my boat my second choice would be a good thermistor. The first would be a depthfinder.

Thermistors are made in hand-held models that give you temperatures when you lower a probe over the side straight down from a stationary boat. They are also made in models that attach to your downrigger cable at the weight and give you constant temperature readouts in the boat. Both work, but the downrigger type are the handiest. They are also the most expensive, costing $500 to $600, compared to $75 to $150 for the hand-held models. Beware of the models that use a plastic-covered downrigger cable to transmit temperature readings to the boat: some of these models are unreliable. The types that radio temperature readouts to the boat through a stern-mounted transducer have worked dependably for me for several years. Fish Hawk manufactures these.

If you use one of Fish Hawk's Thermo-Troll 800 units, it will also give you an alternating digital readout of speed at the downrigger weight along with speed and temperature at the surface.

Depth Sounders (Fish Finders, Bottom Sounders, etc.)

Depth sounders, often referred to as fish finders, are the eyes of the deep-water troller. In combination with a knowledge of water temperature, a depth sounder is an integral part of a trolling rig. Technical advancements in the last few years in depth sounders boggle the mind.

Most depth sounders use either graph recorders or video-monitors. Graph recorders are favored by most trollers, because the good ones have high resolution in deep water and cost less than video recorders. I have used a King 1350 (6-inch paper) recorder for three years now on my boat without a single problem. The King 1060 also has excellent surface-speed and temperature readouts. Recorder graphs made by Furuno, Sitex, and other companies are also excellent.

Improvements in the technology of video recorders combined with decreasing prices may soon make graph recorders obsolete, however. Video recorders, particularly the color videos, appear to be the coming thing in deep-water fish finders. They are quite easy to use and interpret, and they avoid the expense of graph paper. Furuno, Koden, and Sitex all produce outstanding color videos in the higher price ranges.

Flashers, the most primitive of electronic depth sounders, are difficult to interpret, especially for beginners, and are not recommended. LCR (liquid crystal) recorders of the types I have seen are not recommended because they lack good resolution.

Depth sounders should be installed exactly according to the directions supplied with them by the manufacturer to assure optimum performance. For downrigger fishing, adjust the angle of the transducer backward far enough so that the cone of coverage picks up the downrigger weights and close-trolled lures.

One of the questions often asked by fishermen is whether they should purchase a 50-kilohertz or 200-kilohertz graph recorder. The rule of thumb is to use the 50-kHz model for deep-water fishing, and the 200-kHz for shallow water. Many Great Lakes trollers use one of each for different fishing conditions.

Trolling Speedometers

Another essential piece of equipment is a trolling speedometer. Surface trolling speedometers are a valuable aid to the angler who trolls either the surface or deep water. Deep-water speedometers that relay trolling speed from a probe attached to the downrigger cable are the frosting on the cake. These units, like the Fish Hawk Thermo Troll 800, allow deep-water trollers to fine tune speeds to one tenth of a knot or mile per hour. The Datamarine Model LX 50 is an excellent surface-trolling speedometer. Homemade trolling indicators that incorporate a lead weight (4 to 8 ounces) trailed in the water alongside the boat also work.

Speed-Control Devices

Proper trolling speed is crucial to catching trout and salmon. All the trolling speedometers in the world won't do you any good if you cannot adjust the speed of your boat. Faster speeds are seldom a problem, but throttling back to the slower speeds necessary for certain types of deep-water trolling can be tough, especially when a larger horsepower engine is being used.

They say that necessity is the mother of invention, and that is certainly the case with trolling speed-control devices. If you have spent much time on good salmon- and trout-fishing waters you have probably seen almost every contraption imaginable attached to a boat to slow it down. Small-horsepower trolling motors, modified sea anchors designed specifically for trollers, and trolling plates which can be raised or lowered just behind the propellor are probably the most favored speed-control devices on larger boats. I use the large, cast-metal, hydraulically operated Beaver Troll on the outdrive of my inboard/outboard. It works perfectly. Speed is infinitely adjustable with a simple toggle switch located at the helm.

This is one area where smaller boats with smaller engines have a definite advantage. If they troll down slow enough their lucky operator doesn't have to worry about speed control.

Rod Holders

There is an old saying that "You never have enough rod holders on a trolling boat." Keep this in mind when rigging your boat. Each downrigger should have two integrally mounted rod holders. You will need additional rod holders for other purposes.

My boat, the *Fish Doctor,* a 26-foot 4-Winns, is equipped with two rod holders on each of four Riviera downriggers, two adjustable 10-inch Old Pal rod holders mounted astern at the port and starboard corners for wire-line rigs, two 10-inch Old Pals mounted port and starboard for fishing diving planers, three flush-mount Lee rod holders in each of the port and starboard gunnels for fishing lines off planer boards and outriggers, and five side-mount Lee rod holders on the port and starboard sides of the cabin for transporting rods.

If you are just getting started and want to go easy, start with at least one rod holder for each downrigger. You should also install at least two adjustable rod holders, one on each side of the boat. As you gain experience, you will quickly see your additional needs.

Landing Nets

Many once-in-a-lifetime trophies have been lost at the boat because of a landing net that was too small, too weak, or in otherwise bad shape. (We won't mention fish simply missed by the netter.) I'll never forget the day on Paradox Lake in the Adirondack Mountains of New York when I lost the biggest lake trout I ever saw because of a net that was too small. I had been jerklining with a handheld lead-core line and a Pfleuger Record spoon. Late in the day I hooked a horse of a fish. After about a fifteen-minute give-and-take tug of war, I had the huge fish alongside. Its orange-tinged pectoral fins looked as big as my hands. As I slipped it head first into the net it bottomed out with well over half of the fish sticking out of the net. With a bad case of buck fever, I heaved with the net, and the laker thrashed back into the lake. The single hook of the old Pfleuger Record hung in the net, and that huge lake trout was just a picture in my mind.

Make sure you use a strong net big enough to handle the fish of your dreams.

Loran C Units

If you intend to fish your boat on big water like the Great Lakes, you may want to install a Loran C unit for both navigation and safety purposes. These electronic units pinpoint locations on the water, returning you to fishing hotspots or safe harbors with a simple push of a few buttons. They are accurate to about 50 to 200 feet and cost $600 to $1200. They are well worth the price if you do a lot of big-water trolling.

Safety Gear

Meet the requirements of the Navigation Law for safety gear, and you should have everything onboard that you need for emergency situations. Life preservers, fire extinguishers, and other gear are a must. A good tool kit and some spare motor parts like spark plugs, a prop, and fan belts should also be on board. One other thing: be sure you properly fuse all electronic gear installed on your boat. Improperly installed equipment can cause dangerous electrical fires.

Rods, Reels, and Lines: A Matched Outfit

Despite the huge variety of fishing rods, reels, and lines on the market today, selection of a balanced outfit for downrigger fishing is easy. If you are an experienced angler you probably have already made your choice. If you are a beginner just look in a tackle shop for a matched downrigger rod and reel. Downrigger fishing is no longer a new angling technique, and through experience manufacturers have developed many good rods and reels. Selection of a good fishing line is not so easy, and is just as important to downrigger fishing success as either rod or reel.

Line

Monofilament line used for downrigger fishing must be tough enough to stand the abuse of releases and chafing against steel downrigger cables. Most releases (except rubber bands) are hard on line. In addition line takes a beating when fish, especially salmon, streak through downrigger cables on the strike. You can imagine the stress on a line as it grinds away on a steel cable when a big chinook takes off on a blistering 200-foot run.

There are lots of lines on the market, and a number of them are touted as abrasion-resistant. That may be, but the only line used aboard the *Fish*

Doctor, except for some occasional experimenting, is Maxima Chameleon. I use it in 2- to 20-pound test. It's the toughest line made, in my book.

Rods

When selecting a downrigger rod remember that downriggers were developed to avoid the heavy tackle we used to have to use to fish deep water. Why choose a stiff, heavy rod when a lighter rod is more fun and more effective? In most conditions you don't need a heavy rod to land even the biggest chinook salmon.

The traditional downrigger rod is 8 to 8½ feet in length with a medium action, good backbone, and some flexibility through the butt. It should have plenty of ceramic line guides. The rod handle should be long enough to fit well into a rod holder. The fore grip should be large enough to be held comfortably in the hand when fighting heavy fish. Cork handles do not hold up well in some rod holders.

All of the downrigger rods onboard my boat are made by Lamiglas, one of the finest rod builders in the U.S. My rods are either medium-light-

Downrigger rods should be flexible to the butt, with plenty of backbone.

The Penn 320 GTi downrigger reel has plenty of line capacity and a silky smooth drag.

action graphite (Model G 1306) or medium-action fiberglass (Model PSA 85). The graphite rods are used with no heavier than 12-pound-test line. The fiberglass rods are used with up to 20-pound-test line during the late-summer salmon season when heavy terminal tackle like dodgers and squids are the proper recipe, and multiple hookups with big chinooks are common.

Reels

Reels used for downrigger fishing need smooth drags and enough line capacity for whatever size fish you expect to handle. If you tangle with a big chinook you will know in a hurry whether you made the right choice. Although reel manufacturers didn't know it at the time, the level-wind reels developed years ago are perfect for downrigger fishing. If you have even a hint of a doubt about this, check out the reels used by trout and salmon charter captains on the Great Lakes. You will find they use level-wind reels almost exclusively.

There are a number of level-wind reels that have developed around Great Lakes trout and salmon fishing. Some of the best include Penn's new 320 GTi and the Daiwa Sealine 27H and 47H. For light-tackle trolling, I prefer the Daiwa Millionaire 4HM and the 6HM. Whatever your choice in reels, be sure to match them with the right rod and line. You will find that a properly matched outfit is a real pleasure to use.

Locating Fish: How to Find Them

The 18-foot trolling boat eased its way out of Oswego Harbor and headed due north straight out into Lake Ontario. It was a hot, sunny day in early July 1977. Mac Collins and I were searching for big brown trout and lake trout. We were pioneering. There wasn't another offshore fishing boat in sight. Both Mac and I were experienced big-water trollers. Mac was one of the best trout and salmon fishermen in the Finger Lakes. We were starting from scratch here, however, since we had never fished Ontario before, and no one else had cracked the secret of its summer, browns and lakers.

We had done our homework. At the time, I was a fisheries biologist working for the New York State Department of Environmental Conservation in Cortland, New York. Even though I wasn't working on the Ontario salmonid program, I had talked to the biologists who were. They were scratching their heads, because the brown trout and lake trout which provided such an outstanding near-shore fishery in early spring, when water temperatures were cold, seemed to disappear in midsummer. The biologists knew the trout were there, but where? Mac and I decided we would find out. The secret was *fish location*. If we could find them we knew we could catch them.

Find them we did. We had one of the finest, most exciting, and satisfying fishing trips of our lives. Jumbo brown trout up to 12 pounds and some icy-cold lake trout up to 10 pounds were our reward. The simple ingredients of our fish-location recipe were a good fishing water, a knowledge of brown trout and lake trout behavior, a well-equipped trolling boat, water-temperature information, and determination. Let's talk a little more about how they all go together.

Fish Concentrations

Catching fish means fishing good waters with good fish populations. Before Mac Collins and I fished Lake Ontario we checked the trout-stocking records. We knew that thousands of brown trout and lake trout had been stocked in the Oswego Harbor area for several years. Fishermen had been catching nice browns and lakers in the spring when the fish were shallow. Biologists also told us brown trout don't usually roam far, and smelt and alewives were their preferred forage. We were convinced we could locate trout.

Information like this on fish populations, stocking policies, forage fish, and local fishing activity is important in locating fish. Not all waters, and not all areas of lakes—especially large waters like the Great Lakes— support good concentrations of fish. Some areas seem to be preferred by one species of trout or salmon more than another. A good example is the Henderson Harbor area of Lake Ontario, which produces hot fishing for lake trout but slow fishing for browns and steelhead.

In many waters, particularly large waters, seasonal movements of fish result in large concentrations of trout and salmon as well as other game fish like walleyes in certain locations. Learn these movements, and you'll catch more fish. One of the classic examples of huge seasonal concentrations of game fish is the mass gathering of jumbo chinook salmon that gang up in the Mexico Bay area, in the southeast corner of Lake Ontario. This is a prespawning concentration ready to run the Big Salmon River to spawn. It produces some of the wildest fishing for trophy chinooks in the entire Great Lakes.

There are a variety of reasons for the concentrations of fish in specific areas at specific times, including location of stocking or spawning areas, forage-fish concentrations, seasonal water temperatures, habitat selection, and a host of other factors, some of which remain a mystery that only the fish themselves can unwind. The fact is, however, that it is more important for anglers to know these factors exist than to understand why they operate.

Where does a fisherman find this information? Well, sometimes it's easy, and sometimes it isn't. One of the best places to start is with the natural-resource or environmental-conservation agency in the state you plan to fish. Get in touch with the fishery biologist in the district office closest to the lake you plan to visit. Most of these people are competent professionals who know the fisheries in their area. Their business is producing good fishing, and most of them like to talk fishing with anglers. These officials are the best source of information on good fishing.

Once you find a hot lake look for more information at local bait and tackle shops and marinas. Don't be afraid to ask other fishermen for help. Most of them are more than willing to give you a few tips.

Marking Fish Concentrations. Locating good concentrations of active, feeding salmonids in a large lake can be one of the most satisfying experiences in fishing. Losing those fish after finding them and not being able to relocate them can drive even the most abstemious angler to drink! It doesn't have to happen to you, though, because marking fish concentrations is simple. One way to do it is with a marker buoy made from a float, a line, and a small weight or anchor. You can buy these, or you can make them from plastic jugs. If you like the jug idea, tie a premeasured nylon line or cord to the handle of the jug. Store the marker buoys in your boat. When you locate a good concentration of fish or a piece of structure you want to fish over, simply throw your marker buoy overboard after removing the rubber band.

If you want to get a little fancier—and dig a lot further down into your wallet—you can purchase a Loran C unit to keep you on fish. Use Loran C units in combination with Loran maps and hydrographic maps, and your offshore fishing success on big waters like the Great Lakes will skyrocket.

Temperature

Once you have located a water with a good game-fish population and you are fairly certain you are fishing an area with a reasonable concentration of fish, you should be thinking one thing: temperature, temperature, temperature!

Temperature is the key to knowing exactly where to place deep-trolled lures and baits. Without knowing water temperatures and location of the thermocline (Figure 3) you will waste valuable time finding the "strike zone," *even if you are using a good fish locater!* When Mac Collins and I left Oswego Harbor that hot July day on a due-north compass bearing, the first thing we wanted to know was water temperature. We boated out to 100 feet of water, stopped, and lowered a downrigger with a thermistor attached. The surface temperature was in the low seventies. When the counter on the downrigger read 75 feet, however, the needle on the temperature unit fell quickly from the high sixties to 56 degrees. That was the preferred temperature for the brown trout we were seeking. Lakers prefer temperatures a bit colder, but if actively feeding, they would be at 56 degrees too, especially if colder water wasn't too far away.

Individual species of trout, salmon, other game fish, and forage fish like alewives and smelt all have preferred temperatures and temperature ranges where they spend most of their time. That is not to say that a chinook salmon will not move from the comfort zone to warmer or colder water to feed or rest. Generally, though, you can count on finding fish in their preferred water-temperature range. The preferred temperature ranges for various salmonid species are listed in the following temperature table:

Game fish Species	Preferred Temperature (F)	Temperature Range (F)
Brown Trout	56	50–60
Lake Trout	50	45–55
Steelhead	55	50–60
Rainbow Trout	61	58–63
Brook Trout	54	50–58
Splake	52	48–58
Landlocked Salmon	55	50–60
Chinook Salmon	54	50–58
Coho Salmon	54	50–58

Some species have a narrower range of preferred temperatures than others. Domestic rainbow trout in most lakes prefer a 61-degree temperature and can almost always be found in water at that temperature if it is available. Brown trout, on the other hand, seem to have a much wider range of preferred temperature. Browns are commonly taken in water temperatures up into the low sixties, especially if that is where the baitfish are. Lake trout also have a wide range of temperature tolerance, despite what many books say. I have taken them on the surface at temperatures of 61 degrees.

It's important to understand that the smaller, juvenile fish of any species, including lake trout, landlocked salmon, and steelhead, are often found at water temperatures much warmer than those preferred by the larger adults. In the early 1970's on Lake George in northeastern New York, fishing was great for rainbow trout in the summer at 61 degrees. Landlocked salmon were also common at this temperature, but they seldom were larger than 18 inches. If you wanted larger landlocks in the 4- to 10-pound class, you had to fish 55-degree water.

Fish may move among temperature zones in a regular pattern in a single day. Some salmonid species like lake trout and chinook, for example, seem to retire to deeper, colder water to take a little snooze when they aren't active. In today's world of modern electronics many anglers fall into the trap of ignoring water temperature and gluing their eyes to their graph recorder. They see large numbers of fish on the screen in deep water and fish for them with no luck. Other boats in the area fishing at shallower depths with fewer visible fish are doing better. What is happening is that most of the fish in the area are inactive and have moved to deeper water and colder temperatures for whatever reason. Even though there are fewer

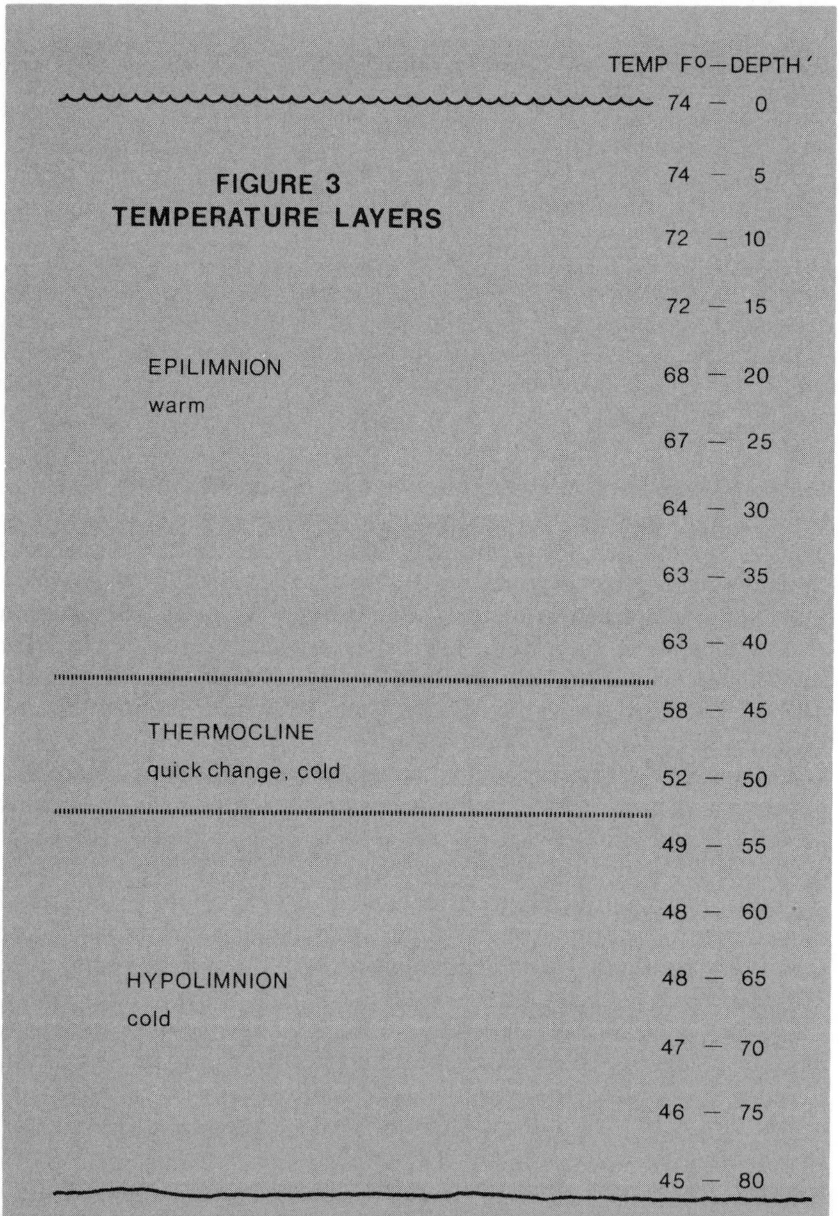

TEMP F°—DEPTH′

~~~~~~ 74 — 0

FIGURE 3
TEMPERATURE LAYERS

74 — 5

72 — 10

72 — 15

EPILIMNION

warm

68 — 20

67 — 25

64 — 30

63 — 35

63 — 40

THERMOCLINE

quick change, cold

58 — 45

52 — 50

49 — 55

48 — 60

HYPOLIMNION

cold

48 — 65

47 — 70

46 — 75

45 — 80

The thermocline, where water temperature drops quickly, is a hotspot for trout and salmon. Shown is a typical temperature profile for July on Lake Ontario.

fish showing on the fish finder at shallow depths the fish there are active and are hitting.

Temperature, temperature, temperature. Know it and remember it, and you will take more fish.

Structure

Underwater structure in a lake is shown on hydrographic maps, which help fishermen quickly locate fish on large lakes.

Certain salmonid species, especially lake trout, orient strongly to structure. Lakers love steep dropoffs, underwater shoals, and areas of rugged bottom. At times lakers are found on structure at depths and temperatures far below those the book says are optimum. In Lake Ontario, in early spring, when lakers are supposed to be in shallow water at their preferred temperatures, I have taken them in depths of 100 to 125 feet near structure.

Lake trout will also suspend off bottom, especially in waters like New York's Finger Lakes, but generally if you're looking for lakers you look for structure. Chinook salmon and especially brown trout also tend to home

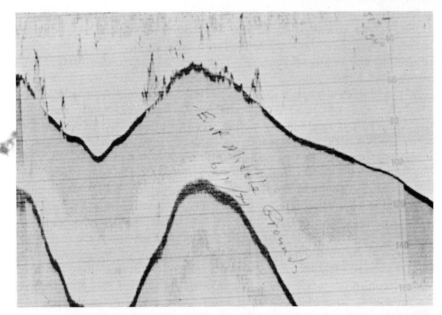

Printout from a fish finder, showing structure and fish. Lake trout often concentrate near structure like this shoal in Lake George.

in on structure. Sonar tagging and tracking studies show that the first place to look for brown trout in deep water is where the thermocline intersects the bottom. Browns will often be located there or just a little deeper and no more than 15 feet or so off bottom.

Other species, like steelhead and cohos, have more of a wanderlust. Structure doesn't mean very much to these species. Water currents, however, seem to attract both steelhead and cohos, and other salmonids as well. Structure sometimes influences water currents, and when it does, you may have found a hotspot.

Deep-Water Lure Presentation: Doing It Right

Lure presentation basically involves the placement of a bait or lure close enough to a fish so that through its senses of sight, hearing, feel, and smell that fish is enticed into striking. If that happens and you have the rest of your act together, lines release and tighten, drags scream, and you're hooked up and battling.

In shallow water it's relatively easy to control your lure, presenting it exactly where you want it. In depths of 20 feet or more the ballgame changes. You may know the temperature and depth where fish are, but controlling the depth of your lure becomes the key to consistently presenting that lure to fish.

In the old days, when I used to row my dad around Adirondack lake trout lakes in an old wooden rowboat day after day, we carefully controlled the depth of our single-hook spoons. We did this mostly by feel and by experience. A good dacron lead-core line was a pretty sensitive instrument in the right hands. The line transmitted the location of the spoon to your fingertips. A soft bottom dulled that vibration, while the spoon clicked on a hard bottom. The only hydrographic map available was the one indelibly engraved in your mind after years of trolling the same areas.

Today things are different, but even with all of the electronic gadgetry and fishing gear available, lure presentation often separates the men from the boys. Controlled-depth trolling is still the name of the game. Downriggers are probably the easiest way to control depth in trolling for trout and salmon in deep water. There are other techniques that are effective for presenting lures to fish in deep water, however. Wire lines, three-way sinker rigs, and diving planers all work. Nevertheless, downriggers are the method of depth control most commonly used by trollers today.

Depth Control

Depth control for effective lure presentation is easy with a downrigger. Just attach the manufacturer's recommended weight of 8 to 12 pounds, adjust the counter on the downrigger to read a depth of 0 feet at the surface, and lower the weight into the water. Watch the counter until it reads the exact depth you want, and presto! You are fishing at exactly the depth you want, right? Well, almost.

Actually you have to consider the angle of your downrigger cable if you want to fish exactly at a certain depth. When your boat is moving as you troll, the resistance of the water against your downrigger cable and weight

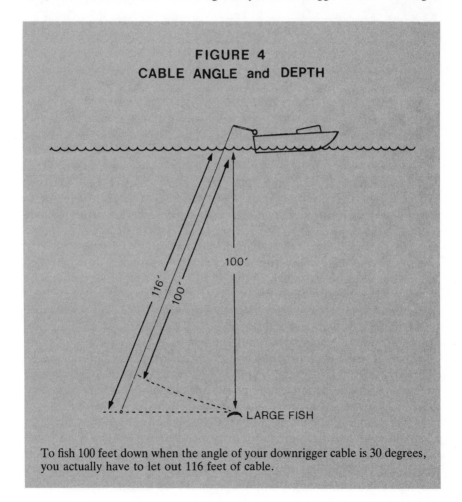

FIGURE 4
CABLE ANGLE and DEPTH

To fish 100 feet down when the angle of your downrigger cable is 30 degrees, you actually have to let out 116 feet of cable.

along with your fishing line and lure force the cable to angle back. The further the cable angles back and the more cable you let out, the less accurate the depth reading on your counter. At higher trolling speeds up to 3 to 4 mph with 100 feet or more of cable out, your lure could actually be fishing up to 10 feet or more shallower than your counter reads. Figure 4 shows how this works and gives you a rule of thumb to help you control depths.

Target Depth (feet)	Cable Angle (degrees)	Cable Length (feet)
50	10	51
50	15	52
50	30	58
50	45	71
100	10	102
100	15	104
100	30	116
100	45	142

Depth control is also important in relation to fish that you see marked on your graph recorder or video fish finder. Fish show up on these fish finders as an inverted V. To fish at exact depths where trout and salmon are being seen on a graph or video recorder, downrigger weights should be set to fish the top of the V-shaped fish marks.

Don't get too hung up on fishing the exact depths where fish are showing up on your fish finder, though. Trout and salmon often prefer to swim up to strike lures presented just above them.

Depth Control Without Downriggers. If you are fishing lead-core or wire line, experience combined with awareness of trolling speed and length of line fished will help control depth. Lead-core line comes from the factory dye-marked with a different color every 30 feet. Wire line can be measured and marked at various intervals with small strips of tape from an adhesive bandage. A measured length of line fishes a certain depth. Speed up and it fishes shallower. Slow down and it fishes deeper.

Diving planers (which force the lure down) and three-way sinker rigs also help control depth. In addition to speed, length of line fished, and line diameter, the size of the diving planer and the weight of the sinker also affect the depth fished.

With a level-wind reel it is simple to estimate the length of monofilament line being used when fishing a diving planer. Just measure the amount of line you let out from the rod tip on one full pass of the level winder. On some reels, like the Penn 320 GTi, this distance is almost exactly 10 feet per pass of the level winder. Depending on your speed and the size and type of diving planer used, 100 feet of line should fish 35 to 50 feet deep.

Lure Control

The simplest way to control a lure fished on a downrigger at a given depth is to keep the distance from the release to the lure short, say 3 to 6 feet. In that way the lure runs almost exactly at the same depth as the weight. Unfortunately trout and salmon won't always hit a lure close to the weight, and thus distance to the lure must be increased up to 100 feet behind the release. This doesn't present much of a problem when fishing lures like flutterspoons, which are very light and seem to ride up. However, if you fish a body bait, like a FASTRAC Rebel or a J-13 Rapala, which may dive 10 feet on 100 feet of line, you must account for this at your downrigger by raising the weight 10 feet above your target depth. This is especially important when you are fishing lures close to bottom.

Presentation of lures can also be controlled in other ways so that more than one lure can be fished on a single line at once. To do this the line from the rod is attached to the downrigger weight in the normal way. The downrigger weight is lowered into the water a few feet. A 6- to 8-foot leader with a lure on one end and a swivel at the other is attached to the main line. A rubber band is snugged up around the main line and then passed through the swivel to hold the leader in place. The swivel is snapped into place and the leader, or "cheater," as it is often called, is locked into position. Spoons fished on "cheaters" 4 to 5 feet above dodgers are very effective for both trout and salmon. If a fish hits the spoon the line snaps from the release and the swivel works down to the lure at the end of the main line (see Figure 5).

Lures fished like this on all downriggers simultaneously create a school effect and often trigger strikes when fewer lures will not. Don't be surprised if you take two fish at once using cheaters. It's common.

Extra lures can be added to your trolling rig by stacking lines (see Figure 6). This is where the second rod holder on your downrigger comes into play. Attach the first line and lure in the downrigger release normally. Lower the weight to a predetermined depth, say 13 feet, and add a second release to the downrigger cable at about 15 feet. Let out your lure behind the boat and snap it into the release. Lower the weight to your fishing depth, and you will be trolling two lures, one 15 feet above the other. To

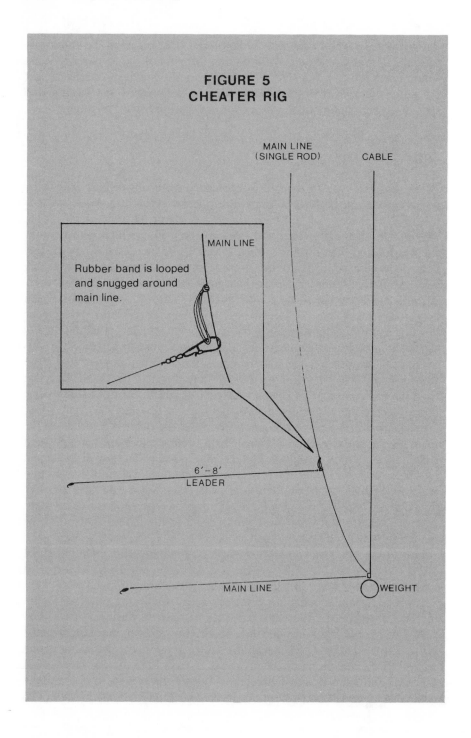

**FIGURE 5
CHEATER RIG**

MAIN LINE
(SINGLE ROD)

CABLE

MAIN LINE

Rubber band is looped
and snugged around
main line.

6′ – 8′
LEADER

MAIN LINE

WEIGHT

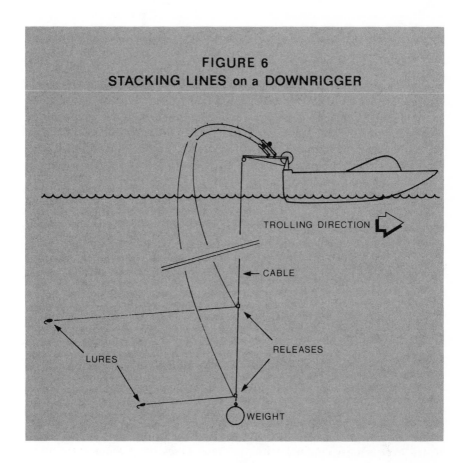

FIGURE 6
STACKING LINES on a DOWNRIGGER

TROLLING DIRECTION

CABLE

RELEASES

LURES

WEIGHT

use a stacker you need a release that will automatically unlock and slide down the cable when it touches the roller tip on the end of the downrigger. The Roemer release works extremely well for this. It locks into place easily, yet unlocks dependably when you retrieve your weight.

Speed Control

Assuming proper depths and temperatures are being fished, speed may be the most important variable involved in taking fish by trolling. Not only do certain lures work best at certain speeds, but certain species of trout and salmon favor lures trolled at certain speeds. Controlling speed is all-important to successful deep-water trolling. To control the speed at which a lure is presented, a fisherman must be able to precisely control boat speed, and he must be aware of any currents present at the depths being fished.

A fishing trip on the morning of May 15, 1987, on Lake Ontario provides a good example of the importance of speed in catching fish by trolling. Surface action for lakers and steelhead had been hot along an offshore thermal bar. My party, from New Jersey, had done well, taking a limit of lakers along with a few steelhead. Just as the sun broke through, we decided to troll inshore for jumbo brown trout. As we reached 100 feet of water, I noticed some large marks on the graph recorder that looked like big chinooks. Four downriggers were lowered. The thermistor read only 42 degrees at 100 feet.

We had been taking lakers and steelhead at 2.9 mph and I had unconsciously locked in on that speed. It wasn't working. After unsuccessfully trolling over the marks for about a half hour, I slowed to 1.5 mph, then gradually worked back up to 2.5. Still no luck. Finally I hit the throttle slightly to position the boat. In seconds a screaming Penn reel on a port downrigger rod gave rude notice that a big chinook was trying to tear our gear apart. Instinctively I checked the thermistor. The digital speed indicator read 3.5 mph. Three 20+-pound chinooks later we knew the right formula was 3.5 mph + 100 feet + a green/black ladder Yeck spoon = Success!

Subsurface Currents. Subsurface currents are generally insignificant on smaller inland lakes, and surface speed is all a fisherman needs to control in order to achieve proper trolling speed. However, on larger lakes like the Great Lakes, the Finger Lakes, and Lake Champlain, studies and experience have shown that heavy currents are something that a deep-water troller must contend with. In some cases deep-water currents of more than 1 knot make proper trolling speed hard to determine from the surface. The secret to this is a good, downrigger-mounted temperature/speed indicator like the Fish Hawk Thermo-troll 800. It's just the ticket for tuning in the speed of your lures at any depth.

Lure Speed and Action

Once you have a handle on speed at the downrigger weight, the next step is to control speed to get optimum performance out of your lure. All lures have a certain range of speed at which they perform best. This speed range is wider for some lures than for others. For instance ultralight flutterspoons like the Number 44 Sutton with a 1/0 single hook have a nice wobbling action from about 2.3–2.8 mph. Go faster, and they spin. Go slower, and they look dead in the water, with little or no action. Spoons

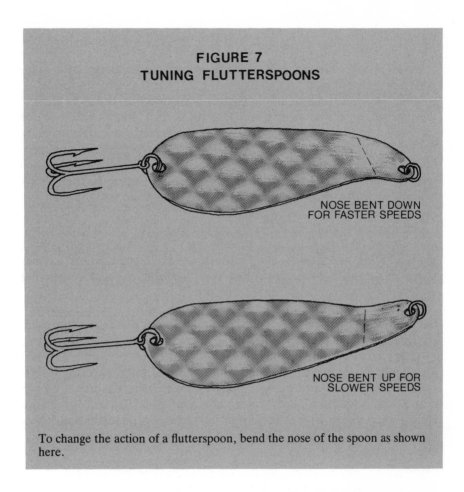

FIGURE 7
TUNING FLUTTERSPOONS

NOSE BENT DOWN
FOR FASTER SPEEDS

NOSE BENT UP FOR
SLOWER SPEEDS

To change the action of a flutterspoon, bend the nose of the spoon as shown here.

like the Eppinger Flutterdevle with an S bend and the Northport Nailer have good action over a wider range of speed, from less than 2.0 mph to just over 3.0. Heavier spoons, like the Eppinger Flutter Chuck, must be trolled at speeds from 3.0–4.0 mph and faster to work properly. Well-tuned plugs, like a jointed Rapala or Rebel, will fish well over a very wide range of speed from less than 1.5 mph to more than 4.0.

To find the optimum trolling speed for a lure, hold it in the water alongside your boat and watch its action as you troll along. If it is rolling over or spinning, your speed is too fast. If it is not working or barely working at all, your speed is too slow. A spoon should generally have a nice side-to-side wobbling action with an occasional kick that flips it over. When you see that action, check the reading on your speedometer. That's the speed at which you should troll that particular spoon. Then try it a little faster and slower to see at what range of speed the lure can be fished. Check the action of plugs the same way. Plugs like a Flatfish can be fished at a snail's pace. Plugs like a Silver Horde can be burned through the water at speeds over 5.0 mph.

Many lures can be "tuned" to run properly at either faster- or slower-than-normal speeds by using a heavier-than-normal swivel or by changing the hook to one size larger. Replacing treble hooks with single, salmon-type hooks is standard for lures on board the *Fish Doctor,* because singles hook and hold fish better. However, there are some spoons, like the Loco and Northern King, that don't seem to work as well when the treble hook is replaced with a single. You can see the difference in the lure, and you can feel the difference in the vibration.

Flutterspoons can be tuned as shown in Figure 7 to run faster or slower than normal or simply to have a better action than they might have out of the box. Plugs like Rapalas can be tuned to have a good action at either faster- or slower-than-normal trolling speeds by sliding a tight clinch knot up or down on the eye in front of the lure.

If the plug wants to swim to the side, bend the wire eye in the direction the plug wants to swim. It doesn't take much, but it makes the plug swim straighter, especially at high speeds.

No matter how well you tune lures some of them just can't be fished together because they are not compatible at similar trolling speeds. Unless you purposely want an Eppinger Flutterdevle to spin, you shouldn't fish it at 3.5 mph with a Flutter Chuck. The same generally holds true with large J-Plugs fished with attractors such as Number 0 dodgers and squids (see "Attractors," below). Be sure the lures fished in your trolling setup work well together.

Speed Preference of Trout and Salmon

Another consideration when determining correct trolling speed is the behavior of the particular species of trout or salmon you are fishing for. Species like steelhead and landlocked salmon generally like a fast-trolled lure. Landlocked salmon fishermen often troll streamers at speeds over 6 mph. Steelhead jump on a lure trolled at 4 mph or more. So do chinook salmon at times. Lake trout and brown trout, on the other hand, generally like a slow-trolled lure, especially when water temperatures are in the low forties. Despite these general behavioral patterns, try to keep an open mind about trolling speed. I say this as I recall catching a lake trout on the surface of Lake Champlain at 6 mph and about fifteen walleyes one

Lure Selection: "Eeny Meeny Miny Mo"

There can't be anyone more confused, yet excited, than a fisherman new to deep-water trolling walking into a well-stocked fishing-tackle shop displaying walls and walls of different trout and salmon lures. This beginner will be awed by the huge selection of plugs, spinners, flashers, and flies in every conceivable color, finish, shape, and size. He must feel sort of like a kid in an old-fashioned penny candy store. Everything looks great, but is it?

Well, not really. You can take an occasional trout and salmon on almost any of thousands of different types of lures if you fish them properly. On the other hand just a handful of good lures that are tried and true will take lots of trout and salmon in most situations. Let's approach lure selection the simple way, starting with just a few of the old favorites.

Most of these plugs, spoons, and spinners can be fished straight, that is with no attractor rigged on the line ahead of them to get the fishes' attention. They can also be fished with an attractor like a dodger, a flasher, or a set of spinners (see below). Attractors can often be used very effectively to take trout and salmon when lures fished straight just will not do the trick. Lures like squids, flash flies, and tinsel flies are meant to be fished behind dodgers and flashers.

Spoons

Of all lures used to troll for trout and salmon, spoons are the most versatile. Spoons are effective in almost every type of trolling situation. One of the reasons for this is the tremendous variety available on the market today: a myriad of sizes, colors, finishes, and actions.

Spoons are a favorite lure of the deep-water troller. In 1987 my fishing records show that spoons were trolled from my boat on every single trip of the charter-fishing season. Spoons were fished straight, in combination with plugs, in combination with dodgers and flashers, and behind attractors. Spoons can be fished effectively in any light conditions and at any reasonable speed from 1.0 to 6.0 mph if the proper spoon is selected.

Spoons can be broken down into three categories: flutterspoons, lightweight spoons, and hard spoons. Flutterspoons are extremely light and pliable and are commonly bent, or "tuned" to modify their action in the water. Flutterspoons include the Eppinger Flutterdevle, Sutton, and Elmer Hinkley, which are often used for slow trolling. Lightweight spoons, like

A selection of favorite Great Lakes plugs. From top clockwise: Wiggle Wart, Fire Plug, Flatfish, Tadpolly, Hot Shot, and Hot-N-Tot.

the Stinger, Evil Eye, and Northport Nailer, are effective at slow to moderate speeds and are seldom tuned by bending. Hard spoons, like the Flutter Chuck, Northern King, and Loco, are generally used at moderate to fast speeds. All of them have their place in a deep-water troller's bag of tricks.

Flutterspoons. Of all spoons flutterspoons may have the widest range and variety of uses. Sutton flutterspoons were developed in the Finger Lakes and are made in a variety of sizes, ranging from the size Number 5, which is about 1 inch long, up to Number 06, which is 6 inches long. My favorites are Number 44, 71, 88, and 38. They are available in beautifully silver plated plain and hammered finishes as well as brass, silver/brass, and silver/copper. Elmer Hinkley spoons are also silver plated, but are available in different sizes from Suttons. My favorite is the size W, an excellent smelt imitation.

The Eppinger Flutterdevle is also a personal favorite. It is available in two sizes, 3100 (3¼-inch) and 3200 (4-inch), and comes in silver plate, brass, and silver in combination with various colors of prism and paint, and a myriad of colors such as chartreuse/fire dot, "Glo 'in," and others. The hammered silver/lemon lime in the 3100 size is one of my favorites for browns and lakers in Lake Ontario in sunny conditions. The Glo 'in, which is a fluorescent red and nickel, is deadly for lake trout and walleyes in Lake Champlain in overcast conditions.

Lightweight Spoons. Lake Ontario and the Upper Great Lakes have been one of the greatest proving grounds in the world for the development of lures. Spoons like the Northport Nailer and Evil Eye, which originated in the Great Lakes, are now standard in every troller's tacklebox. They are made in a wide variety of finishes and colors. They are extremely effective because of their excellent lure action over a wide range of moderate trolling speeds. Another classic, developed on Lake Ontario, which is extremely effective for brown trout, lake trout, steelhead, and spring and summer chinooks, is the Stinger. Try the small, medium-small, and medium sizes in blue/white, green/white, chartreuse/red, chartreuse/green, pink/purple, and black purple.

Hard Spoons. Although hard spoons, like Cleos, Cop-E-Cats, and others, are effective for slow trolling, moderate- to high-speed trolling is generally the name of the game for these lures. Spoons like the Loco troll well at 2.5 to 2.8 mph. Locos are an old favorite on Lake Ontario in chartreuse/silver prism, blue/silver prism, chartreuse/fire dot, and brass/silver prism. They are excellent for brown trout, cohos, and chinook salmon. Spoons like the Flutter Chuck are effective at faster speeds, from 3.0 to 4.0 mph, and are available in all the same finishes, colors, and prism tapes that you can imagine. My favorite is the hammered silver/lemon lime in both magnum (4-inch) and regular (3¼-inch) sizes. Black/purple prism, chartreuse/red ladderback, chartreuse/green diamond, glow green, and green/black ladderback, are also excellent.

Another spoon in this category that took Lake Ontario by storm in 1987 is the Northern King in size 28. In silver plate with blue or red prism, silver/brass, black/purple prism, and black/orange tape, it was a hot number. Another excellent hard spoon is Evil Eye's Perfect Minnow.

Plugs

Plugs can be separated into three categories: wobbling plugs, body baits, and J-plugs. Wobbling plugs like the Flatfish are extremely effective for slow, slow trolling. Body baits like the Hot Shot, Fire Plug, Hot-N-Tot, Wiggle Wart, Wee Wart, Rapala, and Rebel are used over a wide range of speeds. J-plugs are just the ticket for chinooks and cohos at moderate to fast speeds. Each has its place for trout and salmon.

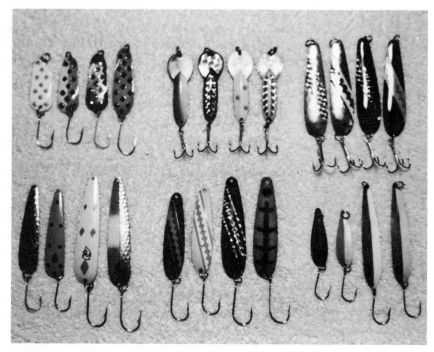

A selection of "hot" spoons. From the top left clockwise: Alpena Diamond, Loco, #28 Northern King, Stinger, Yeck Spoon, and Flutter Chuck.

Wobbling Plugs. Wobbling plugs, like the Flatfish and Fire Plug, are absolutely deadly for lake trout when slow trolled tight to the downrigger weight. On Lake Champlain an F-7 Flatfish fished flat on the bottom 3 to 4 feet behind a three-blade cowbell attached to a downrigger weight is devastating for lakers. The F-7 coach dog, chartreuse/fire dot, chrome/blue and green/ladderback are excellent. The X-5 in gold and the T-4 in pearl are also tops for lakers. In Lake Ontario, the F-7 Flatfish or the Number 20 Fire Plug in chartreuse/fire dot, fished 3 to 4 feet behind a chartreuse weight, are killers for lakers. Fire Plugs have also taken their share of browns, chinooks, and cohos. The lip of a Flatfish can be cut back about ¼-inch to make it more effective at faster-than-normal trolling speeds. The wire eye of a Fire Plug often has to be bent to one side or the other to make it run true at faster speeds.

Body Baits. This group includes a wide variety of plugs from Hot Shots and crankbaits to minnow-like plugs such as the Rebel, Rapala, and Bomber Long A. Plugs like the Hot Shot in size 30, Wiggle Wart, Hot-N-Tot, and Tadpolly have all proven themselves for all species of trout and salmon in the Great Lakes. In the early 1980's, when cohos from 8 to 16 pounds were abundant in the Mexico Bay area of Lake Ontario, Hot-N-Tots, after a few days of fishing, were identifiable only by their shape because coho after coho quickly tore the paint off the plugs. The plugs looked like they had been in a cat fight! Size 30 Hot Shots in chartreuse/fire dot, glow green, and nickel/blue work well.

Although minnow-imitation plugs can be effective in deep water at times, they are not favorites for this type of fishing. One exception is the J-13 Rapala, along with the J-20 and J-30 Rebel, which have been effective for chinooks in spring and fall. The chartreuse J-13 Rapala, along with the chartreuse/green diamond J-20 Rebel, took good numbers of chinooks in early September in Lake Ontario when stacked above dodgers and squids.

J-plugs. J-plugs, Silver Hordes, Tiger Plugs, Grizzlies, and other similar plugs are undoubtedly one of the best lures for chinook and coho salmon in the Great Lakes in late summer and fall. They are also used for both commercial and sport fishing for salmon along the Pacific Coast. There are a variety of effective colors in both the solid and jointed models. These include glow green, glow green/black ladderback, "silver bullet," green or blue prism, and chartreuse/fire dot. The size 3 jointed J-plug in chrome or gold plate has been excellent in Lake Ontario in late summer. The larger size 5 plugs are usually most effective in early fall when salmon concentrate in shallow water off river mouths before spawning.

Attractors

Attractors such as dodgers, flashers, and spinners or cowbells are not meant to catch fish by themselves. As the name implies, their purpose is to attract game fish to a lure like a plug, spoon, squid, or flash fly trailed behind them. Attractors are commonly fished directly off a line on a fishing rod; however attractors attached directly to the downrigger weight are deadly and avoid one of the major disadvantages of large attractors—heavy drag.

Spinners (Cowbells, Christmas Trees). In Lake Champlain, the Great Lakes, the Finger Lakes, and many inland lakes, one of the favorite techniques for taking lake trout is a spinner followed by a wobbling plug or a smelt, alewife, or minnow fished just barely off bottom at a crawl. Rainbow trout in many inland waters are also suckers for spinner rigs trailed by a nightcrawler on a harness.

Spinners are made in a variety of sizes, shapes, and combinations of blades. Good ones for lake trout include the Les Davis Sun Flash, the first three large willow-leaf blades of the Les Davis Odd Ball, and a spinner sold by Big Jon. Spinners made by Pop Geer and Sebago are excellent for rainbows. Chrome, fluted chrome, hammered chrome, brass, and copper spinners are all effective in certain situations. A slash of chartreuse paint or dark green prism can improve their effectiveness.

Dodgers. A dodger is a thin piece of metal that goes ahead of the lure and serves as an attractor and action enhancer. To the Great Lakes fisherman, dodgers and squids are the bread and butter of his salmon-lure selection in late summer. The standard rig is a size-0 dodger with a squid or flash fly trailed 14 to 16 inches back. Favorite dodger colors include chrome; chrome with blue, green, or salmon spectra prism tape; chartreuse; chartreuse/fire dot; chartreuse/green; glow blue; and glow green. Dodgers trolled at proper speeds, say 1.8–2.0 mph for standard Number 0 sizes, have a wobbling action that imparts an enticing, darting motion to a trailing lure. In combination with the right color squid or flash fly, dodgers may have taken more chinook and coho salmon from the Great Lakes in August than any other lure.

Flashers. Flashers, rather than wobble side to side like a dodger, are meant to slowly revolve with a fly or squid trailing 22 to 34 inches behind, depending on the size of the flasher. Flashers are standard fare along the

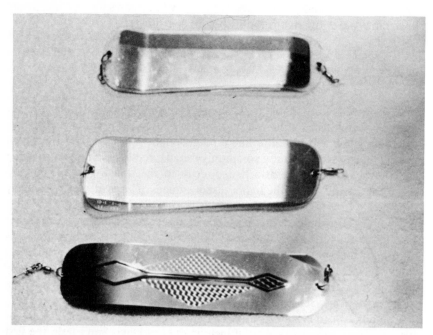

Rotating flashers.

Pacific Coast, where they are a mainstay of the sport and commercial salmon-fishing fleet. They are rarely used on the Great Lakes but are going to catch on there in the next few years. They are hot! In 1987 I used flashers like the Diamond Striker, Oki, and Hot Spot, and on days when nothing else was really working well they took kings. The Number 1 Diamond Striker, especially, was deadly!

Proper speed is critical with flashers. Generally they should be trolled just fast enough to revolve in a full circle. The Number 1 Diamond Striker fished 14 feet behind the downrigger weight rotates properly at 2.5 mph. The Hot Spot and Oki rotate at a slower 2.0 to 2.2 mph. The Diamond Striker and a wide variety of other flashers and dodgers are available through Kingston Marine and Tackle, Kingston, Washington. Dick Johnson, a retired commercial salmon troller, and owner of Kingston Marine and Tackle, theorizes that salmon interpret the movement and vibration of a flasher as another feeding salmon. The squid or fly trailing behind it is simply an easy meal that dropped out of a baitfish school under attack.

Squids and Flash Flies

Squids have been used behind flashers and dodgers by commercial salmon fishermen on the Pacific Coast for years. In the Great Lakes dodger–squid combinations have proven themselves since the salmon fishery began in the 1960's. Popular squid patterns include green, black, chartreuse, chartreuse/green, pink/purple, glow green, and glow blue. Pacific patterns that have worked well in Lake Ontario are Ole's Opal, Surf Smelt, Sunrise Devil, and the Alaska Number 1. With the many combinations of colored beads, tinsel inserts, and spinners used in the various squid patterns, the permutations are endless.

Flash flies are also effective behind dodgers. Ron's Lucky Buck flash flies by Avery Tackle in Marquette, Michigan, are the very finest made. The Lucky Buck in green/black, blue/black, blue/white, black/purple, and pink/purple with a glow or silver prism insert are excellent producers. The red/black Lucky Buck with a prism insert has been hot in combination with a Number 1 white pearl Salmon Spectra dodger, especially in low light conditions.

It is no secret to experienced trollers that the combination of dodger or flasher and squid or fly is more important than the color or finish of either one alone. A pink and purple squid behind a chrome dodger on a given day may be a real dud, but fish it behind a chartreuse/green dodger and you will probably hit paydirt! Another variable is the distance of the squid or fly behind the attractor. Fourteen inches is the proper length of leader for a Number 0 dodger. For active fish the distance to the squid is shortened. Species such as cohos like this fast, erratic lure presentation. For inactive fish it helps to increase the distance to the lure.

Lure Size, Color, and Finish

With the mind-boggling array of different sizes, colors, and finishes of lures available to fishermen today, it isn't any wonder that all of us scratch our heads at times as we try to select a hot lure. To the beginner it probably sounds impossible, but it isn't. Why? Because over the years through trial and error some relatively consistent patterns and recipes have emerged.

Lure Color and Finish. One of the overriding factors involved in the selection of lure color is light intensity. There is no question that color preference changes with varying light conditions. A good example of this is the pattern of lure selection off the mouth of the Big Salmon River in Lake Ontario in early September. Invariably chinooks concentrated there hit glow green Number 5 J-plugs early before the sun rises and then select for chrome or silver plated plugs. In midsummer in Lake Ontario magnum Flutter Chucks in glow green or chartreuse/green diamond work well in overcast conditions. In bright sun, silver-plated Northern Kings with blue prism outfish the others.

Silver-plated flutterspoons work best in bright sun. Paint the belly chartreuse and at times they work even better. However, if you add a quarter stripe of fluorescent red or dark green prism to the back of a silver-plated spoon, it will work well in low-light conditions.

Fluorescent orange, for most species, works best in low-light conditions. Steelhead, however, prefer fluorescent orange almost any time. Lures like the fluorescent orange Number 51 Alpena Diamond and the orange and gold Rebel are proven steelhead producers. Green, green/black ladderback, chartreuse, chartreuse/fire dot, chartreuse/red ladderback, chartreuse/green, and black/chrome or silver, are also effective in low-light conditions. Lake trout, however, hammer chartreuse/fire dot lures in bright sun.

Chrome-plated lures with either a neon blue stripe or scale finish are generally good in the sun. Most chrome lures dressed with either silver or light blue prism also work well in bright light. Blue Rapalas work well when the sun is up, while chartreuse plugs of this type are best when it is overcast. Surprisingly, spoons in black/purple with a white belly are generally excellent in bright-light conditions.

When it comes to selection of colors and finishes of lures, you can never be sure. Color preference in some waters like Lake Champlain is very standard and seldom changes. In other waters like Lake Ontario, trout and salmon are more fickle, with their color preference often changing daily or even hourly. A lure manufacturer's delight!

Start with the standard colors, and if they aren't working, experiment. If you have a VHF radio, listen for patterns nearby fishermen are using, and don't be bashful about asking for information from a charter captain. Don't forget that local information from marinas and fishing-tackle shops is one of the best ways to learn which colors and finishes are hot. I keep a daily fishing log which is invaluable in developing a sixth sense for lure colors.

Lure Size. Another major factor involved in lure selection is lure size. At times small lures are more effective than larger lures. At other times larger lures work best. Without trying to explain why, we know for sure that for deep-water trout and salmon trolling you need a lure assortment in a range of sizes. Your tacklebox should contain flutterspoons, lightweight spoons, hard spoons, and plugs in sizes from small to magnum.

In some cases preferred lure size is definitely related to size of the forage fish trout and salmon are feeding on. In April on Lake Ontario when spawning 5- to 8-inch smelt are concentrated inshore and brown trout are chowing down on them, larger lures like FASTRAC Rebels, Number 71 Suttons, and medium-size Stingers are tops. Later, when smelt have moved offshore and alewives haven't yet moved in, smaller lures like 1/4-ounce Cop-E-Cats, size 2F Evil Eyes, and small Stingers work better than larger lures.

Size of forage fish is not always the link to lure size, however. It's a fact that when fishing gets tough, especially in clear water and bright sun, small lures in bright, fluorescent colors take fish when nothing else will. For example, I have taken lethargic, beer-bellied brown trout on small Stingers and Cop-E-Cats right in the middle of dense schools of 5- to 7-inch alewives which were four times longer than the lures used.

Scents

In recent years a number of different manufacturers have produced a variety of different scents which are said to be highly attractive to various game fish including trout and salmon. In the old days lures drenched with anise oil seemed to be attractive to lake trout and brown trout. Sturgeon fishermen on the West Coast spray dead smelt with WD-40 lubricant and use them for bait.

It's hard to say for sure if scents work, because no carefully controlled scientific studies have ever been done on them. Dr. Juice lake-trout scent, however, in my book is very effective and has produced well for lakers in Lake Champlain, the Finger Lakes, and Lake Ontario. It may also entice an occasional chinook to strike. As long as it doesn't turn fish off, why not use it?

Hooks: A Vital Detail

Sharp hooks are often the difference between success and failure for the deep-water troller, especially the downrigger fisherman. *No hooks on lures straight out of the box are sharp enough to fish with, except for the new chemically sharpened hooks like those made by Gamakatsu.* All standard hooks, including the treble hooks on plugs like Rebels, need sharpening. Hook sharpening can be a frustrating task unless you use the right tool, but with one of the excellent hook hones, like those sold by Luhr Jensen, it's easy. Just hold the point of the hook facing toward you and hone each side and the top of the point lightly in a triangular shape (see Figure 9, Chapter 6).

The Angler: Last, but Certainly Not Least

Anyone who has fished at all is familiar with the old saying, "Ten percent of the fishermen catch ninety percent of all the fish." It seems to be true, but why? Well, if I had to guess, I would say the reason is the attitude of the fisherman involved and his approach to fishing.

Most good fishermen take fishing seriously and work hard to catch fish. They accept fishing as a challenge and have an intense desire to be successful. They study fishing and constantly strive to improve their techniques. They learn all they can about the fish they search for and the waters that support them.

Years ago, when I trolled single-hook spoons on a hand-held lead-core line, everything—including the bait, leader, and swivels—had to be "just so," exactly as the old man had showed me. This attention to detail separates the men from the boys in deep-water trolling—or in any fishing, for that matter. Attention to detail is a characteristic of every outstanding charter captain I know. It is the difference between catching only an occasional fish and consistently taking good catches.

The author with a spring chinook from Lake Ontario.

Another trait of successful fishermen is versatility. The versatile angler does not get into the proverbial rut. He is an experimenter, always willing to try something new. He keeps an open mind, listens to others, and either has a memory like a computer or keeps good records of his fishing trips. The philosophy that there is always a better mouse trap helps a lot. The deep-water troller who restricts himself entirely to downriggers is a *nonversatile* angler. Those who learn to use diving planers, wire and lead-core lines, sinker rigs, and other techniques will catch the most fish.

Commercial fishermen in Alaska have a term for those anglers who almost always catch fish. They call these select few anglers "fishy," but not for the odor that undoubtedly occasionally surrounds them, but because of their uncanny ability to catch fish. Sure, this can undoubtedly be attributed to hard work, versatility, *etc.,* but I will venture a guess that the underlying characteristic of these "fishy" folks is simply a love for fishing.

The bottom line is that fishing is fun, and the better a fisherman you become, the more fun you will have doing it.

Appendix I:
Getting Kids Started
in Fishing

by Todd Swainbank

S tarting a child off fishing the right way can pose quite a challenge to non-angling parents. Indeed for urban families, just finding a suitable location to take the kids for the first angling safari can present almost insurmountable problems. More important, before the students (your kids) can learn anything of fishing, you, the teacher, must have acquired the knowledge necessary to be able to teach them something about the sport.

Above all, fishing with kids must be *productive*. Children must meet with a relatively high degree of success to counteract their tendency toward short attention spans. Let's take a look at how parents can stack the deck in their kids' favor.

The Right Tackle

Push-Button Spin Cast Outfits. This inexpensive and easy-to-use rod-and-reel combination is what millions of children have used on their first fishing excursions. Complete beginners' outfits are offered by companies such as Zebco and Shakespeare. This type of equipment is often used in fishing programs at summer camps, and although it's sturdy and simple, it tends to be outgrown quickly.

Light Spinning Combo. Spinning gear is a little more difficult to learn

Young Matt Butler knows bluegills can't resist a tiny cork popper.

to operate, and it's more expensive, but it's also less likely to be quickly outgrown.

Fly-fishing Combo. Fly gear is an excellent choice for the child lucky enough to grow up in trout country. Flies are deadly on panfish as well. Fly tackle, however, requires more skill of the user than other tackle, and it is important that a child get expert instruction early if the benefits are to be grasped. See "Introduction to Fly-fishing."

The Tacklebox. Nowadays you can go into a discount tackle department and find a whole wall of tackleboxes, some already filled with hundreds of pieces. The problem is that I have never yet seen a prepacked tacklebox that was filled with anything but the cheapest junk.

If you don't know what should be in a tacklebox, get someone at a tackle shop to set one up for you. For the vast majority of early fishing safaris, the following hardware will prove sufficient:

Snelled Hooks. Size-6 and -8, long-shank hooks if bullheads are the quarry. Squeeze down the barbs for safety.

Small Bobbers. To aid in casting and alerting the young angler to a nibbling fish.

Small Sinkers and Split Shot. Split shot should be the reusable kind; you shouldn't need anything heavier than 1/4-ounce.

Needlenose pliers. To aid in unhooking fish.

Lures. Some leadhead jigs with twister-type tails (1-inch and 2-inch tails on lightweight jigheads). Also, some small Mepps spinners, less than 1/4-ounce.

Stringers. Either a chain stringer or the rope-and-spike variety, to keep and transport the catch.

A jackknife and extra spool of monofilament line in 6- to 10-pound test.

The Baits

The right bait can be bought or caught. Here are some baits to be aware of:

Worms. The traditional bait that seems to be able to catch just about anything that swims. Nightcrawlers can be picked up easily on the lawn after dark by using a flashlight. They are especially easy to catch after a rainstorm or by watering the lawn with a hose or sprinkler system. Store worms in a cool place.

Minnows. A deadly bait that can be purchased in a bait shop, seined from ponds, or caught with a minnow trap baited with bread crumbs. Keep them in a minnow bucket and use a small dip net to aid in handling them while baiting up. Keep the water that the minnows are in aerated and cool by using oxygen tablets or a battery-operated oxygenator. Hook the minnows through the lips with a small hook. This will keep the bait lively and swimming freely, and because predator fish swallow minnows head first, you will be more likely to get a good hook set.

Crayfish. Small crayfish are deadly baits for a variety of fish. They look just like tiny lobsters and are found under rocks along shallow shorelines. Hook them through the tail and watch out for the pincers: they can grab hard.

Grasshoppers. Grasshoppers and crickets make excellent bait for panfish and can be caught by hand or by using a butterfly net. Use small hooks.

Other baits. Salamanders and small frogs make deadly baits for many kinds of fish but can be hard to obtain regularly and aren't for use by the squeamish.

Locating Fishing Holes

Finding a perfect fishing hole for you and your kids can be as easy as picking up the telephone and calling the nearest fisheries office in your state's department of natural resources. Fisheries managers will know where and when certain waters are to be stocked, and they keep current with hot angling locations statewide.

Another valuable shortcut to angling success can come from simply reading the local newspaper. Many papers have outdoor columnists who report on local fishing conditions. Outdoor writers are often in contact with tackle shops, marinas, and professional guides and so are in a position to provide helpful advice.

Other spots that are often perfect for fishing safaris are park ponds or golf-course ponds, which are usually stocked with bass, bluegills and bullheads and often forgotten. Farm ponds, boat yards and marina docks all offer angling adventure. Check them out.

Panfish: Their Habits and Habitats

Panfish is a generic term for many members of the sunfish, perch, bass, and catfish families. Heaviest fishing pressure is on bluegills, pumpkinseeds, crappies, rock bass, yellow perch, white bass, white perch, and bullheads. Panfish eat almost anything smaller than they are and despite their small size are strong fighters. They have provided angling for youngsters for centuries.

Sunfish and perch feed heavily on insect larvae, crustaceans, small mollusks, and smaller fish. White bass and crappies are almost exclusively minnow eaters. Food preferences often dictate their habitat and bait. Fishermen can increase their success by studying the feeding preferences of the type of fish being sought.

Yellow perch prefer varying habitats, their choice being dependent on size and sex. Smaller perch, mostly males, are usually found in relatively shallow water, often near weedbeds. Larger females, erroneously called "jacks," are usually found in much deeper water.

Crappies, especially during the spring spawn, are drawn like magnets to sunken brush piles, deadfalls, overhangs and bridge abutments. In summer, however, they may leave shoreline abodes to suspend at mid-depths near the thermocline. Drift fishing with minnows or jigging with small jigs will locate crappie schools in a hurry.

Bluegills spawn in shallow water and can often be seen guarding their nests in the spring. They are easily caught on almost any small bait or lure when they are aggressively protecting the saucer-shaped nest.

White bass are often found in large lakes and are often seen chasing schools of thread-fin shad to the surface. Therefore a common technique in fishing for white bass is to watch for surface commotion and fish where it is found.

Bullheads, smaller cousins of the catfish, prefer ponds, back coves and other slow-moving waters. Because of their tendency to swallow the whole hook, you should use long-shank barbless hooks when fishing for bullheads. Beware, too, of the sharp spines on bullheads and avoid contact with them: they hurt!

Most panfish are very prolific. They grow fast, reproduce early, and produce large numbers of young. They prey on smaller fishes, insects, and other aquatic life, while forming a forage base for larger predators. Since most fishing pressure is on the larger predatory game fish, heavily fished lakes may become overpopulated with panfish, which then become stunted. Removing panfish, therefore, is an excellent management tool to help keep fish populations in balance. Anglers should feel free to keep as many panfish as they wish to eat.

A major part of the fun in panfishing is in eating the catch. Most panfish are excellent table fare if they are carefully handled to retain their quality. For best results, they should be alive and/or on ice until you are ready to clean them. An ice chest is a better choice to preserve the flavor than a stringer.

Many people scale panfish by rubbing a knife blade or scaler against the grain of the scales. I prefer skinning to scaling, because skinning is faster and less messy. A sharp, small fillet knife is all that is necessary. For fish like yellow perch and bluegills, cut the skin along the back from head to tail and peel the skin off by using pliers. Bullheads also require skinning. The time-tested method involves hanging the fish on a mounted spike and pulling the skin off with pliers.

Panfish fillets are generally fried, either in a pan or deep fried in a tempura batter or any favorite coating. Panfish can also be boiled, steamed, poached, or broiled. They can be used in nearly every fish recipe, including chowder.

Some type of panfish can be taken at any time of the year, under any water conditions, and at any time of day. Panfish are abundant and willing, and they offer the beginning angler an easy entry into the lifelong sport of fishing. Study your local waters to build up several locations for different conditions, and give panfishing a try. You may even find that you have as much fun as the kids.

Appendix II: Dream Trips

by Todd Swainbank

Eventually, for every serious angler, the lure of faraway places with strange-sounding names becomes too great, and plans for the fishing trip of a lifetime are made.

In planning a dream trip, today's modern mobile angler can simply pick up any good fishing magazine and peruse the advertisements in the classified section for locations in Alaska, Argentina, and other exotic fishing holes. For the globe-trotting angler, there are even specialty travel agencies such as Frontiers in Wexford, Pennsylvania, whose claim to fame is booking high-quality, totally researched, worldwide angling safaris.

Since a week of fishing at a major sport-fishing lodge in some locations can cost as much as $500 a day, the angler who gets the best value for his money is he who is prepared for the trip.

Aside from the obvious advice to follow the gear requirements listed in the brochures sent to the angler interested in booking a dream trip, I feel it necessary to mention some points about such adventures that evidently are not universally covered by the term "common sense."

Extra Preparation

First, if the fishing game you will be playing is going to require skills that you don't exercise regularly, then you had better practice before you set out. If you will be required to make accurate casts and long casts, then work on developing those skills. Don't depend on your guide to turn you into a finished angler in one day; he will undoubtedly help, but his obligations can spread pretty thin with his other duties.

Take the time to get checked out by a professional (not the guy at the discount store). At Orvis in Manchester, Vermont, where I am one of the fly-fishing instructors, we teach students who are going on fishing trips all over the world. We get letters and photos regularly from students at all skill levels, mentioning key words such as "developed confidence," and "much improved casting ability." Usually the letters include a photograph of a big fish and a very happy angler. Such a course can rapidly aid in developing angling skills.

If time doesn't permit a two-and-a-half day course such as the one Orvis teaches, you might do well to rent some of the many angling and casting videos now available for playing on a VCR.

An even better idea, however, is to at least get out in the back yard, local park, or nearby pond and *practice* casting. Set up targets and obstructions; learn to cast standing, crouching, sitting down, and kneeling with an overhand cast, sidearm, and backhand. You will be ready to fish, and your guide will love you.

Ultra-Light Tackle

I am a big fan of light-tackle fishing, and for some applications even ultra-light tackle. Unfortunately, I've seen several instances, in several locations, where ultra-light tackle was responsible for creating problems.

If you will be doing any drift-boat fishing, such as is often done on snag-filled wilderness Alaskan rivers, leave the ultra-light gear behind. If you don't, you will spend most of the day hung up, losing line and lures, retying knots with cold fingers, losing fish, wasting time, and irritating the others on board.

Another item to be aware of is that extremely lightweight gear so prolongs the battle with a big fish that reviving a hard-fighting fish becomes difficult, if not impossible. If your tackle kills a fish that should not have died, then you as a sportsman have broken a fundamental rule of fair chase. Use the right tackle for the job, and if you have any doubts, ask questions.

What Do Professional Guides Do?

Dream trips to distant places generally mean you are fishing with a guide. You need to know how to make the most out of this very special relationship—that of guide and client. A guide's duties depend on location

Former Alaskan guide Roy Gray will long remember his dream trips. He guided the rivers of Bristol Bay for three seasons.

and whether or not he is independent or employed by a lodge or marina. First off, all guides should see to it that you have whatever gear is required of you, and that means selling, renting, loaning, or giving it to you.

Guides should help you rig up, improve your casting and handling of tackle and lures, and extend your understanding of the waters and the fish available in the areas where they guide. While showing you a good time enjoying the pursuit and capture of the fish you are both out to catch, a guide should be able to answer questions relating to the fishery and the natural history of the area. If you are at one of the lodges in Alaska, your guide should be able to prepare a sumptuous shore lunch of freshly caught fish from jealously guarded secret recipes.

Most important, guides are responsible for the group's safety and welfare and for the performance of the equipment necessary to get the job done. The guide must be alert to possible danger and deft at handling, landing, and releasing fish. By the time you step in a guide's boat, he should have acquired the ability to be cool, confident, and capable in foreseeing and dealing effectively with the unexpected. And all of his duties should be done with style, grace, and a sense of humor, because for a guide to be worth his salt, he has to be able to salvage a good showing under even the bleakest of conditions, and *that* is all part of what you are paying for. When it all works, it's magic!

What Should Clients Do When out with a Professional Guide?

Generally speaking, if clients followed the advice of the guide in the same spirit they show in heeding advice from the family doctor and trusted mechanic, the world would be a better place. The guide starts out the day on your side; whether or not he's still on your side at the end of the day will no doubt depend on *your* performance.

No one ever won an argument with an umpire. Rumor has it that even fewer people win arguments with professional guides. If you don't want to wind up stuck in some dead-end, mosquito-infested slough with a dead motor and no insect repellent, then remember who the guide is and who the client is, and let the guide do his job. After all, the guide works for you.

A client really interested in learning something from a guide will engage him in conversation rather than merely taking a boat ride. Remember, in many areas, if a guide does too good a job, one day he will likely find his secret spots being fished by ex-clients and their friends. The competition factor definitely exists, and no guide wants to put himself out of business.

If clients are interested enough to ask questions, a guide will give them answers. And generally a guide will have much information to impart. He will have very specific reasons for using certain tackle or techniques that he has found to be effective. Also the guide's feeling for what the fish have been doing and will be doing can be discerned by the client from the guide, and this communication is essential to success in fishing.

Be in the Right Boat

Occasionally, due to unforeseen events, guides will be moved around to accommodate certain circumstances. I have seen this occur at the fly-out lodges in Alaska. Generally a proficient guide can quickly adapt to a new location by communicating with other guides on the major topics of concern, such as specific fishing hotspots, tackle, and techniques. *Really* learning new spots, however, still takes some time.

If at all possible, make sure that you wind up with the guide who has spent the most time on the body of water to be fished. And should you discover that you are with a guide new to your territory, then endeavor to make a switch if you aren't catching enough fish. Generally the ideal time to inquire about switching boats is either before you start out the day or at shore-lunch time, when plans for the rest of the day are discussed.

Bring the Right Attitude

Booking certain weeks at the best lodges often means planning way into the future. Both of the lodges I worked at in Alaska are 50–75% booked a year in advance, so make your reservations early—really early.

If you intend to book a certain week that is supposed to be peak time to catch a specific glamour species, and due to the mysteries of nature that species hasn't yet arrived to where it's supposed to be, try not to let that ruin your whole trip. Roll with the punches and keep your perspective.

I recall a group of anglers who were very hot to catch king salmon one year when the runs were late. Although it was true that the kings were late, the rainbow trout, Dolly Varden, grayling, and northern pike were big, ready, and willing. Some anglers enjoyed their week, and others didn't. A good wilderness fishing trip includes much more than just fishing. The scenery and wildlife, the good food and quietude, the camaraderie of a shared adventure, all should contribute toward a lifetime of pleasant memories.

Other Things to Consider

If an expensive wilderness trip is your idea of the ultimate fishing adventure, and you want to get maximum enjoyment from your dream trip, you might want to keep a few things in mind.

Having parents that are avid anglers is a wonderful opportunity for a child to learn about the lifelong sport of fishing. However, if your kids are too young to have the coordination and necessary attention span to be able to enjoy themselves without driving dad and the guides nuts, then leave them behind another year until they are mature enough to handle the trip. And don't be in too big a hurry to force a trip on your spouse, either. Join a fishing club, go out and meet fisherfolk and go on a trip with the right people, or go it alone. Then you can hang out the sign that says what it means and have a great time:

GONE FISHING!

Index

Baits. *See under* various species of fish;
  Live bait
Bass, largemouth
  baits 14, 24–33
  boats 33
  factors in locating 11–14
  fishing tactics 16, 17, 20, 22, 34–35
  fly-fishing 122, 125, 136
  forage 13, 14–15
  in artificial lakes 20–23
  seasonal patterns 23–24
  tackle 33
Bass, smallmouth
  baits 44–48
  boats 39
  factors in locating 38–39, 48–53
  fishing tactics 54–59
  fly-fishing 104, 122, 125, 136
  hotspots 54–59
  in rivers 58
  life history 37
  range 36
  seasonal patterns 48–53
  tackle 42–44
  world record 37
Big-lake fishing 38–42, 128–30, 186–87
  See also Trolling
Boats
  bass 33–34, 39
  northern pike 86–87
  trolling 189

Carp
  as game fish 99
  baits 100
  fishing tactics 100–101
  life history 98–99
  tackle 100
  world record 99
Casting. *See* Fly-fishing: how to cast, casting refinements
Cayuga Lake 38, 50–51, 52, 54, 56
Crankbaits

history 29–30
northern pike 87–88
smallmouth bass, 45–47, 49–51, 52, 54,
  56
specific crankbaits 30, 46–48, 217–19
surface 31
walleye 63, 64, 68

Depthfinder 33, 40, 55, 57, 62, 194
Downrigger. *See under* Trolling

Finger Lakes 12, 38, 51, 52, 128, 140,
  167, 212
Flies
  dry (duns) 119–20, 121, 152–53,
    172
  emergers 121, 122, 158–59
  nymphs 119–20, 122
  stillborns 121, 158–60
  wet 119–20, 171–73
  See also Streamers; Nymphs
Fly-fishing
  casting refinements 114–17, 123–25,
    162–65
  baitfish 128, 131, 132, 134, 136
  how to cast 105–14
  in lakes and ponds 125
  in streams 122–25, 129–37, 143–45
  striking and playing 126–27, 130–31,
    133
  tackle 102–104, 125, 138–40
  wind fishing 128–30
  See also Nymphs; Salmon, landlocked;
    Streamers

Grubs and jigs
  largemouth bass 30–31
  northern pike 89
  smallmouth bass 45, 49, 50, 53, 56,
    58
  specific baits 45
  walleye 66, 68
Guides 233–36

Hook removal
  from fish 90, 95
  from people 95–96

Jigging 30–31, 42–44
Jigs. *See* Grubs and jigs

Knots 118

Lake Champlain 12, 38, 52, 54, 59, 167,
  212
Lake Ontario 38, 167, 200, 201, 204, 212
Lakes
  artificial 13, 20–23
  bottom topography 14, 17–19, 205–206
  currents 212
  food zones 14–15
  northern pike 78–84
  sizes and types (related to bass) 12, 38–
    39, 48–53
  temperature 13, 23–24, 48, 52, 185,
    188, 202–205
Lines
  bass 13, 44, 50
  fly line 103–104, 117, 128, 139–40, 152,
    154–55, 170–71
  northern pike 87
  trolling 197–98
  walleye 64
Live bait
  panfish 229
  walleye 64–68

Motors 33, 39–40, 86–87, 195
Muskellunge 72, 91

Nets 41, 89, 196
Northern pike
  around islands 81–82
  attack on bait 71–72
  baits 87–89
  best times for fishing 84–86
  boats 86–87
  fishing tactics 72, 75, 80, 91–95
  fly-fishing 104, 122, 125, 136
  forage 75–76
  hotspots 74–84
  in lakes 78–84
  in rivers 74–78
  life history and habitat 70–72

tackle 87, 89
  world records 71
Nymphs, floating
  fishing tactics 162–65
  history 147–48
  matching the hatch 123, 149, 160–61
  patterns 149, 150–51, 155–60
  tackle 149, 152–54
  timing 165–66
Nymphs, submerged
  fishing tactics 143–44
  for big fish 138, 145, 153–54, 172
  patterns 141–43
  striking 144

Oneida Lake 12, 48–50, 52

Pickerel 122, 125, 135
Plugs. *See* Crankbaits
Panfish
  finding fish 230
  fly-fishing 103, 122
  life histories 230–31
  tackle 227–29

Reels
  bass 33, 43–44
  carp 100
  fly reels 104, 170
  northern pike 87
  trolling 199–200
  walleye 61–62
Reservoirs. *See* Lakes, artificial
Rivers and streams
  largemouth bass 18, 58
  northern pike 74–78
  trout 122–23, 129–31, 132–36
Rods
  bass 33, 42, 44
  carp 100
  fly rods 103–104, 138–39, 149, 152
  landlocked salmon 169
  northern pike 87
  trolling 198–99
  walleye 61–62

Salmon, landlocked
  fishing tactics 130, 169, 175–80
  flies 104, 122, 128, 171–75
  habitat 169–70, 185, 188, 203

life history 168
playing 180–82
range 167·
striking 177, 180
tackle 169
Spin casting 43, 227
Spinnerbaits
  how to fish 27–29
  northern pike 89
  smallmouth bass 47, 51
  specific baits 47
  walleye 64
Spoons
  bass, 31–33, 47, 51
  modifying 213
  northern pike 87
  specific spoons 47, 55, 87, 215–17
Streamers
  bait imitations 121
  fishing tactics 130–31, 136–37
  for big fish 122, 125
  in lakes 128–29
  in streams 130–31
  salmon 172–73
  selection 136–37
Streams. *See* Rivers and streams
Structure
  bottom contour 13–14
  largemouth bass 14–23
  smallmouth bass 17, 50–53
  trout 188, 205–206
  walleye 64
Sunlight, effect on fish 13

Tail-spinners 47, 51
Thermocline 188
Topographic maps 14, 41
Trolling
  attractors 219–22
  back trolling 64–68
  boats 189

defined 185
depth 207–209
downriggers 186, 189–93, 206
equipment 189, 193–97
finding fish 201–206
hooks 224
lure action 209–14
lures 47–48, 222
northern pike 78–84
scents 223–24
smallmouth bass 51, 52–53
specific lures 48, 213, 215–19
tackle 197–200
walleye 62–68
Trout
  brown 133, 200–201, 203
  in lakes 128–30, 186–89
  in streams 122–23, 130–31, 132–34
  lake trout 188, 200–201, 203, 205
  playing 127
  rainbow 128, 134, 188, 203
  spawning 145–46
  striking 126
  tackle 104
  See also Fly-fishing; Nymphs

Ultra-light tackle 233

Water temperature 13
  See also under Lakes
Walleye pike
  baits 64–68
  forage and schooling 61
  life history 60–61
  range and abundance 60, 68
  seasonal patterns 64, 201
  tackle 61
  world record 61
Weeds 13, 16–19, 53, 74–84
Worms
  plastic 25–26
  real 67, 100, 229

Fish and Game Books Available from The Countryman Press

The Countryman Press, long known for its fine books on the outdoors, offers a range of practical and readable manuals for sportsmen and women—from fly tying to wild game cooking.

Fishing and Hunting
The Fisherman's Companion, by Frank Holan, $6.95
Getting the Most from Your Game and Fish, by Robert Candy, $16.95
Taking Freshwater Game Fish: A Treasury of Expert Advice, edited by
  Todd Swainbank and Eric Seidler, $14.95

Fly Tying
Bass Flies, by Dick Stewart, $12.95 (paper), $19.95 (cloth)
The Hook Book: A Guide for Fly Tyers by Dick Stewart, $8.95
Universal Fly Tying Guide, by Dick Stewart, $8.95

Cookbooks
Fish and Fowl Cookery: The Outdoorsman's Home Companion, by Carol
  Vance Wary with William G. Wary, $10.95
Wild Game Cookery: The Hunter's Home Companion, Revised and Expanded Edition, by Carol Vance Wary, $12.95

We also publish books about canoeing, hiking, walking, bicycling, and ski touring in New England, New York State, and the Mid-Atlantic states.

Our titles are available in bookshops and in many sporting goods stores, or they may be ordered directly from the publisher. Please add $2.00 per order for shipping and handling. To order or obtain a complete catalog, please write The Countryman Press, P.O. Box 175, Woodstock, Vermont 05091.